Platform Supply Chains in the AI Era

Platform Supply Chains in the AI Era

Baofeng Huo • Yuxiao Ye • Minhao Gu •
Siyu Li • Min Tian

Platform Supply Chains 4

Platform Supply Chain Integration

Springer

Baofeng Huo
School of Management
Zhejiang University
Hangzhou, China

Minhao Gu
College of Management and Economics
Tianjin University
Tianjin, China

Min Tian
School of Management
Shandong University
Jinan, China

Yuxiao Ye
Business School
University of Nottingham Ningbo
Ningbo, China

Siyu Li
School of Management
Xi'an Jiaotong University
Xi'an, China

ISSN 3091-4795 ISSN 3091-4809 (electronic)
Platform Supply Chains in the AI Era
ISBN 978-981-92-0132-7 ISBN 978-981-92-0133-4 (eBook)
https://doi.org/10.1007/978-981-92-0133-4

This Springer imprint is published by the registered company Springer Nature Singapore Pte Ltd.
The registered company address is: 152 Beach Road, #21-01/04 Gateway East, Singapore 189721, Singapore

"Platform Supply Chains" Project Committee

Director:

Yugang Yu, University of Science and Technology of China

Deputy Director:

Xinyu Zhang, Chinese Academy of Science
Jia Shu, University of Electronic Science and Technology of China
Baofeng Huo, Zhejiang University
L. Jeff Hong, University of Minnesota

Member:

Shengming Zheng, University of Science and Technology of China
Jiahui Zou, Capital University of Economics and Business
Yongzhen Li, Southeast University
Yuxiao Ye, University of Nottingham Ningbo China
Lin Tian, Fudan University

Competing Interests The authors have no competing interests to declare that are relevant to the content of this manuscript.

Contents

Chapter 1
Introduction

Abstract This introductory chapter defines platform supply chains as customer-centered, technology-enabled networks in which coordination is mediated by a platform. It explains why platformization makes supply chains harder to control even as it expands scale and visibility: participation becomes multi-sided and dynamic, interdependence spreads beyond immediate partners, and small misalignments can cascade into system-wide failures. The chapter motivates the book's central argument that integration is valuable because it removes recurring value-creation bottlenecks—cost-center pressures, continuous demand upgrading, and fragile network effects—through coordinated design and governance. It clarifies scope and key definitions, positions integration as an interrelated set of design choices inseparable from governance, and previews a four-pillar framework built around supplier, customer, technology, and logistics integration.

Keywords Platform supply chain · Integration · Platform governance · Value creation · Bottlenecks

1.1 Motivation

Platform-based business has moved beyond being a digital sales channel. It has become an organizing logic for end-to-end operations. Firms such as Amazon, Alibaba, JD.com, and Haier increasingly coordinate supply, production, distribution, and consumption through platforms rather than through stable, dyadic relationships. In this setting, a platform supply chain is not a chain with a clear upstream and downstream. It is a customer-centered, technology-enabled network in which platform owners, suppliers, service providers, IT partners, retailers, and consumers jointly participate in value creation (Fig. 1.1). This shift creates a familiar managerial paradox. Platformization promises scale, speed, and scope. It enables end-to-end visibility, richer data, and faster learning, making operating models such as reverse customization and precision marketing feasible at scale. At the same time, the features that generate these benefits make platform supply chains harder to

B. Huo et al., *Platform Supply Chains 4*, Platform Supply Chains in the AI Era,
https://doi.org/10.1007/978-981-92-0133-4_1

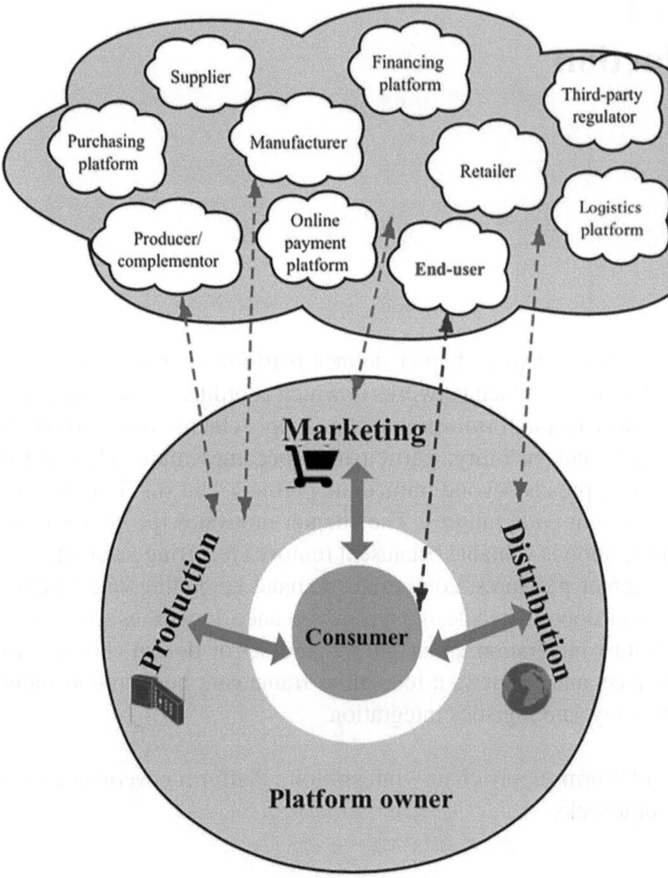

Fig. 1.1 Structure of platform supply chain

control. Once transactions and coordination are mediated by a platform, the system becomes open, dynamic, and multi-sided. Interdependence expands from immediate partners to a broader ecosystem. Coupling becomes looser, autonomy rises, and outcomes become less predictable.

Some examples may illustrate why platform supply chain management is challenging. A consumer electronics platform can launch a new product line quickly by mobilizing multiple suppliers and contract manufacturers. Yet a small mismatch in component availability, quality standards, or after-sales responsibilities can propagate across the ecosystem. The platform may see a surge in complaints, returns, and negative reviews within days, even if each individual partner believes it met its own obligations. The operational problem is not one supplier's failure. It is misaligned coordination across actors. A second example comes from fast fashion marketplaces. Platforms can translate real-time browsing and purchase data into rapid replenishment decisions. However, if suppliers are not integrated into the same cadence of planning and quality control, the platform experiences short-lived spikes followed by stockouts, inconsistent sizing, and higher return rates. Demand becomes visible, but supply cannot respond in a disciplined way.

These examples highlight a core implication: integration can no longer be treated as a generic practice. In conventional supply chain research, integration often refers to internal integration, supplier integration, and customer integration, supported by information sharing, collaborative planning, and relational governance. Platform supply chains add problems that traditional supply chains do not fully address, including multi-actor participation, competing complementors, platform-specific uncertainty, cross-side network effects, and rapid shifts in consumer demand and engagement. The platform owner does not simply coordinate a chain. It orchestrates interactions among multiple sides and shapes multilateral flows of information and resources.

The motivation for this book starts from a straightforward observation: platform supply chains rarely fail because a single function underperforms. They fail because value creation becomes bottlenecked at points where cross-actor coordination is required but governance is weak, incentives are misaligned, or capabilities are fragmented. We refer to three bottleneck factors that repeatedly constrain platform supply chain performance: the risk of becoming a cost center rather than a profit center, the pressure of continuous demand upgrading, and the challenge of building and sustaining positive network effects.

The cost-center bottleneck is not merely an accounting issue. Many platforms subsidize participation, invest heavily in digital infrastructure, and expand logistics capacity to improve delivery speed and coverage. These moves are often necessary for growth, but they also raise the cost base. Without integration, the platform cannot convert scale into efficiency. Instead, it accumulates operational redundancy: duplicate inventory buffers across sellers, inconsistent packaging and labeling standards that increase handling costs, repeated quality inspections, and avoidable last-mile failures that increase reverse logistics costs. In such settings, integration is the mechanism that pools resources, standardizes interfaces, and coordinates processes so that growth does not automatically translate into escalating costs. A practical case is marketplace fulfillment. When a platform offers a unified fulfillment promise, it must decide how to integrate sellers into consistent service levels. If sellers remain loosely connected, the platform pays for service recovery through refunds, expedited shipping, and customer support. Some platforms respond by tightening seller onboarding rules, enforcing packaging standards, or shifting more transactions into platform-managed fulfillment. These are integration choices that determine whether the platform can deliver a consistent service promise while controlling unit costs.

Demand upgrading is structural rather than temporary. Platform customers do not only demand lower prices and faster delivery. They expect personalization, transparency, responsive service, and involvement in product and service design. In many categories, customers also shape supply-side decisions through search patterns, clicks, reviews, and community interactions. This demand-side dynamism can trigger frequent reconfiguration of product offerings, production plans, and service bundles. Consider consumer-to-manufacturer (C2M) models in home appliances or apparel. Customers may select features, colors, or bundles online, and the platform aggregates these signals into production instructions. If supplier integration is weak, customization increases complexity without improving performance. Lead times rise, component shortages become frequent, and quality variation increases. If customer integration is weak, the platform may misread demand signals and overreact to short-term noise, resulting in costly swings in production and inventory. Technology can reveal demand patterns, but it cannot translate signals into coordinated action unless supplier and customer integration align incentives, standards, and decision rights.

Network effects are both a growth engine and a coordination challenge. Platform ecosystems become valuable because more consumers attract more complementors, and more complementors attract more consumers. Yet network effects do not arise automatically, and they can reverse quickly. They depend on rules, incentives, and credible enforcement that protect participation quality. A small failure can cascade. A data outage may halt transactions and damage trust. A wave of counterfeit products can deter customers and harm legitimate sellers. A logistics disruption can amplify negative reviews and reduce purchase intention, which then discourages high-quality suppliers from staying on the platform.

In each case, the platform faces a governance problem: how to maintain participation and quality when actors are autonomous and switching costs are low. This is why integration is crucial in platform supply chains. Integration is not only about connecting processes; it is also about shaping behavior and creating value. The book elaborates value-creation based on a precise sense: it treats integration as a theory of how platform supply chains remove value-creation bottlenecks through coordinated design and governance across interlocking pillars. We classify value creation into several activity domains—supply, production, distribution, and consumption—and then ask how integration enables value creation in each domain.

A second motivation is grounded in academic literature. Research on platforms and ecosystems has built strong foundations around multi-sided markets, boundary resources, complementor governance, and network effects. Supply chain scholarship, in parallel, has developed rich theories of coordination, integration, and interfirm governance. Each stream is mature on its own terms, yet platform supply chains sit at their intersection. As a result, existing studies often illuminate one part of the system while leaving the cross-pillar logic implicit. Platform studies frequently treat the platform as a market design problem and examine participation incentives and rule-setting, often abstracting away from operational dependencies across supply, production, distribution, and consumption. Supply chain studies typically assume stable buyer–supplier ties and focus on coordination and adaptation within relatively bounded networks. Platform supply chains are open systems with various supply chain participants, cross-side externalities, and continuous reconfiguration. Operational outcomes therefore depend on how design choices interact across multiple actor groups and functional domains.

The practical dilemmas faced by platform firms reveal the academic gap. Managers must decide how open the platform should be to suppliers, how to screen and discipline supplier behavior, how to translate demand discovery into supply responsiveness, how to govern logistics service providers while enabling service innovation, and how to convert data into operational advantage. These choices are interdependent and often involve trade-offs that cannot be resolved within a single theoretical lens. Stricter supplier screening may improve quality and reduce fraud, but it can narrow variety and weaken growth on the supply side. More open access may expand variety and stimulate competition, but it raises monitoring costs and increases the risk of opportunism. Stronger logistics control can improve reliability and customer experience, but it may reduce complementor autonomy and dampen innovation in service offerings. Treating these decisions as isolated governance problems or isolated operational optimizations produces partial solutions, and partial solutions are fragile in platform settings.

For researchers, the same problem appears. Many studies describe platform features, yet struggle to translate them into operational constructs. Even when empirical results are strong, they are often tied to one pillar, one actor group, or one functional slice of the system. What remains underdeveloped is an overarching integration logic that specifies (i) which elements of the platform supply chain must be co-designed, (ii) how governance and capability choices shall be designed in one pillar, and (iii) how they remove value-creation bottlenecks across supply, production, distribution, and consumption. Without such a framework, it is difficult to accumulate knowledge, compare findings across contexts, or generate design implications that remain robust when the ecosystem reconfigures. This book responds by offering an overarching integration framework grounded in value creation. It organizes dispersed insights into a coherent set of pillars and explains how governance choices shape value-creation paths and performance. It also provides roadmaps that connect design rules and governance options to operational outcomes, so that both scholars and practitioners can diagnose bottlenecks, anticipate trade-offs, and design integration solutions that fit the platform supply chain.

1.2 Scope and Definitions

Building on the motivations outlined in Sect. 1.1, this book develops a value-creation–based framework for platform supply chain integration. We focus on platform firms and platform ecosystems in which a platform mediates operational interactions among multiple actor groups and supports end-to-end flows of products, services, information, and logistics capabilities. The central concern is whether the platform fundamentally reshapes how coordination, governance, and value creation are organized across the supply chain.

In this book, a platform is understood as an organizing architecture that enables interactions among multiple sides, establishes participation rules, and provides shared standards and tools that support transactions and value creation. This definition covers a wide range of contexts, including e-commerce platforms, industrial internet platforms, B2B procurement platforms, and consumer-to-manufacturer

(C2M) platforms, as well as hybrid models that integrate online and offline activities. What unifies these settings is not the industry or technology per se, but the platform's role in structuring interactions among heterogeneous participants.

A **platform supply chain** refers to a customer-centered and technology-enabled network of actors involved in value creation through a platform. Unlike traditional supply chains, coordination in this setting is mediated by a platform that structures interactions among multiple participants rather than through linear upstream–downstream relationships. The platform shapes how actors connect, exchange information, and participate in value creation. This definition also clarifies the scope of the book. We do not examine platforms that operate purely as digital content or social media platforms without substantive supply, production, or logistics activities. Nor do we treat every IT-enabled supply chain as a platform supply chain. The defining criterion is whether a platform mediates interactions among multiple autonomous actors and, in doing so, alters the structure and governance of value creation.

Within this setting, **integration** takes on a more specific meaning than in much of the traditional supply chain literature. In this book, integration refers to the deliberate design of mechanisms that reduce boundary frictions among actors and processes, pool and align resources, and enable coordinated action for value creation in platform supply chains. These mechanisms may involve shared interfaces and standards, information sharing and analytics, relational arrangements, or formal governance instruments such as incentives and enforcement rules. Crucially, integration in platform settings cannot be separated from governance. Because participants are autonomous and the platform lacks full hierarchical control, integration depends on how rules, incentives, and coordination mechanisms are designed and enforced. Integration is therefore a system of interrelated design choices that must fit the platform's strategic objectives and operating environment. Its relevance is ultimately judged by its contribution to overcoming value-creation bottlenecks such as cost pressures, demand upgrading, and the fragility of network effects.

Value creation provides the unifying lens of the framework. Here, value creation refers to improvements in efficiency, responsiveness, quality, innovation, and sustainability outcomes that arise from coordinated activities across the platform supply chain and generate superior performance for both the ecosystem and its participants. To make this concept operational, the book organizes value creation around three activity domains: supply/production, distribution, and consumption. This decomposition reflects the empirical reality that many performance problems in platform supply chains arise at the interfaces across these domains. Demand information generated on the consumption side may not translate into supply-side capability. Marketing campaigns may outpace logistics capacity. Supplier quality governance may conflict with customer experience objectives. An integration framework that does not explicitly account for these interfaces risks treating symptoms rather than underlying coordination failures.

The core of the book is developed around four interlocking pillars: suppliers, customers, technology, and logistics. These pillars capture the key elements through which integration and governance shape value creation in platform supply chains. **Supplier integration** and **customer integration** form the two ends of the system.

They determine how supply is formed, how demand is articulated, and how effectively the platform matches the two under conditions of uncertainty and autonomy. Supplier integration focuses on managing open and dynamic supplier networks, improving visibility and coordination. Customer integration focuses on attracting, engaging, and retaining customers through mechanisms such as precise marketing, service responsiveness, and community interaction, enabling customers to participate more actively in value creation rather than remaining passive recipients. **Technology integration** and **logistics integration** play a supporting but indispensable role. Technology integration provides the infrastructure for data fusion, knowledge integration, end-to-end visibility, and intelligent decision-making that allows the platform supply chain to function at scale despite its complexity. Logistics integration governs relationships with logistics service providers, pools logistics resources, supports service innovation, and enables reliability and sustainability in distribution. These definitions and scope choices establish the foundation for the chapters that follow.

1.3 How to Use This Book

This book is intended to serve both as a conceptual reference and as a practical guide. Readers may approach it sequentially or selectively, depending on their objectives. The chapters are structured to support systematic learning, theory development, and problem-oriented application in platform supply chain settings.

The book is written for a broad range of audience. It is primarily intended for advanced students and researchers in operations management, supply chain management, information systems, and related fields who seek a coherent conceptual vocabulary and an integrative framework grounded in platform realities. It also addresses managers and decision-makers in platform firms who are responsible for strategy, operations, procurement, and ecosystem governance, as well as professionals in logistics and technology management whose roles increasingly unfold within platform-based supply chains. While these audiences differ in their immediate goals, they face a common challenge: understanding how integration and governance choices shape value creation in complex, multi-actor systems.

Readers interested in conceptual foundations and theory development are encouraged to begin with Chaps. 1 and 2. These chapters establish the motivation, definitions, and theoretical framework that organize the rest of the book. Subsequent chapters are structured around the four integration pillars. Readers may focus first on supplier integration or customer integration, which form the two ends of the platform supply chain and directly shape supply formation, demand formation, and matching efficiency. Cross-references across chapters are designed to highlight how mechanisms in one pillar depend on enabling conditions in the others. For research design and empirical work, the framework can be used to identify focal integration mechanisms, identify value-creation bottlenecks, and translate abstract platform concepts into constructs and performance outcomes across supply, production, distribution, and consumption.

Practitioners in platform firms may adopt a more problem-driven reading strategy. After reviewing Chap. 1 to understand the overall logic, they can move directly to the pillar chapters that correspond to their most pressing challenges. Each pillar chapter is written to support diagnosis as well as design. The framework can be used as a structured lens to assess where value creation is constrained, whether by supplier opportunism, weak customer engagement, limited data integration, or fragmented logistics services. By tracing how bottlenecks emerge across pillars, managers can identify which governance mechanisms require redesign and where capability investments are most likely to yield system-wide performance improvements.

For instructors, the book is suitable for graduate-level courses on digital operations, supply chain strategy, or platform ecosystems. Chapter 1 provides a unifying narrative that introduces the platform supply chain as an object of analysis. Chapters on supplier and customer integration can serve as core modules, while the technology and logistics chapters can be positioned as enabling components, depending on course emphasis. The structure of the book allows instructors to combine conceptual discussion with applied analysis of platform-based cases.

1.4 Contributions and Roadmap

This book makes three contributions that speak to theory development, governance design, and practical application in platform supply chains. Together, they advance an integrated understanding of how value is created, constrained, and unlocked in platform-based operational systems.

The book develops a theory of platform supply chain integration that moves beyond fragmented treatments of platforms and supply chains. The theory begins with the core elements that shape integration design in platform supply chains and clarifies their roles in value creation. Specifically, it identifies four interlocking pillars—suppliers, customers, technology, and logistics—as the fundamental building blocks of integration. These pillars capture both actor-side mechanisms, which shape participation and behavior, and capability-side mechanisms, which enable coordination and execution under complexity. Supplier and customer integration constitute the ends of the system because they directly shape supply formation, demand formation, and the platform's ability to match the two under conditions of uncertainty and autonomy. Technology and logistics integration play a supporting role by determining the platform's coordination capacity, enabling end-to-end visibility, scalable execution, and reliable service delivery. The theory further anchors integration in value creation across four pillars. Integration acts as a mechanism through which platform supply chains remove bottlenecks that constrain value creation in these domains. Supplier integration governs open and dynamic supplier networks, reduces opportunism, and enables coordinated responses to demand signals. Customer integration shapes how customers are attracted, engaged, and retained, and whether they participate actively in value creation. Technology integration supports data fusion, intelligent decision-making, and knowledge integration that allow the system to function despite complexity. Logistics integration coordinates service providers and resources, supports service innovation, and underpins efficiency and sustainability. Taken together, these paths form a coherent explanation of how platform supply chains move from fragmented coordination toward sustained value creation.

Beyond conceptual development, the book translates the framework into actionable roadmaps for integration decisions. Each pillar chapter concludes with a structured approach to diagnosing and addressing value-creation bottlenecks. Rather than prescribing universal best practices, the roadmaps guide readers to identify where value creation is constrained, which pillar represents the binding constraint, and how governance mechanisms and capability investments can be combined to relieve that constraint without undermining ecosystem participation or adaptability. In doing so, the book helps bridge the gap between abstract platform concepts and concrete operational decisions.

The remainder of the book follows a clear and cumulative structure. Chapter 2 establishes the conceptual foundation by formalizing the platform supply chain as a customer-centered, technology-enabled complex network and introducing the four-pillar integration framework and the bottleneck logic. Chapters 3 and 4 focus on supplier and customer integration, examining how governance and integration choices at the two ends of the platform supply chain shape participation quality, coordination, and value co-creation. Chapters 5 and 6 turn to the supporting pillars, showing how technology and logistics integration enable scalable coordination, service innovation, and sustainable performance. The final chapter synthesizes insights across all pillars and outlines a future research agenda that reflects complexity, co-evolution, and value creation in platform supply chains.

Chapter 2
Platform Supply Chain Integration

Abstract Chapter 2 builds the conceptual foundation for platform supply chain integration. It first reviews conventional supply chain integration, highlighting its governance and information-processing logic and its typical focus on bounded partner sets and relatively stable dyads. It then explains how platforms change the unit of coordination. From this shift, the chapter defines platform supply chain integration as the design and governance of mechanisms that enable coordinated value creation at the ecosystem level. It also articulates three value-creation mechanisms—coordination, allocation, and governance—operating across supply/production, distribution, and consumption. The chapter concludes by introducing a four-pillar framework and clarifying how the pillars interact to relieve value-creation bottlenecks under complexity and scale.

Keywords Supply chain integration · Platform ecosystems · Coordination · Allocation · Governance

This chapter develops the theoretical logic of platform supply chain integration with a focus on value creation. We begin by revisiting the concept of supply chain integration in its conventional form, clarifying what is being integrated and why integration has been viewed as a source of performance improvement. We then introduce the rise of platform-based organizing and explain why the traditional integration logic becomes insufficient in platform supply chain settings. Building on this shift, we articulate how platform supply chain integration creates value through distinct but interrelated pathways. Finally, we synthesize these arguments into a four-pillar integration framework that specifies the key elements, their roles, and their contribution to value creation.

B. Huo et al., *Platform Supply Chains 4*, Platform Supply Chains in the AI Era,
https://doi.org/10.1007/978-981-92-0133-4_2

2.1 Supply Chain Integration

Supply chain integration (SCI) has long been regarded as a foundational mechanism through which firms coordinate interdependent activities and improve system-wide performance. As supply chains expanded across organizational and geographic boundaries, fragmentation in decision-making, information flows, and operational execution became a central concern. Supply chain integration emerged as a response to this fragmentation, aiming to align processes, resources, and incentives across firms so that the supply chain could function as a coherent value-creating system rather than a collection of loosely connected entities. Across the literature, SCI is commonly defined as the extent to which firms strategically collaborate with supply chain partners and jointly manage inter- and intra-organizational processes to achieve efficient, responsive, and reliable flows of products and information (Flynn et al., 2010; Wong et al., 2011). Although definitions vary, three core ideas are consistent. First, SCI is intentional and design-oriented, reflecting managerial choices rather than incidental interaction. Second, integration extends beyond transactional exchange to encompass process alignment and joint decision-making. Third, the ultimate purpose is value creation, typically reflected in improved operational performance, customer satisfaction, and competitive advantage.

As the field matured, scholars increasingly recognized SCI as a multidimensional construct. A dominant view distinguishes between internal integration and external integration, with the latter commonly divided into supplier integration and customer integration (Swink et al., 2007; Flynn et al., 2010). Internal integration focuses on cross-functional coordination within the firm, aligning procurement, production, logistics, marketing, and product development. External integration emphasizes close collaboration with upstream suppliers and downstream customers, enabling information sharing, joint planning, and coordinated execution. This structure has become the backbone of empirical research and provides a parsimonious way to capture how integration operates across organizational boundaries.

The theoretical foundations of SCI are similarly diverse but converge on a common logic. From a resource-based and knowledge-based perspective, integration enables firms to access and combine complementary resources and knowledge distributed across supply chain partners, thereby creating value that cannot be generated in isolation (Barney, 1991; Grant, 1996). Transaction cost economics highlights the governance role, viewing integration as a means to mitigate opportunism, reduce uncertainty, and economize on coordination and monitoring costs without resorting to full vertical integration (Williamson, 1979). Information processing theory emphasizes the role of enhancing information processing capacity, allowing firms to cope with uncertainty by improving information quality, timeliness, and dissemination (Galbraith, 1973). Relational and social capital perspectives further stress trust, joint investment, and relational rents as mechanisms through which integration enhances performance (Dyer & Singh, 1998). Together, these perspectives frame SCI as a coordination and governance capability that transforms dispersed activities into a unified value-creation system.

Building on these foundations, a substantial body of empirical research has examined the performance implications of SCI. Numerous studies report positive associations between SCI and operational efficiency, delivery reliability, flexibility, innovation, and financial performance (Frohlich & Westbrook, 2001; Flynn et al., 2010; Leuschner et al., 2013). However, this relationship is rarely linear or unconditional. Scholars have identified important contingencies, including environmental uncertainty, supply chain complexity, technological infrastructure, and relational maturity (Van der Vaart & Van Donk, 2008; Wong et al., 2011). Excessive or poorly aligned integration can generate coordination overload, rigidity, and diminishing returns, particularly when integration practices are adopted without appropriate governance mechanisms. These findings shift the focus of SCI research from the question of whether to integrate toward the question of how integration should be designed, combined, and governed. Integration is no longer viewed as a single practice or a binary choice, but as a system of interrelated decisions. The effectiveness of SCI depends on how internal and external integration reinforce one another, how integration practices are sequenced, and how they are aligned with the broader supply chain context. Figure 2.1 summarizes extant studies on the relationship between SCI and performance. This insight has motivated more recent work that emphasizes complementarities, configurations, and interaction effects among different integration dimensions (Gimenez et al., 2012; Zhao et al., 2013).

Despite its richness, the traditional SCI literature is largely grounded in a linear and relatively stable view of the supply chain. Most studies assume identifiable focal firms coordinating a bounded set of suppliers and customers through repeated interactions. Governance mechanisms are typically examined in dyadic or small-network settings, and integration is often operationalized as the intensity of collaboration within these predefined relationships. While this framing has generated important insights, it becomes increasingly strained as supply chains evolve toward more open, digital, and networked forms of organization. In contemporary settings, supply chains are increasingly embedded in digital platforms that mediate interactions among multiple actor groups. Supplier bases expand, customer demand becomes more heterogeneous and data-driven, and coordination increasingly relies on shared digital infrastructures rather than bilateral relationships. Under these conditions, integration cannot be reduced to aligning a fixed set of partners or synchronizing sequential processes. Instead, it involves designing coordination and governance mechanisms that operate at the system level, enabling value creation across a complex and evolving network. The foundational logic of SCI remains highly relevant. The emphasis on coordination, governance, and value creation provides a critical starting point for understanding integration in platform supply chains.

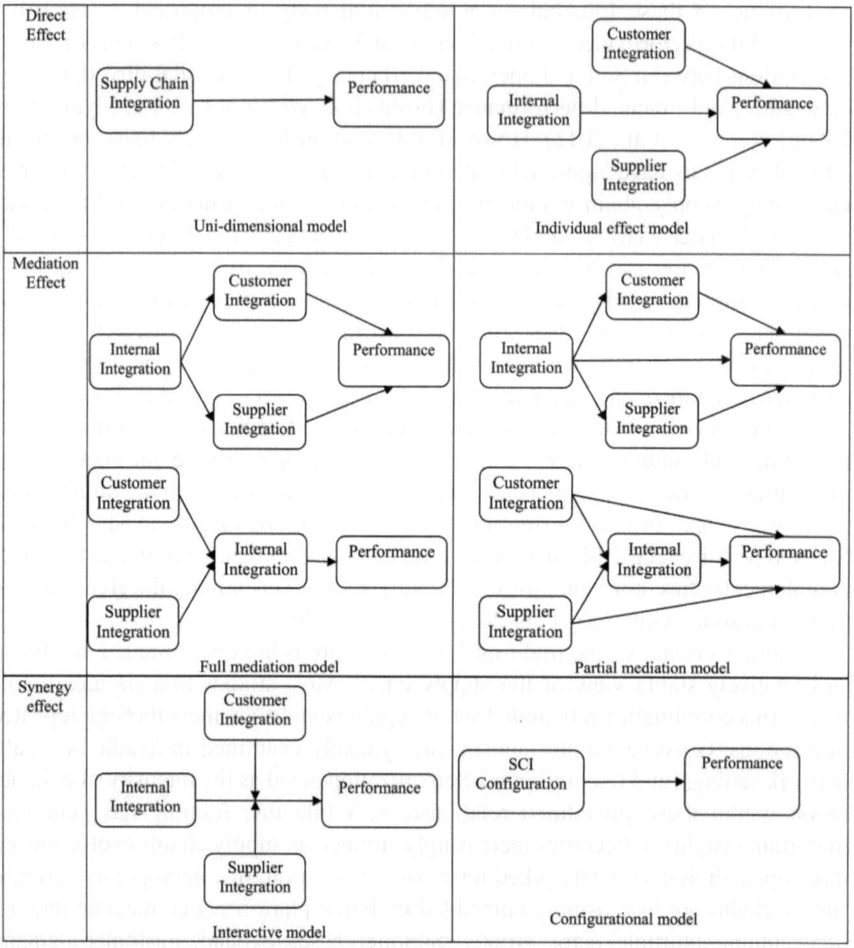

Fig. 2.1 SCI-performance relationships

2.2 Platform Supply Chain Integration

Platforms fundamentally reshape how supply chains are organized and governed. Instead of coordinating transactions through a sequence of bilateral exchanges, platforms mediate interactions among multiple actor groups within a shared infrastructure. Suppliers, service providers, logistics partners, and customers interact through the platform, often in real time and outside traditional hierarchical relationships. Coordination therefore no longer relies primarily on stable dyads or linear process alignment. It depends on platform-enabled mechanisms that orchestrate dispersed and autonomous participants at scale.

As supply chains become embedded in platforms, several structural transformations redefine the nature of integration. First, the supply chain becomes explicitly customer-centered. In traditional supply chains, demand is typically treated as an outcome observed at the downstream end and transmitted upstream through planning and forecasting routines. In platform settings, demand signals are continuously generated through customer search behavior, transactions, reviews, and usage data. These signals do not merely inform downstream replenishment decisions; they actively shape upstream choices such as production planning, supplier selection, and product or service customization (Hagiu & Wright, 2015; Parker et al., 2017). Demand thus becomes an endogenous driver of coordination rather than an exogenous input.

Second, technology's supporting role is becoming more central. In conventional supply chains, information systems primarily facilitate coordination among predefined partners by improving information quality and timeliness. In platform supply chains, digital systems constitute the core infrastructure through which interactions occur. They enable multilateral data flows, real-time visibility, and algorithmic decision-making across actors who may not have direct contractual relationships with one another (Tilson et al., 2012; Yoo et al., 2012). Technology therefore shapes not only how information is processed, but also who can participate, how coordination is executed, and how rules are enforced.

Third, the supply chain takes the form of a complex network rather than a linear chain. Actors are no longer confined to fixed upstream–downstream positions. They can connect with multiple counterparts, bypass intermediaries, and reconfigure relationships dynamically through the platform. Complementors retain a high degree of autonomy, yet their actions are tightly coupled through shared infrastructures and interdependencies (Jacobides et al., 2018). This networked structure expands scale and flexibility, but also increases coordination complexity and systemic risk.

These structural shifts expose the limits of traditional supply chain integration concepts. In much of the conventional literature, integration is understood as alignment between predefined partners through information sharing, joint planning, and relational governance. The focal firm and its immediate suppliers or customers typically form the unit of analysis. Such an approach assumes relatively stable relationships, clear role boundaries, and governance through contracts or long-term relational ties. In platform supply chains, by contrast, integration becomes a system-level problem. The platform firm assumes the role of system architect rather than hierarchical controller, shaping participation rules, interaction patterns, and coordination mechanisms across a network rather than along a chain. Actors remain autonomous and may multi-home across platforms or exit with limited friction. As a result, integration cannot be achieved simply by intensifying collaboration with a fixed set of partners. It requires mechanisms that enable coordination among heterogeneous actors while preserving openness, adaptability, and participation incentives. Integration and governance therefore become inseparable.

Table 2.1 summarizes these differences between traditional and platform supply chains, highlighting contrasts in ownership, structure, configuration, complexity, coordination patterns, technology use, visibility, and complementor autonomy. These differences imply a fundamentally different integration logic. Where

Table 2.1 Differences between traditional and platform supply chain

Dimensions	Traditional supply chain	Platform supply chain
Owner	None	Platform firm
Structure	Hierarchical	Network
Design and configuration	Linear and relatively stable structures	Non-linear and dynamic structures
Complexity	Low	Extremely high
Operations	Predictable and stable	Unpredictable and dynamic
Coordination and interaction	Dyadic	End-to-end
Technology use and digitalization	Low	High
Visibility	Low	High
Complementor autonomy	No	Yes

traditional integration emphasizes dyadic alignment and process synchronization, platform integration emphasizes network orchestration and rule-based coordination.

Against this background, **platform supply chain integration** can be defined as the design and governance of mechanisms that enable coordinated value creation across a platform-mediated supply chain network. Integration extends beyond operational alignment to include the design of rules, interfaces, and incentives that structure interaction among participants. It operates at the network level rather than the dyadic level, addressing interdependencies that span multiple actors and activities. Furthermore, integration is evaluated by its contribution to value creation under conditions of complexity, autonomy, and scale. A critical change is that what is being integrated in platform contexts. Integration no longer concerns only processes or information flows between known partners. Instead, it involves the integration of participants, resources, activities, and decision rights across the platform ecosystem. Unlike traditional supply chains, where integration often assumes hierarchical influence or long-term relational commitment, platform supply chains are characterized by voluntary participation and low switching costs (Hagiu & Wright, 2015). Integration therefore cannot rely solely on relational trust or contractual enforcement. It must be embedded in governance mechanisms that balance openness with control and flexibility with reliability.

From this perspective, platform supply chain integration is inherently intertwined with governance. Governance defines access rules, standards, incentive structures, monitoring mechanisms, and dispute resolution processes that shape behavior within the platform (Tiwana, 2013). Integration mechanisms are effective only to the extent that governance aligns individual incentives with system-level value creation. For example, increasing openness to suppliers may expand variety and innovation, but without appropriate governance, it may also increase quality variance and opportunism. Similarly, deeper customer integration through data collection and personalization may enhance responsiveness, but it also raises concerns related to data ownership, privacy, and trust.

2.3 Value Creation from Platform Supply Chain Integration

A defining feature of platform supply chains is that value creation is inherently distributed. Suppliers and manufacturers contribute production capacity, technical expertise, and innovation potential. Customers contribute demand signals, usage data, and participation that shape market outcomes. Logistics providers contribute distribution capabilities that determine service reliability and responsiveness. Technology provides the infrastructure through which these contributions are connected, coordinated, and recombined. The platform occupies a central but non-hierarchical position in this system. It enables value creation by structuring how resources and participants interact. Integration determines whether these contributions remain isolated or become mutually reinforcing. When integration is weak, resources exist but are poorly matched to needs, participants act on partial information, and coordination costs escalate. Platforms then risk becoming cost centers rather than value-generating systems, as investments in technology, logistics, and ecosystem expansion fail to translate into performance. When integration is well designed, the platform aligns participation and resource deployment, allowing scale, diversity, and autonomy to generate value rather than instability. As illustrated in Fig. 2.2, platform supply chain integration transforms autonomous participants and dispersed resources into system-level value through platform-enabled coordination, allocation, and governance mechanisms that effectively manage interdependencies across supply, production, distribution, and consumption.

The first mechanism operates through coordination, understood as the alignment of interdependent decisions among autonomous actors. Platform supply chains involve multiple participants whose actions are tightly coupled but not hierarchically controlled. Suppliers determine production scope and capacity, logistics providers allocate distribution resources, and customers decide when and how to engage. Without integration, these decisions are made independently, based on partial information and local objectives, resulting in misalignment across supply,

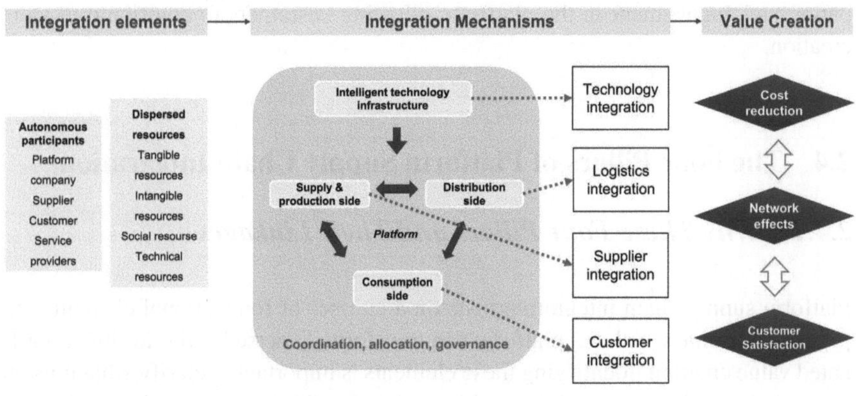

Fig. 2.2 Platform supply chain integration conceptual framework

production, and distribution. Platform supply chain integration addresses this coordination problem by structuring participation through shared rules, standardized interfaces, and visibility. By reducing coordination frictions, integration allows platforms to manage scale and complexity without a proportional increase in managerial or transactional costs.

The second mechanism concerns allocation, specifically the allocation of resources and decision attention across activities and actors. In platform supply chains, integration determines how resources such as production capacity, logistics services, and operational effort are distributed in response to changing environments. Value creation depends on whether integration mechanisms enable coordinated adjustments across supply, production, and distribution. When integration is effective, resources are allocated in a way that matches operational capabilities with realized demand and service requirements. When integration is weak, resources may be abundant but poorly deployed, leading to mismatches, delays, or underutilization.

The third mechanism operates through governance, defined as the design of rules and incentives that shape participation and behavior within the platform. Platform supply chains rely on voluntary participation and grant actors substantial autonomy. While this openness supports flexibility and innovation, it also introduces risks related to opportunism, quality variation, and instability. Integration contributes to value creation by embedding governance mechanisms that align individual behavior with system-level objectives. Through access rules, incentive structures, and enforcement mechanisms, the platform governs how actors participate and how interdependencies are managed. Effective governance stabilizes interactions over time, enabling coordination and allocation mechanisms to function reliably.

These mechanisms operate across three interrelated activity domains: supply and production, distribution, and consumption. On the supply and production side, integration supports visibility, coordination, and capability alignment among suppliers/manufacturers and the platform company. On the distribution side, integration enables the pooling and orchestration of logistics resources, improving reliability and responsiveness. On the consumption side, integration deepens customer participation and engagement in the platform, allowing customers to contribute to value creation.

2.4 The Four Pillars of Platform Supply Chain Integration

2.4.1 Why These Four Pillars and Their Linkages

Platform supply chain integration rests on a number of foundational elements that jointly determine whether a platform can transform dispersed activities into coordinated value creation. Identifying these elements is important to clarify what must be integrated, and how integration enables value creation across supply, production, distribution, and consumption. This book advances a four-pillar view of platform supply chain integration: supplier integration, customer integration, technology integration, and logistics integration. These pillars capture the actors and capabilities whose integration is necessary for value creation in platform supply chains.

The choice of these four pillars follows directly from the defining characteristics of platform supply chains. First, platform supply chains are multi-actor systems in which value creation depends on the participation of heterogeneous and autonomous actors. Suppliers and customers represent the two primary actor groups on the supply and demand sides of the system. Their participation determines the scope, diversity, and intensity of economic activity on the platform. Second, platform supply chains are end-to-end systems that connect supply, production, distribution, and consumption. Logistics therefore plays a critical role in translating coordination into operational outcomes and service performance. Platform supply chains are technology-enabled systems. Finally, digital infrastructures are not peripheral support tools but the primary means through which interactions are organized, information is processed, and decisions are coordinated. This distinction between actor-side and capability-side pillars is important. In traditional supply chains, integration often focuses on aligning processes and information flows among a relatively stable set of partners. In platform supply chains, integration cannot be achieved solely by tightening relationships among existing partners. It requires mechanisms that structure participation, enable coordination among unknown or weakly connected actors, and support scalable interaction. The four pillars jointly address these challenges.

The four pillars also map naturally onto the core activity domains of value creation. Supplier integration primarily concerns the supply and production domains. It governs how suppliers and manufacturers are selected, coordinated, monitored, and connected to demand. Customer integration primarily concerns the consumption domain, shaping how demand is generated, articulated, and fed back into upstream activities. Logistics integration primarily concerns the distribution domain, determining how products and services are delivered, returned, and supported. Technology integration spans all four domains by providing the infrastructure that connects actors, activities, and decisions across the system. Their value-creation effects arise through interaction rather than isolation. Supplier integration without technology integration may fail to generate visibility or coordination. Customer integration without supplier integration may improve demand sensing but not supply responsiveness. Logistics integration without governance mechanisms may enhance capacity but create conflicts among service providers. Technology integration without actor integration may result in underutilized infrastructure and fragmented data.

Focusing on these four pillars allows the book to develop a cumulative and coherent theory of platform supply chain integration. Each pillar represents a distinct integration domain with its own logic, challenges, and mechanisms. At the same time, all four pillars contribute to a shared objective: enabling value creation under conditions of complexity, autonomy, and scale. By examining each pillar in turn and then synthesizing them, the book moves beyond fragmented insights from platform research, supply chain management, and digital operations.

2.4.2 Supplier Integration

Platform supplier integration refers to the mechanisms through which a platform structures, coordinates, and governs the participation of suppliers that contribute to the supply and production side of the platform supply chain. In this book, suppliers are not limited to upstream component providers. They may include manufacturers and production partners that directly participate in platform-mediated production and fulfillment activities. Supplier integration therefore concerns how the platform connects dispersed production capabilities to demand.

A defining characteristic of platform supplier integration is openness. Unlike traditional supply chains, where supplier bases are relatively stable and bounded, platform supply chains often rely on open or semi-open supplier networks. Entry and exit are more fluid, and suppliers may participate in multiple platforms simultaneously. This openness expands variety and capacity, but it also weakens bilateral control and increases coordination challenges. Supplier integration in platform contexts therefore cannot depend on standardized interfaces, transparent participation rules, and platform-level mechanisms that enable coordination. Supplier integration plays a critical role in value creation by enabling coordination and allocation on the supply and production side. Through integration, the platform improves visibility into supplier capabilities, capacity, and performance, allowing production and supply decisions to be aligned with downstream requirements. At the same time, supplier integration serves a governance function. By defining access conditions, performance criteria, and incentive structures, the platform mitigates risks related to opportunism, quality variation, and supply instability.

2.4.3 Customer Integration

Platform customer integration refers to the mechanisms through which a platform connects customers to supply chain activities, enabling their participation in value creation. In platform supply chains, customers actively shape production, distribution, and service outcomes through their engagement with the platform. Customer integration, therefore, concerns how the platform structures and leverages customer participation within the broader supply chain system.

A key characteristic of customer integration in platform settings is continuity of interaction. Customer engagement extends beyond discrete purchase decisions to include search behavior, feedback, customization choices, and post-purchase interaction. These interactions generate information and coordination requirements that differ fundamentally from those in traditional supply chains, where customer demand is often treated as an exogenous input. By integrating customers into the platform supply chain, the platform can allocate production, inventory, and service resources in ways that better reflect realized demand and usage conditions. Effective customer integration enables the platform to connect consumption patterns to operational decisions, improving responsiveness while reducing mismatches between supply and demand. At the same time, customer integration supports governance by shaping participation quality on the demand side. Through rules, incentives, and interface design, the platform influences how customers engage, provide information, and contribute to value creation.

2.4.4 *Technology Integration*

Platform technology integration refers to the integration of digital infrastructures that enable coordination, information processing, and decision-making across the platform supply chain. In platform contexts, technology is not a supporting tool added to existing relationships. It constitutes the core infrastructure through which interactions occur and integration is enacted. Technology integration, therefore, concerns how digital systems connect actors, activities, and decisions across supply, production, distribution, and consumption.

A defining characteristic of technology integration in platform supply chains is scalability under complexity. Platforms must coordinate a large number of heterogeneous actors whose interactions change over time. Technology integration provides shared interfaces, data standards, and analytical capabilities that allow coordination to occur. Technology integration contributes to value creation by enabling coordination, allocation, and governance at scale. By integrating data across actors and activity domains, the platform enhances system-wide visibility and supports timely adjustment of supply, production, and distribution decisions. Technology integration also underpins learning and adaptation by allowing the platform to process information generated through participation and interaction.

2.4.5 *Logistics Integration*

Platform logistics integration refers to the mechanisms through which a platform coordinates and governs the provision of logistics services within the supply chain. In platform supply chains, logistics is rarely internalized within a single firm. Instead, it is provided by multiple service providers that vary in capability, scope, and strategic orientation. Logistics integration therefore concerns how the platform orchestrates distributed logistics resources to support end-to-end value creation.

A key characteristic of logistics integration in platform settings is multi-provider coordination. Platforms often rely on a network of logistics partners rather than a single integrated provider. This structure increases flexibility and coverage, but it also introduces coordination challenges related to service consistency, reliability, and accountability. Platform logistics integration must balance decentralization with coordination, allowing service providers to operate autonomously while aligning their actions with platform-level performance requirements. Logistics integration contributes to value creation by translating coordination and allocation into operational outcomes. Through integration, the platform aligns logistics capacity with production and consumption requirements, improving delivery reliability and responsiveness. Logistics integration also supports governance by defining service standards, performance metrics, and incentive mechanisms that stabilize interactions among logistics providers. In this sense, logistics integration ensures that value created through supplier and customer integration is realized in distribution and service execution.

References

Barney, J. (1991). Firm resources and sustained competitive advantage. *Journal of Management, 17*(1), 99–120.

Dyer, J. H., & Singh, H. (1998). The relational view: Cooperative strategy and sources of interorganizational competitive advantage. *Academy of Management Review, 23*(4), 660–679.

Flynn, B. B., Huo, B., & Zhao, X. (2010). The impact of supply chain integration on performance: A contingency and configuration approach. *Journal of Operations Management, 28*(1), 58–71.

Frohlich, M. T., & Westbrook, R. (2001). Arcs of integration: An international study of supply chain strategies. *Journal of Operations Management, 19*(2), 185–200.

Galbraith, J. K. (1973). Power and the useful economist. *American Economic Review, 63*(1), 1–11.

Gimenez, C., Van Der Vaart, T., & Pieter van Donk, D. (2012). Supply chain integration and performance: The moderating effect of supply complexity. *International Journal of Operations & Production Management, 32*(5), 583–610.

Grant, R. M. (1996). Toward a knowledge-based theory of the firm. *Strategic Management Journal, 17*(S2), 109–122.

Hagiu, A., & Wright, J. (2015). Multi-sided platforms. *International Journal of Industrial Organization, 43*, 162–174.

Jacobides, M. G., Cennamo, C., & Gawer, A. (2018). Towards a theory of ecosystems. *Strategic Management Journal, 39*(8), 2255–2276.

Leuschner, R., Rogers, D. S., & Charvet, F. F. (2013). A meta-analysis of supply chain integration and firm performance. *Journal of Supply Chain Management, 49*(2), 34–57.

Parker, G., Van Alstyne, M., & Jiang, X. (2017). Platform ecosystems. *MIS Quarterly, 41*(1), 255–266.

Swink, M., Narasimhan, R., & Wang, C. (2007). Managing beyond the factory walls: Effects of four types of strategic integration on manufacturing plant performance. *Journal of Operations Management, 25*(1), 148–164.

Tilson, D., Sorensen, C., & Lyytinen, K. (2012). Platform complexity: Lessons from mobile wireless.

Tiwana, A. (2013). *Platform ecosystems: Aligning architecture, governance, and strategy*. Newnes.

Van der Vaart, T., & Van Donk, D. P. (2008). A critical review of survey-based research in supply chain integration. *International Journal of Production Economics, 111*(1), 42–55.

Williamson, O. E. (1979). Transaction-cost economics: The governance of contractual relations. *The Journal of Law and Economics, 22*(2), 233–261.

Wong, C. Y., Boon-Itt, S., & Wong, C. W. (2011). The contingency effects of environmental uncertainty on the relationship between supply chain integration and operational performance. *Journal of Operations Management, 29*(6), 604–615.

Yoo, Y., Boland, R. J., Jr., Lyytinen, K., & Majchrzak, A. (2012). Organizing for innovation in the digitized world. *Organization Science, 23*(5), 1398–1408.

Zhao, L., Huo, B., Sun, L., & Zhao, X. (2013). The impact of supply chain risk on supply chain integration and company performance: A global investigation. *Supply Chain Management: An International Journal, 18*(2), 115–131.

Chapter 3
Platform Supplier Integration

Abstract Chapter 3 examines platform supplier integration as the capability to embed heterogeneous suppliers into a coordinated service system that delivers consistent end-to-end outcomes. It characterizes supplier integration along technical, operational, and behavioral layers, and argues that governance is integral because supplier effort, security practices, and resilience investments are only partially observable. The chapter develops a governance perspective that combines relational mechanisms, especially ability and goodwill trust, with formal contracting. It then uses data breaches as a revealing context to show how shocks update beliefs about supplier reliability and trigger security-driven portfolio adjustments. The chapter closes by synthesizing managerial implications for scaling supplier networks, and by outlining research directions on how supplier governance architectures evolve under external uncertainty.

Keywords Supplier integration · Trust · Contracts · Data breaches · Supplier switching

3.1 Overview of Platform Supplier Integration

3.1.1 Definition and Scope

Platform supplier integration refers to the arrangements through which a platform incorporates external suppliers into a coordinated service system that delivers consistent outcomes at scale. In platform environments, integration is frequently described in the language of digital connectivity, marketplace access, or transaction enablement, but these descriptions capture only the surface layer of what is at stake. The deeper issue is that platform customers experience performance as an end-to-end outcome that they attribute to the platform brand, even though that outcome is produced through a network of independent organizations. Integration therefore concerns how external suppliers are embedded in the platform's service architecture so that their contributions can be combined reliably with adjacent modules,

B. Huo et al., *Platform Supply Chains 4*, Platform Supply Chains in the AI Era,
https://doi.org/10.1007/978-981-92-0133-4_3

governed under shared standards, and corrected through structured routines when variability or failures occur. Under this definition, integration is not a one-time act of linking a supplier to an interface, but a continuing capability for organizing interdependence across organizational boundaries. It sets the conditions under which heterogeneous suppliers can behave like parts of a single operational system rather than a collection of loosely coupled contractors. This scope is broad by necessity, because the platform's promise to users rests on system performance rather than on the performance of any single supplier.

The concept is multidimensional, spanning technical, operational, and behavioral dimensions that jointly determine whether multiparty service delivery can be made dependable. Technical integration aligns interfaces, data standards, interoperability specifications, and access control rules so information and control signals can move across boundaries without ambiguity or degradation. It also encompasses cybersecurity and compliance protocols, including authentication requirements, permissions, logging practices, and audit trails, because security and reliability failures are often rooted in the weak governance of shared data and shared control surfaces. Operational integration aligns workflows, handoffs, exception handling procedures, service recovery routines, and escalation paths so that execution is repeatable rather than improvised, especially when disruptions emerge under time pressure. Behavioral integration aligns incentives, expectations, and accountability through performance obligations, compliance routines, monitoring, and enforcement mechanisms, because critical supplier decisions about effort, reliability, and security investment are only partially observable. These dimensions cannot be treated as separate checklists, since a platform can have strong interface standards but still be fragile if recovery routines are weak, and it can have well documented workflows but still be exposed if suppliers have incentives to underinvest in resilience or to delay disclosure during incidents. Treating integration as a system rather than a set of disconnected components clarifies why platforms often struggle even after achieving technical connectivity.

Integration is challenging because platforms orchestrate interdependence under limited observability. Unlike a bilateral buyer-supplier relationship in which performance can be evaluated at a single interface, platforms assemble multiple specialized suppliers into a shared architecture where responsibilities are distributed and outcomes are jointly produced. Suppliers often possess private knowledge about their capabilities, their operational processes, and their security practices, and they control effort and investment choices that the platform cannot fully verify in real time. This information asymmetry becomes especially consequential when suppliers manage components that interact with shared customer data, core service logic, or critical operational routines, because small weaknesses can create disproportionate exposure. Interdependence creates spillovers, since failures can propagate through shared interfaces, shared workflows, and shared customer journeys, turning localized problems into ecosystem wide incidents. The platform bears reputational costs even when the immediate source of failure is a supplier, because the customer's attribution logic is end to end and brand based. The platform therefore confronts not only classic outsourcing hazards such as moral hazard and underinvestment, but also systemic externalities that arise because one supplier's shortcuts impose costs on the entire ecosystem.

As integration deepens, platforms also face stickiness and switching constraints that make the governance problem more acute. Integration typically produces co-specialized routines, customized interfaces, and accumulated data dependencies that raise switching costs and reduce the platform's credible threat of exit. A supplier's module may become intertwined with adjacent components, and replacement may require recertification, data migration, retraining, and operational reconfiguration that risks service disruption. These constraints can produce a misalignment between the platform's exposure and its formal contractual power, because legal exit may be feasible while operational exit is costly and risky. This misalignment increases the temptation for suppliers to shift risk to the platform by meeting minimum contractual metrics while underinvesting in less observable reliability and security practices. It also increases the likelihood that vulnerabilities accumulate over time, because weaknesses can remain latent until a shock reveals them. The practical implication is that integration should be understood as an ongoing discipline of governance and adaptation rather than a one-time onboarding exercise. A platform that treats integration as static connectivity will tend to discover fragility only when it is stress tested.

These features make governance integral to integration rather than an auxiliary managerial layer that can be added after connectivity is achieved. Because contracts are incomplete and monitoring is imperfect, platforms rely on both relational and formal governance to make supplier participation governable. Ability-based trust reduces friction by enabling the platform to form credible expectations about supplier competence and execution reliability, which is essential when coordination depends on discretion and judgment. Goodwill trust supports cooperation in situations where formal requirements cannot anticipate contingencies, including exception handling, timely disclosure, and willingness to prioritize ecosystem continuity when local incentives diverge. Contracts provide the backbone of accountability by specifying responsibilities and liabilities, service level expectations, reporting and audit rights, and escalation levers that deter opportunistic behavior. The design problem is configurational, because excessive reliance on formal safeguards can induce defensive compliance, while excessive reliance on trust can leave the platform exposed to free riding and underinvestment. This motivates the remainder of the chapter, which examines how platforms combine relational mechanisms such as trust with formal mechanisms such as contracts to make supplier participation governable, and how these governance arrangements are stress tested and adjusted when shocks such as data breaches reveal hidden vulnerabilities.

3.1.2 How Platform Supplier Integration Creates Value

Platform supplier integration creates value when it converts dispersed external capabilities into ecosystem performance that is scalable, dependable, and aligned with the platform's service promise. The value of platforms depends on more than transaction efficiency or the breadth of supplier participation, because customers experience platform performance as a single service and update beliefs about the platform based on that end-to-end experience. Failures are therefore value relevant not only because they impose direct costs, but also because they threaten trust, participation, and the network effects that underpin platform growth. Integration becomes economically meaningful when it strengthens the platform's ability to coordinate interdependent suppliers under uncertainty and to limit the probability that localized deviations become systemic shocks. This logic shifts attention away from integration as a cost-saving device and toward integration as a capability for producing dependable performance under complexity. It also implies that the value of integration is realized through both average performance improvements and reductions in downside exposure. The challenge for the platform is to design integration in a way that supports scale without sacrificing control and accountability.

On the technical dimension, integration creates value by stabilizing interfaces and information flows across organizational boundaries, thereby reducing coordination ambiguity and preventing errors from compounding across modules. Shared standards for data formats, interoperability specifications, and access control rules reduce the likelihood of mismatches that produce delays, rework, and service failures. Technical integration also creates observability through logging, audit trails, and standardized reporting, which supports monitoring and diagnosis when anomalies arise. Cybersecurity protocols are an essential part of this layer because suppliers often interact with shared customer data and shared infrastructure, and small weaknesses can become pathways for widespread exposure. By defining clear boundaries and control surfaces, technical integration allows the platform to enforce minimum security requirements, to detect suspicious behavior, and to coordinate remediation across parties. This is a direct value creation mechanism because it reduces both the frequency of everyday coordination failures and the tail risk of severe incidents. It also supports comparability across suppliers, which strengthens the platform's ability to evaluate performance, to allocate work, and to justify switching decisions when necessary.

On the operational dimension, integration creates value by turning coordination into routine-based execution that can scale without proportional increases in managerial oversight. Platforms often operate in environments where variability is unavoidable, including demand surges, exceptions in fulfillment, service disruptions, and compliance incidents. Operational integration reduces the cost of handling variability by standardizing handoffs, defining escalation paths, and establishing service recovery playbooks that coordinate response across organizational boundaries. When these routines are institutionalized, disruptions are detected earlier, responsibility boundaries are clearer, and response times are shorter, which reduces the probability that small incidents become platform-wide failures. Operational integration also supports learning by generating comparable data on incidents, root causes, and resolution outcomes, which can be used to refine standards and improve resilience over time. These routines create a disciplined cycle of detection, containment, and improvement that is difficult to sustain in loosely coordinated ecosystems. The value mechanism is therefore not only efficiency, but the creation of reliable coordination capacity that supports growth while preserving service consistency. A platform that scales supplier participation without scaling routines often experiences erosion in service quality, whereas integrated routines reduce the marginal coordination cost of adding suppliers and expanding categories.

On the behavioral dimension, integration creates value by aligning incentives and accountability so supplier decisions remain compatible with ecosystem reliability under limited observability. Many high consequence choices, such as investments in resilience engineering, patching discipline, and incident disclosure, are difficult to measure continuously and cannot be fully verified through audits. Trust and contracts therefore become central channels through which integration affects supplier behavior. Trust supports cooperation under uncertainty by enabling discretionary effort during exceptions, timely sharing of sensitive information, and rapid coordination when formal obligations are ambiguous. Ability-based trust is particularly valuable when supplier competence can be demonstrated and remains stable, because it reduces the need for costly monitoring and allows coordination to rely on credible expectations. Goodwill trust becomes salient during stress, when incentives to delay or to shift blame are strong, and when cooperative action is necessary to contain cascading failures. Contracts complement trust by defining responsibilities, allocating liability, specifying reporting and audit rights, and establishing enforcement levers that increase the credibility of accountability. The platform's challenge is to configure these mechanisms so that formal safeguards discourage opportunism without undermining goodwill and cooperative adaptation, since defensive compliance can itself create fragility by slowing response and discouraging transparency.

The interaction of these dimensions yields three broad value outcomes that matter to platform performance, even when the platform's objective is framed narrowly as operational efficiency. First, integration improves execution quality and efficiency by reducing delays, errors, and rework through standardized interfaces, synchronized workflows, and predictable behavioral expectations. Second, integration enables scalable growth by making onboarding repeatable and modular, allowing supplier expansion across categories and geographies without proportional increases in coordination costs or erosion of customer experience. Third, integration improves risk-adjusted performance by reducing the probability and impact of severe negative events that can destabilize the ecosystem, because integrated monitoring, incident routines, and governance structures strengthen detection, containment, and recovery. This third outcome becomes particularly visible when shocks reveal hidden vulnerabilities and force platforms to update beliefs about supplier reliability. A data breach is not simply an operational failure, but an information event that reveals weaknesses in controls, compliance routines, and supplier behavior. Platforms respond by tightening standards, increasing monitoring, revising contractual safeguards, reallocating activity toward suppliers with stronger security capability, and, in some cases, replacing suppliers. Integration is valuable because it makes these responses feasible without jeopardizing service continuity. This motivates the remainder of the chapter, which examines how platforms adjust governance mechanisms and supplier portfolios when shocks such as data breaches make ecosystem risk salient.

3.1.3 Chapter Framework

This chapter is organized to move the reader from a definition of platform supplier integration to the governance foundations that make integration workable, and then to the mechanisms through which integration becomes value relevant when shocks reveal hidden vulnerabilities. The ordering reflects the claim that connectivity alone does not produce dependable ecosystem performance, because platform service delivery depends on coordinated behavior across interdependent suppliers whose actions are only partially observable. Integration is framed as a capability that allows platforms to render supplier relationships governable by ensuring suppliers can be effectively coordinated, monitored, and held accountable, ultimately driving the operational reliability and performance of the entire ecosystem. Governance is not presented as a purely legal or contractual idea, but as an operational property of the ecosystem that depends on standards, routines, and governance mechanisms working together. By framing integration as a capability that coordinates suppliers, this chapter connects micro-level governance mechanisms, such as trust-building and contracting, to macro-level outcomes, including enhanced system reliability, trust, increased participation, and network effects, all of which drive platform success. It creates a coherent conceptual bridge between how platforms manage suppliers and how platforms sustain value creation over time. The goal of the chapter is to develop this bridge in a way that clarifies why integration choices matter most when ecosystems are stress tested. This argument is synthesized in Fig. 3.1, which presents the chapter's core framework: integration as a three-stage orchestration process. It begins with the foundational Integration Elements—the autonomous participants and dispersed resources that constitute the ecosystem's raw material. The platform, as the orchestrator, must then enact a suite of Integration Mechanisms—governance, coordination, and allocation/reconfiguration—to shape behaviors, align workflows, and manage the supplier portfolio. The effectiveness of this orchestration is ultimately realized as multi-dimensional Value Creation, including technical robustness, operational efficiency, and risk-adjusted performance. The chapter is structured to unpack this framework.

Section 3.1 establishes the conceptual foundation for this bridge. It defines platform supplier integration as more than linking suppliers to a digital interface or enabling transactions, emphasizing integration across technical, operational, and behavioral layers that jointly shape end-to-end service outcomes. It also motivates why integration is inherently value relevant in platform settings: because

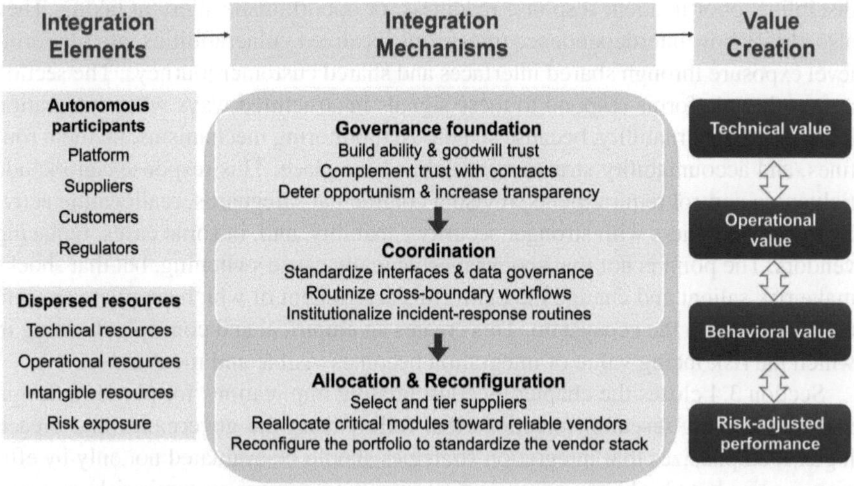

Fig. 3.1 Framework for Platform Supplier Integration and Value Creation

interdependence can amplify small failures into system-wide exposure, integration matters not only for average efficiency and scalability, but also for risk-adjusted performance and the credibility of the platform's service promise. This section sets the stage for understanding how integration mechanisms (governance, coordination, and reconfiguration) interact to create value, particularly in the face of shocks. By establishing the value logic early, we clarify how these mechanisms contribute to improved performance, resilience, and long-term platform success.

Section 3.2 develops the governance foundations that make platform supplier integration workable. It reframes integration as a joint problem of coordination and control in a networked environment where suppliers are interdependent, heterogeneous, and only partially observable. Governance plays a dual role: it enables cooperation across interdependent suppliers to ensure efficient end-to-end performance, and it prevents opportunism by creating mechanisms that limit discretion and expose potential risks. The section explains why governance is necessarily multi-layered. Relational mechanisms support cooperation and adaptation under uncertainty, whereas formal mechanisms clarify responsibilities, create credible accountability, and provide enforcement levers when incentives diverge. Trust and contracts are treated as configurations rather than simple substitutes, because their interaction shapes whether suppliers cooperate, comply defensively, or exploit ambiguity. This vocabulary equips the reader to understand why some integration efforts scale smoothly while others accumulate conflict, fragility, and escalating monitoring costs.

Section 3.3 shifts from governance foundations to integration outcomes under shock, using data breaches as a revealing context for platform supplier integration. A breach is treated as an information event that forces platforms and organizations to update beliefs about supplier reliability and to reassess the risk embedded in their supplier portfolio. Breaches reveal vulnerabilities that may have remained latent under normal conditions, such as weak access controls, inadequate patching discipline, poor incident response readiness, or opportunistic shortcut taking. They also clarify how interdependence transforms localized vulnerabilities into platform-level exposure through shared interfaces and shared customer journeys. The section argues that platforms respond to these signals in structured ways when integration has created governability, because standards, monitoring mechanisms, incident routines, and accountability structures are already in place. This response can include tightening control requirements, revising contractual safeguards, reallocating activity toward suppliers with stronger security capability, and, in some cases, replacing vendors. The point is not that shocks mechanically cause switching, but that shocks make risk salient and change the platform's assessment of which suppliers are safe to rely on within the ecosystem. This creates an empirical and conceptual setting in which the risk facing value of integration becomes visible and measurable.

Section 3.4 closes the chapter by consolidating implications for platform design and by outlining research directions that follow from the governance and breach logic. It emphasizes that integration strategies should be evaluated not only by efficiency gains but also by the ecosystem's capacity to manage systemic risk, preserve trust, and sustain participation over time. It also highlights tradeoffs that platforms face as they scale, such as the tension between openness and control, the balance between modular expansion and concentration around highly capable suppliers, and the choice between flexibility in supplier participation and discipline in security requirements. These tradeoffs motivate open questions about how governance architectures evolve as platforms learn from incidents, how compliance and cybersecurity pressures reshape supplier ecosystems and selection criteria, and how platforms design integration to preserve the ability to reconfigure without destabilizing service continuity. The chapter's framework thus sets up a coherent agenda in which supplier integration is treated as a capability for managing interdependence under uncertainty rather than as a technical feature of platform infrastructure. It also positions shock contexts as revealing events that expose latent fragilities and illuminate the governance mechanisms that distinguish robust ecosystems from fragile ones. The next step is therefore to specify the governance foundations in detail, since those foundations determine whether integration produces scalable reliability or scalable exposure.

3.2 Governance of Platform Suppliers

In this section, we will examine the governance mechanisms that play a crucial role in ensuring the effective integration and management of platform suppliers. Governance in the context of platform supplier integration refers to the systems, rules, and practices that guide the interactions between platforms and their suppliers, ensuring that these relationships are productive, efficient, and aligned with the platform's strategic objectives. Effective governance mechanisms help mitigate risks such as supplier opportunism, maintain operational stability, and foster long-term partnerships that create value for both the platform and its suppliers.

We begin by discussing the role of trust and contracts as key governance mechanisms. Following this, we will explore the specific ways in which these mechanisms interact and influence supplier relationships in the platform ecosystem.

3.2.1 Ability and Goodwill Trust

In platform supplier governance, trust is widely recognized as a central mechanism for fostering cooperation, reducing opportunistic behavior, and minimizing transaction costs. Since Williamson (1985) seminal articulation of transaction cost economics, scholars have emphasized that trust serves as a critical informal governance mechanism that compensates for contractual incompleteness and bounded rationality (Das & Teng, 1998). This role becomes particularly salient in platform-based business models, where repeated interactions and long-term collaboration are essential for sustained value creation (Williamson, 1985; Oliveira et al., 2025). By shaping expectations about partner behavior, trust reduces platforms' reliance on excessive contractual safeguards, enabling more efficient coordination with suppliers. Trust, thus, serves not only as an instrument for risk mitigation but also as a means for fostering the relational embeddedness necessary for effective governance in platform ecosystems (Beer et al., 2018).

Consistent with the relational governance literature, trust is commonly conceptualized as comprising two distinct but complementary dimensions: Ability Trust and Goodwill Trust, each reflecting different cognitive and motivational assessments of exchange partners (Poppo et al., 2008; Lumineau, 2017). Ability Trust addresses the perception that a supplier has the necessary competencies to execute tasks, whereas Goodwill Trust focuses on the supplier's intention to act in the best interests of the platform. This distinction is crucial because it allows platforms to address two different types of uncertainty inherent in platform-supplier relationships: execution uncertainty and behavioral uncertainty. Ability Trust primarily mitigates the former, focusing on whether suppliers can fulfill their roles, while Goodwill Trust mitigates the latter, ensuring that suppliers will act cooperatively and avoid opportunistic behavior.

Ability Trust refers to the platform's confidence in a supplier's competence to fulfill contractual obligations, meet performance standards, and deliver products or services of expected quality. This form of trust is grounded in assessments of suppliers' technical expertise, operational capabilities, and prior performance records, aligning with transaction cost economics' emphasis on capability evaluation under conditions of bounded rationality (Williamson, 1985). When platforms perceive suppliers as highly capable, they are less inclined to engage in intensive monitoring or detailed ex ante specification, thus lowering governance and coordination costs (Poppo et al., 2008). This shift from direct monitoring to competence-based trust allows platforms to allocate fewer resources to operational oversight and more toward strategic activities, such as exploring new market opportunities or building ecosystem capabilities.

Importantly, Ability Trust mitigates execution uncertainty, regarding whether suppliers are technically and operationally able to perform as required, rather than uncertainty about suppliers' intentions (Li, 2013). In platform ecosystems, where suppliers often enjoy substantial operational autonomy, such execution-focused trust allows platforms to economize on direct supervision while still maintaining confidence in performance outcomes. As a result, governance attention can be reallocated from routine oversight toward higher-level coordination and system integration, which is vital for fostering inter-organizational collaboration at scale.

In platform business models, suppliers frequently occupy a pivotal role in delivering core offerings that directly shape the platform's value proposition. Trust in suppliers' operational competence therefore has implications that extend beyond dyadic efficiency. As Liu et al. (2009) argue, confidence in a partner's capabilities allows focal firms to shift managerial attention away from routine supervision toward strategic activities such as market expansion, ecosystem orchestration, and innovation. High levels of Ability Trust thus enable platforms to respond more flexibly to market changes, as confidence in supplier competence reduces the perceived need for continuous oversight and renegotiation. This shift is particularly important in environments where suppliers' abilities are critical to innovation and maintaining competitive advantage in rapidly evolving markets (Chen et al., 2016).

Moreover, in multi-sided platform ecosystems, Ability Trust facilitates scalability. As platforms expand their supplier base, it becomes increasingly impractical to apply uniform, intensive monitoring mechanisms. By relying on competence-based trust, platforms can grow without proportionally increasing governance complexity, thus sustaining efficiency at scale. This scalability is crucial in platform-based models, where the growth of the platform is often dependent on network effects and the expansion of supplier networks.

The importance of Ability Trust becomes even more pronounced in environments characterized by rapid technological change. Prior research highlights that, under conditions of technological turbulence, firms increasingly depend on external partners' specialized knowledge and adaptive capabilities (Carson et al., 2006). In such contexts, detailed contractual specifications often become obsolete quickly, making rigid control mechanisms less effective. Trusting suppliers' abilities to innovate and adapt allows platforms to cope with uncertainty without resorting to overly prescriptive contractual control, a pattern documented in buyer–supplier relationships operating under high task complexity (Cao & Lumineau, 2015).

At the same time, technological turbulence amplifies the strategic value of suppliers' capabilities, increasing platforms' exposure to dependency risks. Ability Trust therefore plays a dual role: it supports adaptive coordination while simultaneously shaping how platforms perceive and tolerate performance deviations during periods of change (Andrade-Rojas et al., 2024). In a highly dynamic technological environment, where suppliers' innovative capacity directly influences platform competitiveness, Ability Trust fosters a collaborative atmosphere that allows both parties to adapt jointly to shifting market conditions without relying on overly stringent contracts.

While Ability Trust focuses on what suppliers can do, Goodwill Trust centers on what suppliers intend to do. Drawing on social exchange theory and relational governance perspectives, Goodwill Trust reflects the platform's belief that suppliers will act in good faith, refrain from opportunistic behavior, and prioritize the long-term interests of the relationship even when formal safeguards are incomplete (Malhotra & Murnighan, 2002; Lumineau, 2017). This dimension of trust emphasizes suppliers' integrity, benevolence, and commitment to fairness rather than their technical competence.

Goodwill Trust thus addresses behavioral uncertainty, which arises when suppliers possess discretion and asymmetric information (Oliveira et al., 2025). In platform settings, such discretion is pervasive, as suppliers often retain control over internal processes, data usage, and innovation decisions. By shaping expectations about suppliers' intentions, Goodwill Trust reduces concerns that such discretion will be exploited for short-term gain. This, in turn, enables platforms and suppliers to engage in more flexible, collaborative behavior, particularly when challenges arise that fall outside of strict contractual boundaries.

Goodwill Trust is especially salient in long-term platform–supplier relationships, where not all contingencies can be contractually specified ex ante. Weber and Mayer (2011) note, relational expectations about fair dealing often substitute for detailed contractual provisions when uncertainty is high. In situations involving market volatility, regulatory shifts, or unexpected technological disruption, suppliers perceived as high in goodwill are more likely to communicate transparently, share information proactively, and collaborate on adaptive solutions, even in the absence of explicit contractual obligations. This relational orientation ensures that, even in the absence of formal controls, suppliers act in ways that benefit the relationship in the long term, reducing the risk of opportunistic behavior.

Such cooperative behavior contributes not only to dyadic stability but also to ecosystem-level resilience. In platform environments where suppliers are interdependent, goodwill-driven coordination helps prevent localized disruptions from cascading across the network (Bakshi & Kleindorfer, 2009). In platform ecosystems, where the interdependence among suppliers creates a networked system, Goodwill Trust contributes to collective resilience, stabilizing the broader ecosystem.

Although analytically distinct, Ability Trust and Goodwill Trust are deeply intertwined in platform supplier governance. Prior research emphasizes that effective governance rarely relies on a single dimension of trust; rather, it emerges from the interaction of competence-based and intention-based assessments (Poppo et al., 2008). When Ability Trust is high, platforms are confident that suppliers can meet performance expectations; when Goodwill Trust is also strong, platforms are willing to share sensitive information and grant greater discretion, thereby deepening collaboration.

This interaction becomes particularly consequential in volatile environments. Under technological turbulence, while Ability Trust ensures that suppliers possess the necessary expertise to adapt, Goodwill Trust enables rapid coordination and joint problem-solving when unforeseen contingencies arise (Carson et al., 2006). Together, these two forms of trust allow platforms and suppliers to navigate uncertainty more effectively, aligning short-term adjustments with long-term relational goals and preparing the relational foundation upon which subsequent contractual governance mechanisms are constructed.

3.2.2 *The Role of Contracts*

While trust plays a crucial role in platform-supplier governance, contracts are indispensable tools that provide formal structures for managing complex, uncertain relationships between platforms and suppliers. Contracts in platform ecosystems are not just formal agreements or enforcement mechanisms; they also serve as framing devices that shape how parties interpret, process, and respond to uncertainty. By framing the governance structure and defining expectations, contracts help platforms and suppliers navigate risks and maintain long-term cooperation despite uncertainty and changing conditions (Weber & Mayer, 2011; Fahn & Zanarone, 2022).

In platform ecosystems, where multiple suppliers with varying levels of dependency and capabilities interact, uncertainty is pervasive. Contracts, according to information processing theory (IPT), function as framing devices that guide how both platforms and suppliers interpret and manage uncertainty in their relationships. This framing aspect of contracts is crucial because it influences supplier behavior and performance evaluation within the context of platform operations (Malhotra, 2004). When both the platform and supplier face rapidly changing market conditions, technological disruptions, or competitive pressures, contracts allow for a shift in focus from rigid compliance to more adaptive governance structures (Weber & Mayer, 2011).

The framing function of contracts goes beyond providing operational guidelines; it also shapes how both parties perceive their mutual dependence and responsibilities. This aspect is particularly important in platform ecosystems, where interdependence increases the risk of opportunism and misunderstandings. By clearly outlining responsibilities, contracts help align both parties' goals and facilitate smoother coordination across organizational boundaries. In highly dynamic markets, contracts act as dynamic tools that can evolve as circumstances change, ensuring that the governance framework remains relevant and responsive to emerging risks (Weber & Mayer, 2011).

For instance, platforms often operate in environments characterized by technological turbulence, where innovation and change are constant. In such contexts, contracts play a critical role in ensuring that suppliers remain aligned with platform goals while retaining the flexibility to adapt to unforeseen challenges. Coordination contracts, in particular, are designed to facilitate joint problem-solving and information sharing, allowing for ongoing adjustments in response to environmental shifts. These contracts do not impose rigid rules but instead establish guidelines for collaboration, mutual adjustment, and adaptive governance that evolve as circumstances change (Malhotra & Murnighan, 2002; Mooi & Ghosh, 2010). Flexibility is crucial in such settings, as rigid contracts might result in missed opportunities or an inability to pivot when external factors change rapidly. Therefore, coordination contracts offer a more nuanced approach, encouraging responsiveness while maintaining core commitments.

Control contracts are designed to address execution uncertainty, which is particularly relevant in platform ecosystems where suppliers' actions are difficult to monitor and outcomes are hard to specify in advance (Poppo et al., 2008; Schepker et al., 2014). These contracts typically include detailed provisions regarding performance standards, penalties for non-compliance, and delivery timeframes. Control contracts enforce specific behaviors by setting clear rules and consequences for deviations from agreed-upon terms (Poppo et al., 2008).

In platform governance, control contracts are especially useful when suppliers' actions are difficult to observe or when platforms face high risks of opportunism. For example, when platforms depend on suppliers for crucial components, software, or services that directly influence the platform's value proposition, control contracts ensure that suppliers meet performance standards and deadlines without exploiting their market position or the platform's dependency on them (Cao & Lumineau, 2015). These contracts effectively reduce opportunism by setting clear boundaries and formalizing expectations. However, platforms must balance the degree of control they impose to prevent diminishing supplier motivation and trust. Excessive enforcement can inadvertently create a competitive disadvantage by stifling the creative autonomy of suppliers, which is particularly important in platform ecosystems where innovation is a key competitive advantage.

Execution uncertainty refers to the risk that a supplier may fail to meet agreed-upon standards or deviate from performance expectations. By clearly defining these expectations and penalties for non-compliance, control contracts address this risk directly. However, execution uncertainty is not static; it fluctuates with market conditions and the strategic importance of specific suppliers within the broader platform ecosystem. For instance, in more stable market conditions, the risk of execution failure may be low, and platforms may not need as strict a contractual framework. However, during periods of high market volatility or technological disruption, these contracts serve as critical mechanisms to ensure suppliers remain committed to the platform's operational requirements, even when external pressures might induce opportunistic behavior (Cao & Lumineau, 2015).

However, while control contracts are highly effective in reducing opportunism, they also have certain limitations. The detailed and prescriptive nature of control contracts can constrain supplier autonomy and reduce their ability to innovate, leading to lower levels of collaboration and mutual trust. When platforms impose excessive control, suppliers may feel restricted and less motivated to take risks or propose innovative solutions. As a result, control contracts, while preventing short-term opportunism, can limit long-term relational development by narrowing the scope for creative contributions from suppliers (Lumineau, 2017). Over-control can ultimately harm the very relationships it aims to protect by reducing suppliers' willingness to invest in collaborative ventures, particularly in rapidly changing technological landscapes.

In contrast to control contracts, coordination contracts are designed to promote flexibility, innovation, and long-term collaboration between platforms and suppliers. Rather than providing highly detailed specifications or penalties, coordination contracts are more general and emphasize joint problem-solving and collaborative adaptation. These contracts provide platforms and suppliers with the latitude to adjust their roles and responsibilities as market conditions change, while still maintaining a shared understanding of their strategic objectives (Mooi & Ghosh, 2010; Feng et al., 2013).

Coordination contracts are particularly important in platform ecosystems where innovation, co-development, and shared knowledge creation are critical. In these settings, contracts focus on fostering long-term relationships and ensuring that suppliers are incentivized to collaborate rather than simply comply. These contracts may include collaborative provisions, such as joint development agreements, sharing of intellectual property, and co-investment in new projects, to enable innovation and mutual adaptation to changing circumstances. The primary advantage of coordination contracts is that they allow both parties to remain aligned without rigidly specifying all aspects of the relationship in advance (Poppo et al., 2008; Oliveira et al., 2025).

Coordination contracts do not merely focus on minimizing risks; they are oriented toward fostering innovative collaboration and enhancing the adaptability of the partnership. By encouraging knowledge sharing and long-term investments, these contracts create a shared understanding that helps both parties navigate technological uncertainty and market volatility. In platform ecosystems where competition is based not just on product offerings but on continuous innovation, such coordination mechanisms allow platforms and suppliers to align their strategic goals, ensuring the long-term success of both parties.

However, the success of coordination contracts relies heavily on strong goodwill trust. Without goodwill trust as a foundation, these contracts can become ineffective, as suppliers may perceive flexibility as an opportunity to exploit the platform or act opportunistically. Therefore, coordination contracts are most effective when goodwill trust has already been established, allowing both parties to engage in collaborative innovation and risk-sharing (Lumineau, 2017). Goodwill trust, in this sense, is a crucial enabler of flexibility, as it reduces the risks of opportunism that might arise in the absence of strict monitoring.

3.2.3 Supplier Opportunism Governance Design in Platforms

Trust and contracts are both essential governance mechanisms in platform–supplier relationships, and their interaction is often what determines whether integration curbs opportunism and supports collaboration. Under high uncertainty or market volatility, contracts do more than specify obligations. They shape how trust is enacted by framing expectations about disclosure, responsiveness, and acceptable performance, thereby steering supplier behavior toward outcomes that protect platform objectives. From an information processing perspective, contracts function as moderating devices that condition the behavioral consequences of Ability Trust and Goodwill Trust. High Ability Trust increases the platform's confidence in a supplier's execution capability, which can make control-oriented provisions more attractive for securing reliability and meeting performance standards. When Goodwill Trust is also strong, platforms can rely more on coordination-oriented provisions that organize joint problem solving and mutual adaptation, because cooperative intent reduces the risk that flexibility will be exploited. This contractual moderation helps platforms maintain a workable balance between execution reliability and behavioral cooperation, enabling adaptation without inviting opportunistic exploitation (Carson et al., 2006). The need for such calibration becomes sharper under asymmetric dependence, where suppliers with greater bargaining power can leverage informational advantages and discretion, including renegotiating terms, withholding operationally critical information, or shading performance in ways that are difficult to verify (Li, 2013). In these conditions, governance effectiveness hinges on configuring contractual safeguards and relational mechanisms so that accountability remains credible while coordination retains enough flexibility to function under uncertainty.

Information asymmetry also exacerbates the risks of opportunism. In many cases, suppliers hold proprietary knowledge about their operations, capabilities, and constraints. This information asymmetry gives suppliers the power to make decisions that favor their own interests, potentially at the platform's expense. For example, suppliers might overstate their capabilities to gain favorable terms in contracts or hide performance failures, knowing that the platform is unable to fully verify their claims. This can be particularly damaging in rapidly evolving markets, where a supplier's claimed expertise may not align with actual performance. Without effective governance mechanisms, these actions can cause significant harm to the platform, especially in highly competitive or rapidly evolving markets, where being misled by a supplier can have severe consequences for market positioning and future growth.

To effectively address opportunism, platform operators must design governance structures that minimize risks and align incentives between the platform and its suppliers. As noted by Williamson (1985) in his seminal work on transaction cost economics, governance mechanisms can take many forms, ranging from formal contracts to informal trust-based relationships. However, relying on any single governance mechanism in isolation can be detrimental. A combination of formal governance (contracts) and informal governance (trust) is necessary for mitigating opportunism in platform ecosystems. The dual approach ensures that platform suppliers are held accountable, while also promoting long-term cooperation and mutual adaptation in response to changing market conditions.

Contracts are one of the most powerful tools for formalizing expectations, specifying supplier obligations, and creating mechanisms for accountability. Contracts in platform ecosystems must be designed to reduce both execution uncertainty and behavioral uncertainty. Execution uncertainty arises when suppliers are unsure about how to meet performance standards, or when the platform is unsure whether the supplier will deliver as expected. Behavioral uncertainty occurs when there are doubts about the supplier's intentions, i.e., whether the supplier will act opportunistically to exploit the platform for short-term gain.

Control contracts are often used to address execution uncertainty. These contracts are highly detailed and prescriptive, specifying performance targets, penalties for non-compliance, and deadlines. Control contracts are particularly effective in reducing the risk of delayed deliveries, substandard goods, or failure to meet service level agreements (SLAs). However, as Poppo et al. (2008) point out, these contracts can be rigid and limiting, restricting the supplier's autonomy and preventing innovation. Over-reliance on control contracts may stifle creativity and prevent suppliers from making adaptive changes when faced with new opportunities or challenges. For instance, strict contracts might hinder suppliers' ability to innovate or experiment with new solutions that could benefit both parties in the long run.

On the other hand, coordination contracts help address behavioral uncertainty by promoting collaboration and information sharing between the platform and its suppliers. These contracts are less detailed and more flexible, allowing for ongoing adjustments to the terms as market conditions change. Coordination contracts emphasize joint problem-solving, fostering an environment of mutual trust and cooperation rather than mere compliance. Coordination contracts allow platforms and suppliers to adapt to changes in technology, market demands, and external factors without renegotiating the entire contract (Mooi & Ghosh, 2010; Feng et al., 2013) trust must work in tandem to ensure that suppliers remain committed to the platform's long-term goals while also being held accountable for performance (Cao & Lumineau, 2015). The interaction between trust and contracts plays a central role in managing opportunism in platform-supplier relationships. In situations of high uncertainty or market volatility, contracts serve as moderators that influence how trust is enacted. IPT suggests that contracts not only clarify the rules of engagement but also shape how trust-based behaviors manifest. In platforms where ability trust is high, control contracts are often preferred to ensure performance reliability. However, in platforms where goodwill trust is strong, coordination contracts may be more effective, as they emphasize collaboration and mutual adaptation over rigid enforcement (Carson et al., 2006).

This dual approach of leveraging both trust and contracts allows platforms to manage both execution and behavioral risks simultaneously. Contracts provide the formal structure needed to address execution uncertainty, while trust fosters a collaborative environment that encourages long-term, mutually beneficial relationships (Moshtari, 2016). As such, governance design in platform ecosystems must integrate both formal and informal mechanisms to address the complexities of supplier opportunism and ensure sustainable cooperation. Effectively mitigating supplier opportunism requires a comprehensive governance approach that combines formal and informal mechanisms. Control contracts help manage execution uncertainty, while coordination contracts foster innovation and long-term collaboration. Trust, especially goodwill trust, enhances the effectiveness of these contracts by reducing the need for excessive monitoring and increasing flexibility in the relationship. The interaction between contracts and trust is crucial to managing opportunism and fostering a cooperative environment in platform ecosystems. By leveraging both governance mechanisms, platforms can ensure that suppliers remain aligned with the platform's strategic goals while adapting to dynamic market conditions and technological changes. This holistic approach to governance provides a strong foundation for sustainable innovation, adaptability, and long-term success in platform ecosystems.

3.3 Value Creation: Security-Driven Supplier Selection After Data Breaches

This section explores the value creation mechanisms that emerge from security-driven supplier selection, particularly in the wake of data breaches. The rise of digital platforms and increased reliance on data-driven services has made information security a crucial factor in vendor selection. When platforms experience data breaches, they are forced to reassess their supplier relationships and make strategic adjustments to safeguard customer data, maintain regulatory compliance, and restore trust.

We begin by discussing the impact of data breaches on supplier selection, exploring how breaches influence the decision-making process and what strategic shifts occur in the aftermath. We also examine the mechanisms of value creation that emerge from these strategic changes, focusing on how platforms can use the experience of data breaches to strengthen supplier relationships and enhance operational resilience.

3.3.1 Introduction

In today's rapidly evolving digital landscape, data breaches have emerged as one of the most critical risks for organizations, particularly for those operating in interconnected platform ecosystems. With the increasing reliance on third-party suppliers for essential services and data management, information security has become an integral component of supply chain management. The rise in data breaches has exposed significant vulnerabilities within platform supply chains, prompting businesses to reconsider their supplier relationships and security measures. This chapter explores the impact of data breaches on supplier selection within platform supply chains, specifically focusing on how these shifts in supplier choices contribute to long-term value creation. It examines the connection between security-driven supplier changes and broader strategic outcomes such as operational resilience, financial stability, and the preservation of customer trust.

Platform ecosystems are inherently vulnerable to disruptions caused by data breaches. These ecosystems rely heavily on third-party vendors for a variety of services, ranging from data storage to customer management, making them particularly sensitive to security threats. Supplier selection in these ecosystems has traditionally been driven by factors such as cost, quality, delivery times, and service reliability (Verma & Pullman, 1998). However, as platforms become more digitized and data-dependent, the risks associated with information security breaches have grown significantly. Organizations are increasingly realizing that the criteria used to select suppliers must evolve to reflect the growing importance of data security and its direct impact on the entire platform ecosystem.

A data breach does not solely affect the organization that experiences it but can have a ripple effect throughout the interconnected network of suppliers, customers, and partners that form the platform's ecosystem. When a data breach occurs, it exposes vulnerabilities not only in the affected company but also in its entire supply chain. The risks of compromised customer data, operational downtime, regulatory fines, and reputational damage can disrupt the platform's entire ecosystem (Dhillon et al., 2016; Ghadge et al., 2020). For platform operators, minimizing these risks requires a fundamental reassessment of supplier relationships, with a renewed emphasis on security. This shift towards more secure suppliers is not just an operational necessity; it is a proactive strategy to mitigate future risks and create sustainable value for the entire platform ecosystem.

When a platform experiences a data breach, the immediate reaction often includes re-evaluating the security practices of current suppliers. This process of reallocation, shifting spending from high-risk, less secure vendors to those with stronger security measures, directly impacts the platform's overall risk profile. By making these changes, platform operators can lower the expected cost of failures, which could arise from poor product quality, non-compliance with regulatory standards, or legal disputes. Suppliers with poor security practices are more likely to experience breaches, which can result in data loss, legal challenges, and substantial financial penalties. The costs associated with these failures go beyond immediate financial losses and can damage the platform's reputation, erode customer trust, and undermine service reliability.

In contrast, by selecting vendors with robust security systems, platforms can effectively reduce these risks and safeguard their operational integrity. This proactive shift in supplier choices is a key element of value creation. It allows platforms to protect service reliability, prevent future operational disruptions, and preserve customer trust, all of which contribute to long-term sustainability and growth. The reliability of service is particularly crucial in the platform economy. Service disruptions caused by security breaches can lead to downtime, lost business opportunities, and long-term customer attrition. By ensuring that vendors adhere to stringent security measures, platforms mitigate the risk of such disruptions, leading to more stable service delivery and reducing the likelihood of future security failures (Benaroch & Chernobai, 2017).

Customer trust is an invaluable asset in platform ecosystems. Data breaches significantly undermine this trust, as customers become increasingly concerned about the security of their personal information. Switching to suppliers with proven security measures helps restore confidence in the platform, thereby reducing the likelihood of customer churn and improving retention rates. The ability to preserve customer trust in the wake of a data breach is vital to the platform's continued success. In the long term, maintaining this trust contributes to the platform's ability to scale, attract new users, and maintain a competitive edge in the market. This process of restoring trust and ensuring service continuity through better supplier selection is a fundamental mechanism for value creation in the platform economy.

The reallocation of resources to more secure vendors is not merely a reaction to a crisis; it represents a strategic investment in the long-term sustainability of the platform. By selecting vendors with better security measures, platforms reduce their exposure to downside risks, including the significant financial costs that can arise from security failures. These risks include regulatory fines, customer compensation, and reputational repair, all of which can be particularly damaging in the context of platform-based businesses, where customer loyalty and trust are crucial for long-term success (Sullivan, 2010). Reducing these risks helps stabilize cash flows, ensuring that the platform operates in a more predictable and financially secure environment. This stability is essential in platform ecosystems, where unpredictable disruptions, whether from data breaches or operational failures, can cause significant volatility. By prioritizing secure suppliers, platforms protect their financial stability, ensuring consistent revenues even in the face of external shocks.

The stabilization of cash flows becomes a key mechanism through which platforms create long-term value. It provides the financial foundation necessary for future investments, expansion, and innovation, while also ensuring that the platform remains resilient to future challenges (Kannan & Tan, 2002; Chai & Ngai, 2020). When a platform successfully manages its security risks and maintains stable service delivery, it not only protects itself from immediate disruptions but also strengthens its long-term sustainability. These actions enable platforms to foster continued growth and innovation, ensuring that the platform can adapt to new market conditions and emerging challenges without being undermined by recurring security failures.

One of the most significant ways in which security-driven supplier selection contributes to long-term value is through the enhancement of network effects. Network effects are critical to platform-based businesses, where the value of the platform increases as more users, suppliers, and partners join the ecosystem. The more participants there are, the more valuable the platform becomes for each individual user. However, these network effects can only be sustained if the platform operates securely and reliably. Data breaches, by introducing vulnerabilities into the system, can undermine the integrity of the platform and disrupt the very network effects that drive growth. By ensuring that suppliers meet robust security standards, platforms can protect the sustainability of their network effects, ensuring that the ecosystem continues to grow without being undermined by external security threats.

The platform's ability to maintain its ecosystem sustainability is closely tied to the stability and trustworthiness of its supply chain. When platforms select suppliers based on their ability to meet stringent security standards, the entire ecosystem becomes more resilient to future risks. This resilience is critical not only for maintaining current network effects but also for fostering new growth opportunities.

Secure supplier relationships enable the platform to onboard new users and partners without introducing additional risks into the ecosystem, thereby expanding the network and reinforcing the platform's competitive advantage in the market (Kim et al., 2006; Ghadge et al., 2020).

Thus, the strategic shift in supplier selection following data breaches is not merely a defensive action but is integral to value creation within platform ecosystems. By reallocating spend from high-risk suppliers to more secure ones, platforms can reduce the expected costs of failure, protect service reliability, and preserve customer trust, each of which contributes to long-term value. These risk-adjusted gains enhance the platform's financial stability, support its network effects, and ensure the sustainability of the ecosystem. In essence, the process of supplier selection, driven by the imperative to manage security risks post-breach, is a fundamental mechanism of value creation for platform-based businesses. Therefore, platform operators must consider information security not just as a compliance requirement but as a central element of their supplier selection strategy, driving both short-term resilience and long-term growth.

3.3.2 Hypotheses

Platform supply chains increasingly depend on third-party technology and service suppliers to deliver core functions that users experience as a single, integrated service. In contemporary platform ecosystems, suppliers do not merely provide standardized inputs at arm's length. They operate inside the platform's service architecture through APIs, shared data pipelines, identity and access management layers, and tightly coupled operational routines. This embeddedness creates a distinctive governance problem: external suppliers often possess specialized knowledge and retain discretion over practices that matter for reliability and security, yet failures are attributed to the platform as the accountable orchestrator. Supplier governance in platform supply chains therefore goes beyond contracting for performance. It concerns how interdependence is rendered governable under limited observability so that the platform can preserve service continuity, protect stakeholder trust, and sustain scaling.

Data breaches are a particularly revealing shock in this environment because they turn latent risk into salient, system-wide exposure. Beyond immediate operational disruption, a breach signals that the platform's safeguards and oversight routines have not prevented vulnerabilities from materializing, and it raises concerns that similar weaknesses remain embedded in the broader supplier ecosystem. From an attention-based view of the firm, such expectancy-violating failures redirect managerial attention away from routine objectives and toward the threatened domain, making information security a focal issue rather than a background constraint (Ocasio, 1997; Sullivan, 2010; Benaroch & Chernobai, 2017). Breaches can puncture an organization's false sense of security, reveal hidden vulnerabilities, and heighten decision-makers' concern with security performance, thereby encouraging more decisive remediation actions (Nikkhah & Grover, 2022). Consistent with this logic, organizations often overweight cost and routine performance in vendor selection under normal conditions, but security incidents can shift priorities toward risk containment and governance credibility when security becomes salient.

A breach also changes the informational environment in which supplier selection occurs. Security capability and incident response discipline are difficult to observe ex ante. Platforms can audit and specify minimum requirements, yet many behaviors remain unverifiable until stress-tested, including incident disclosure speed, transparency in sharing forensic information, patching discipline, and coordination during recovery. This opacity matters because supplier security standards are often not outwardly visible, so decision-makers must rely on cues to infer security performance when reconfiguring supplier relationships under uncertainty (Gomulya & Mishina, 2017). When risk becomes salient, supplier selection becomes a governance lever rather than a procurement routine: platforms can redraw boundaries of privileged access, tighten accountability, simplify incident response coordination, and provide credible signals of corrective action to external stakeholders.

In this setting, breaches are expected to trigger systematic changes along three conceptually distinct dimensions of supplier selection. The first is whether platforms discontinue incumbent supplier relationships, reflecting governance escalation through relationship discontinuation. The second is the direction of switching conditional on change, reflecting a preference for suppliers whose security capability is more credible and legible under uncertainty. The third is whether platforms redesign sourcing structure toward greater concentration, reflecting a structural response aimed at reducing complexity and improving controllability. Distinguishing these dimensions is important because they represent different governance actions. A platform can replace a supplier without simplifying its overall architecture, or it can consolidate suppliers to improve oversight even if individual suppliers are not replaced.

A breach elevates the expected cost of maintaining the status quo supplier arrangement. These costs include direct disruption and remediation, but also indirect exposure through trust erosion, compliance scrutiny, and reputational spillovers that the platform must absorb as the accountable orchestrator. When security performance becomes salient, decision-makers are more likely to reassess the security capabilities and qualifications of their incumbent suppliers and actively seek alternatives with superior security capability (Ocasio, 1997; Sullivan, 2010). In addition, a breach can trigger broader organizational change. Adverse events are often followed by adjustments in governance practices, process redesign, and strategic reorientation, implying that supplier replacement is a plausible form of post-failure reconfiguration rather than a rare exception (Crossan & Berdrow, 2003; Sosna et al., 2010; Benaroch & Chernobai, 2017; Dahlin et al., 2018). Put differently, breaches can motivate platforms to reset accountability and reduce perceived vulnerability. This logic yields a straightforward prediction about supplier reconfiguration: after a data breach, platforms are more likely to replace incumbent suppliers (H1).

Supplier replacement alone does not specify which suppliers a platform will choose. After a breach, platforms face a selection problem under uncertainty: they need suppliers that can plausibly reduce future risk and help restore stakeholder confidence. Because candidate suppliers' security standards are not readily observable, decision-makers often search for cues that enable inference about security performance (Gomulya & Mishina, 2017). One salient cue is third-party recognition. External evaluators and ranking organizations can serve as certifying intermediaries, and when such third parties disseminate positive evaluations, clients' trust and perceptions of the endorsed products or services tend to increase (Allen, 1984; Bapna et al., 2016). When the relevant rankings explicitly incorporate security- and privacy-related aspects, "star" suppliers that earn prestigious awards become particularly legible indicators of strong security capability under uncertainty.

Two mechanisms further strengthen the post-breach attractiveness of star suppliers. First, the reputational visibility of awards makes capability claims more defensible to stakeholders, reducing information asymmetry in supplier selection. Second, award-winning suppliers tend to institutionalize control procedures and accumulate security-related experience through a larger client base, which can translate into more mature security routines and improved ability to manage security risks (Fernández-Gámez et al., 2016). Their broader experience can also support client learning during crisis response, as highly recognized suppliers may share relevant insights on how similar incidents have been handled elsewhere. As security concerns dominate attention after a breach, third-party recognition becomes a more valuable cue for inferring security capability, making star suppliers disproportionately attractive among available alternatives. The testable implication is that, conditional on supplier change, platforms are more likely to switch to star suppliers in the post-breach period (H2).

Breaches can also reshape the structure of the supplier portfolio, not just the identity of suppliers. Multi-sourcing is often adopted to leverage diverse external capabilities and reduce lock-in, and it has become increasingly common in many technology-intensive sourcing domains (Levina & Su, 2008; Davies & Joglekar, 2013; Handley et al., 2022). Yet multi-sourcing can amplify security exposure and governance costs. Each additional supplier relationship expands the set of privileged access points, creating more potential sources of leakage and increasing security vulnerabilities relative to single-sourcing. Multi-sourcing also increases the monitoring and coordination burden because platforms must maintain consistent security oversight across multiple suppliers, which becomes more difficult as the number of vendors grows.

Operational complexity can further translate into security disadvantage. Integrated multi-vendor systems often involve multiple independent applications tailored to end-user requirements, complicating security operations and standardization tasks such as identity, login, and access control across modules. When a breach occurs and security becomes the dominant concern, these governance frictions become more salient. Platforms may therefore rationally trade off some diversification benefits to gain controllability. Consolidating suppliers can reduce the number of privileged relationships, simplify oversight, and clarify responsibility for security outcomes. This logic implies an observable restructuring of the supplier portfolio after breaches: platforms should shift away from multi-sourcing toward

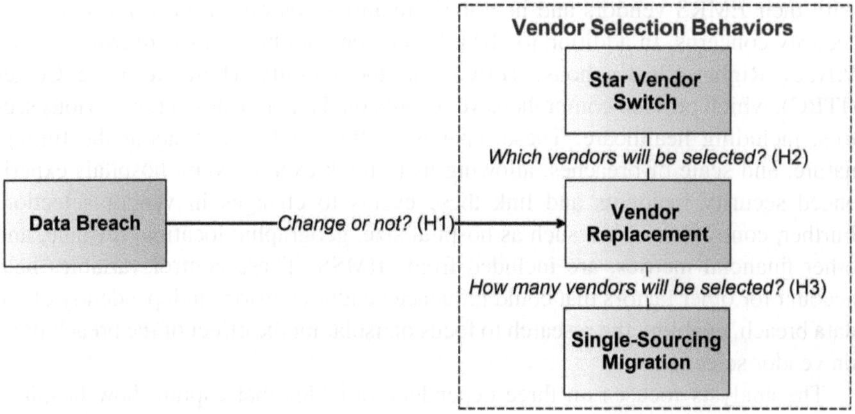

Fig. 3.2 Conceptual framework

more concentrated configurations, including single-sourcing where feasible, for breach-relevant services (H3). Figure 3.2 summarizes the conceptual framework, organizing the post-breach supplier reconfiguration logic into supplier replacement, star-supplier switching, and sourcing concentration.

3.3.3 Methodology

A longitudinal research design is employed to investigate the impact of data breaches on supplier selection, specifically focusing on hospital Electronic Medical Record System (EMRS) outsourcing. The primary aim is to explore how hospitals reassess their relationships with existing vendors and adjust their supplier choices in the wake of data breaches. Given the critical role of data security in industries like healthcare, where breaches can significantly affect patient trust, regulatory compliance, and operational continuity, understanding how hospitals change their supplier selection processes in response to such incidents is essential.

By leveraging quantitative analysis with longitudinal data, this research captures the shifts in hospital vendor behavior over time. The dataset spans a 12-year period (2006–2017), which allows for the observation of vendor selection decisions and a comparison of pre- and post-breach periods. This enables an understanding of whether hospitals are more likely to replace vendors or adopt new sourcing strategies after experiencing a data breach.

The data used in this research are sourced from several reputable databases, each contributing unique information. The Healthcare Information and Management Systems Society (HIMSS) database is central to this study, as it tracks EMRS adoption across U.S. hospitals. HIMSS provides detailed data on the vendors supplying EMRS solutions, as well as hospital characteristics such as size, revenue, and operational data. This information is essential for understanding how hospitals interact with their EMRS vendors and how these relationships evolve in response to data security concerns. In addition to HIMSS, data on data breaches is drawn from the Privacy Rights Clearinghouse (PRC) and the Identity Theft Resource Center (ITRC), which provide comprehensive records on data breaches across various sectors, including healthcare. These databases offer vital details about the timing, nature, and scale of breaches, allowing us to track exactly when hospitals experienced security incidents and link these events to changes in vendor selection. Further, control variables, such as hospital size, geographic location, revenue, and other financial metrics, are included from HIMSS. These control variables help account for other factors that could influence vendor decisions independently of the data breach, enabling the research to focus on isolating the effect of the breach itself on vendor selection.

The analysis focuses on three dependent variables that capture how hospitals reconfigure their EMRS supplier base after a data breach: vendor replacement, star-vendor switching, and the move toward single-sourcing. Vendor replacement records whether a hospital changes its incumbent EMRS vendor in the period following a breach, reflecting an escalation in governance when the existing arrangement is perceived as insufficient for heightened security requirements. Star-vendor switching captures the direction of that change by indicating whether the hospital, conditional on switching, selects a vendor with externally recognized security capability and a strong reputation for safeguarding sensitive data. The shift to single-sourcing measures whether hospitals consolidate their EMRS sourcing configuration by reducing the number of distinct vendors they rely on, thereby simplifying oversight and strengthening control of security practices across integrated modules. Table 3.1 provides illustrative calculations that show how Replacement, Star Switch, and Single-Sourcing are operationalized from year-to-year changes in EMRS sourcing configurations.

The occurrence of a data breach serves as the key independent variable in the analysis. It is coded as 1 for hospitals that experienced a breach during the study period and 0 for those that did not. This allows for a clear investigation into the relationship between data breaches and changes in vendor selection behavior.

To estimate the causal effect of data breaches on vendor selection, the Difference-in-Differences (DiD) methodology is employed. The DiD approach compares the changes in outcomes, such as vendor replacement, the selection of star vendors, or the adoption of single-sourcing, before and after the data breach. This methodology allows for isolating the effect of the breach from other factors, such as industry trends or hospital-specific characteristics that could also influence vendor decisions.

The DiD model can be expressed as follows:

$$Y_{it} = \alpha + \beta_1 \left(Post_t \times Treated_i \right) + \gamma_i + \delta_t + \epsilon_{it}$$

In this model, the dependent variable represents the outcome for a particular hospital at a given point in time, such as whether the hospital replaced its vendor, selected a high-security vendor, or decided to consolidate its suppliers into a single source.

Table 3.1 Example calculations for outcome variables

		Operationalizing replacement		Operationalizing Star Switch		Operationalizing single-sourcing		
Year	EMRS sourcing configuration (CDR-CDS-CPOE-OE-PD)	Module-level replacement? (CDR-CDS-CPOE-OE-PD)	Variable value	Module-level Star Switch? (CDR-CDS-CPOE-OE-PD)	Variable value	Distance from single-sourcing configuration	Reducedcompared withlast year?	Variable value
2006	A-B-C*-D-D	Null	Null	Null	Null	Null	Null	Null
2007	A-B-C*-C*-D	No-No-No-Yes-No	1	No-No-No-Yes-No	1	3	No	0
2008	B-B-C*-C*-D	Yes-No-No-No-No	1	No-No-No-No-No	0	3	No	0
2009	B-B-C*-C*-C*	No-No-No-No-Yes	1	No-No-No-No-Yes	1	2	Yes	1
2010	B-B-C*-C*-C*	No-No-No-No-No	0	No-No-No-No-No	0	2	No	0
2011	B-C*-C*-C*-C*	No-yes-no-no-no	1	No-yes-no-no-no	1	1	Yes	1
2012	B-C*-C*-C*-C*	No-No-No-No-No	0	No-No-No-No-No	0	1	No	0
2013	B-C*-C*-C*-C*	No-No-No-No-No	0	No-No-No-No-No	0	1	No	0
2014	C*-C*-C*-C*-C*	Yes-No-No-No-No	1	Yes-No-No-No-No	1	0	Yes	1
2015	C*-C*-C*-C*-C*	No-No-No-No-No	0	No-No-No-No-No	0	0	No	0
2016	C*-C*-C*-C*-C*	No-No-No-No-No	0	No-No-No-No-No	0	0	No	0
2017	C*-C*-C*-C*-C*	No-No-No-No-No	0	No-No-No-No-No	0	0	No	0

The variable indicating whether the observation occurs after the breach is coded as a binary value, with 1 representing the post-breach period. Another key variable identifies whether the hospital was affected by the breach during the study period. Additionally, the model accounts for hospital-specific effects, which control for characteristics of each hospital that do not change over time, such as its size or market position. To ensure that year-specific factors, which could influence all hospitals simultaneously, are also considered, the model includes year-specific effects. The error term captures all other unobserved factors that may influence the outcome.

The DiD model helps to identify the causal impact of data breaches on vendor selection by comparing the differences in outcomes between hospitals that experienced breaches and those that did not. By focusing on changes in vendor behavior in the pre- and post-breach periods, the model isolates the effect of the data breach on vendor decisions.

To ensure that the treatment and control groups are comparable before the breach, Coarsened Exact Matching (CEM) is used. This matching technique reduces biases by grouping hospitals based on observable characteristics such as hospital size, revenue, and prior vendor relationships. By matching the treatment and control groups more closely, CEM improves the internal validity of the analysis, ensuring that the differences observed in vendor selection are attributable to the breach rather than to pre-existing differences between the groups.

Several robustness checks are performed to validate the findings. Placebo tests are conducted to confirm that there were no significant pre-existing differences in vendor selection between the treatment and control groups, ensuring that the observed effects are truly caused by the breach. Additionally, the severity of the data breach is analyzed to determine whether larger breaches lead to more significant shifts in vendor selection behavior. This analysis provides further insight into how the scale of the breach influences hospital decisions.

Finally, a post-hoc analysis investigates the moderating role of relationship maturity in vendor selection. It is hypothesized that hospitals with long-standing relationships with their vendors may be less likely to switch suppliers after a breach due to inertia or the costs associated with transitioning to new suppliers. This post-hoc analysis offers a deeper understanding of the factors that influence vendor decisions in the wake of a data breach.

While the methodology is robust, it is important to consider the limitations of this approach. The study is based on data from U.S. hospitals, which may limit the generalizability of the findings to healthcare systems in other countries. Moreover, the focus is specifically on EMRS vendor selection and the effects of data breaches in the healthcare sector, meaning the results may not apply directly to other industries. However, the methodology can be adapted to other platform ecosystems, allowing for broader application across various sectors.

3.3.4 Results

The results reveal significant insights into how hospitals adjust their vendor selection in the aftermath of a data breach. When a breach occurs, hospitals respond not just as a reactive measure to mitigate immediate risks, but as a strategic move to align their vendor relationships with their security priorities. These changes highlight the value creation process driven by more security-focused vendor selection and consolidated supply chain strategies. Table 3.2 reports the baseline difference-in-differences estimates of the effect of data breaches on hospitals' EMRS vendor selection behaviors.

In the wake of a data breach, hospitals are significantly more likely to replace their EMRS vendors. Data from the analysis show that approximately 30% of hospitals that experienced a breach replaced their vendor within 1 year of the incident, compared to only 5% of hospitals in the control group. This indicates that the experience of a breach prompts hospitals to re-evaluate their supplier relationships, with a noticeable shift in priorities toward security. Hospitals, now acutely aware of the vulnerabilities exposed by the breach, seek vendors who can provide more robust security measures, ensuring that the future risk of similar breaches is minimized. This trend reflects a broader strategy of allocating resources away from vendors

Table 3.2 Impact of data breach on vendor selection behaviors

Variables	Replacement	Star Switch	Single-sourcing	Replacement	Star Switch	Single-sourcing
	(1)	(2)	(3)	(4)	(5)	(6)
After breach × breach	0.360***	0.576***	0.670***	0.344***	0.521**	0.619***
	(3.01)	(2.74)	(3.48)	(2.86)	(2.46)	(3.20)
Hospital size				0.257	−0.116	0.344
				(1.00)	(−0.26)	(0.83)
Revenue				−0.004	−0.005	−0.074**
				(−0.18)	(−0.15)	(−2.14)
Profit margin				−0.008	−0.030	0.182**
				(−0.27)	(−0.51)	(2.42)
IS expense intensity				8.201***	3.039	9.943*
				(2.83)	(0.59)	(1.86)
System size				0.071	0.147	0.201
				(0.83)	(0.94)	(1.22)
Hospital-fixed effects	Yes	Yes	Yes	Yes	Yes	Yes
Year-fixed effects	Yes	Yes	Yes	Yes	Yes	Yes
Number of observations	6129	3437	3221	6129	3437	3221
Pseudo R^2	.069	.073	.101	.072	.077	.113

perceived as risky and toward those that can better meet heightened security requirements.

The shift in vendor selection post-breach is not merely about replacing one vendor with another. It is, in fact, a shift toward star vendors—those with a reputation for superior security capabilities. These vendors are often certified for their compliance with industry standards, and their track record for protecting sensitive data makes them highly attractive to hospitals looking to restore trust and ensure compliance in the wake of a breach. About 40% of the hospitals that switched their vendors post-breach selected star vendors, a stark contrast to just 15% in the control group. This preference for high-security vendors illustrates how the breach increases the perceived value of vendors with superior security features. The decision to select such vendors signals a strategic alignment with risk management, as hospitals look to prevent future breaches by partnering with those who can offer a higher level of data protection.

Moreover, the data indicates that hospitals that replaced their vendors were also more likely to consolidate their supplier base into a single-sourcing arrangement. The shift to single-sourcing reflects hospitals' desire to streamline vendor management and increase control over security practices. By moving to a single vendor, hospitals can ensure tighter integration and coordination, making it easier to enforce security standards. Approximately 30% of the hospitals that replaced their vendors after a breach adopted a single-sourcing strategy, compared to just 10% in the control group. This consolidation reduces the complexity of managing multiple suppliers and allows hospitals to better oversee the implementation of security measures. It also reflects a broader trend of reducing operational risk by simplifying the vendor base and strengthening oversight of a single supplier.

The evidence points to a clear change in how hospitals manage EMRS vendors after a data breach. Vendor decisions appear to shift from routine procurement logic toward security-centered portfolio reconfiguration. Hospitals are not merely reacting by swapping providers; they are re-optimizing the vendor set around tighter security capability and stronger oversight. This reconfiguration is economically meaningful because it reduces longer-horizon exposure that typically follows breaches, including compliance risk, litigation and settlement costs, operational disruption, and reputational damage that can undermine patient trust and stakeholder confidence.

The baseline estimates indicate a pronounced increase in vendor replacement after breach events, consistent with hospitals reassessing incumbent relationships once security failure becomes salient. Conditional on switching, hospitals display a stronger tendency to select star vendors, suggesting that externally legible security capability becomes more valuable when decision-makers must justify vendor choices to regulators, boards, and affected stakeholders. Hospitals that change vendors also exhibit a higher propensity to consolidate their vendor base into single-sourcing arrangements, which aligns with a governance logic that prioritizes controllability and coordination in security-critical services, even at the cost of reduced diversification.

These patterns remain robust across additional checks. Placebo analyses show no comparable shifts in vendor selection behavior in the pre-breach period, strengthening the interpretation that the observed reconfiguration is triggered by the breach rather than by pre-existing trends. The results also vary systematically with breach severity. More severe incidents, such as those involving larger record counts or more sensitive information, are associated with stronger post-breach responses, including higher replacement likelihood and a more pronounced tilt toward star vendors, consistent with heightened perceived downside risk and intensified external scrutiny.

Relationship history further conditions the response. Hospitals with more mature vendor relationships are less likely to replace incumbents, consistent with relational inertia, switching frictions, and embedded integrations that make change costly even when risks increase. However, this dampening effect weakens when breaches are more severe, implying that sufficiently salient failures can override inertia and prompt decisive supplier reconfiguration. The implication is that post-breach vendor choice reflects a tradeoff between continuity benefits from established relationships and the need to restore security credibility and reduce future exposure.

From a platform supply chain perspective, these findings make vendor strategy part of value creation rather than a narrow compliance exercise. Replacing incumbents, upgrading to star suppliers, and consolidating sourcing can simultaneously lower expected downside costs and stabilize service reliability, which helps preserve trust among users and regulators. In settings where confidence in data protection and uninterrupted service underpins ongoing participation, security-driven supplier reconfiguration supports the conditions for sustained adoption and, by extension, the network effects that platforms rely on for growth.

3.3.5 Implications for Platform Supplier Management

The findings underscore a practical but often underappreciated feature of platform supply chains. Once external technology and service suppliers are embedded in the platform's service architecture, supplier management becomes inseparable from how the platform preserves continuity, governs interdependence, and sustains value creation. Vendors operate through privileged access, shared data infrastructures, and tightly coupled operating routines, so their security practices shape the reliability users experience as a single end-to-end service. When a breach occurs, the platform bears the reputational and regulatory consequences as the focal point of accountability. The breach therefore does not only interrupt operations; it converts previously latent exposure in the supplier portfolio into a salient, decision-relevant liability. The managerial problem that follows is to restore credibility and stabilize service delivery by reconfiguring supplier relationships in ways that reduce future exposure without eroding the platform's capacity to scale.

Against this backdrop, the heightened propensity to replace suppliers after a breach can be interpreted as governance escalation rather than an ad hoc procurement response. Over time, platform–supplier relationships accumulate technical interfaces and informal exceptions that expand access privileges and create opaque dependencies, many of which remain difficult to audit under normal conditions. A breach forces these arrangements into the open and creates a rare window to redesign integration boundaries and accountability assignments. Replacement is costly, yet it provides leverage to reset risk boundaries by narrowing access rights, strengthening monitoring and reporting requirements, formalizing disclosure and escalation rules, and clarifying responsibility for security outcomes in ways that external stakeholders can recognize as credible. The implication is not that platforms should reflexively switch vendors after every incident, but that supplier stickiness is not neutral. Preserving continuity with legacy integrations may protect short-term stability, but it can also prolong long-term exposure when access is overly permissive and transparency is weak.

What platforms switch to matters as much as whether they switch. The observed tilt toward star suppliers following breaches highlights a recurring platform challenge: security capability is difficult to observe ex ante and even harder to verify continuously, so post-breach selection occurs under heightened uncertainty. Legible external signals of security quality become strategically valuable because they allow the platform to justify supplier choices to regulators, partners, and users precisely when trust is fragile. Beyond signaling, suppliers with widely recognized security capability are often perceived as having more mature routines for monitoring, patch management, disclosure discipline, and incident coordination. These routines reduce both the likelihood of recurrence and the cost of recovery when incidents occur. In platform ecosystems, where trust shapes willingness to transact, share data, and integrate complementary services, capability upgrading thus functions as a governance move that also repairs the economic foundations of participation.

The implications extend beyond individual supplier choices to the architecture of the supplier base. A post-breach shift toward more concentrated sourcing suggests that platforms sometimes treat complexity reduction as part of their security strategy. Multi-sourcing can provide flexibility and reduce lock-in, but it also expands privileged access points, multiplies interfaces that must be secured, and raises the monitoring and coordination burden during incident response. In crisis moments, fragmented responsibility across vendors can slow containment and amplify uncertainty, which is exactly what damages trust. Consolidation can simplify oversight, clarify accountability, and standardize response routines, making recovery faster and more executable. At the same time, dependence risks rise as sourcing becomes more concentrated. Concentration is therefore most defensible where services are security-critical and tightly coupled to the platform's core customer journey, whereas more modular functions can preserve multi-sourcing without creating systemic exposure.

More broadly, the evidence indicates that security-driven supplier management is a pathway through which platforms preserve and amplify value aftershocks by making interdependence more governable and coordination more reliable. Replacement, upgrading toward security-capable suppliers, and selective consolidation are not merely portfolio adjustments; they are governance moves that reshape access boundaries, tighten obligations for monitoring and disclosure, reduce coordination frictions in incident response, and reassign accountability across organizational interfaces. Value is created through these mechanisms because they improve risk-adjusted performance and reinforce the credibility of the platform's service promise. Downside exposure declines as the expected costs of future failures fall, including downtime, remediation expenditures, regulatory penalties, and litigation risks, and as the probability of cascading disruption across interconnected services is reduced. Service continuity improves because fewer and better-governed interfaces make standards easier to enforce and response routines faster to coordinate, raising end-to-end reliability that users attribute to the platform. Trust is stabilized because supplier choices act as observable commitments to corrective action, supporting retention and willingness to share data. These effects accumulate into scale advantages: in platform environments where adoption and network effects depend on confidence in uninterrupted service and responsible data stewardship, improved governability and coordination translate into more stable participation on both sides of the market and deeper ecosystem integration, keeping the platform's growth engine viable even under heightened security risk.

3.4 Chapter Conclusions and Future Directions

Platform supplier integration is often described as a technical or operational accomplishment: interfaces are built, service levels are tracked, and vendors are onboarded. A more consequential interpretation treats integration as a governance problem with direct implications for value creation. Platforms mobilize external capabilities to scale, but that advantage remains fragile unless governance mechanisms can sustain cooperation, curb opportunism, and absorb shocks without eroding ecosystem trust. Governance becomes the connective tissue between supplier integration and platform value because it determines whether distributed supplier actions can be translated into consistent end-to-end service outcomes that users attribute to the platform.

Governability must be designed rather than assumed once suppliers are embedded in the platform's service architecture. Relational and contractual governance address different uncertainties that arise from interdependence under limited observability. Trust reduces friction and enables coordination when contracts are incomplete and when execution relies on discretion, exception handling, and timely information sharing. Trust is not monolithic: competence-based confidence and goodwill-based expectations operate through different channels and confront different hazards. Contracts provide the backbone of accountability by clarifying responsibilities, reporting and audit rights, escalation procedures, and enforcement levers when incentives diverge. The core implication is configurational. Dependable integration emerges when trust and contracts are aligned so that formal safeguards remain credible while relational cooperation is preserved for adaptation under uncertainty. Misalignment can produce defensive compliance, ambiguity exploitation, and escalating monitoring costs.

Integration is also dynamic, with its value becoming most visible when shocks reveal hidden vulnerabilities. Data breaches are a revealing context because they make risk salient, disrupt optimistic beliefs about supplier reliability, and redirect managerial attention toward security performance and accountability. In response, organizations often reconfigure supplier portfolios by replacing incumbents, upgrading toward suppliers with stronger and more legible security capability, and selectively simplifying sourcing structures to improve oversight and incident coordination. These moves are not merely procurement adjustments. They reshape access boundaries, tighten monitoring and disclosure obligations, clarify accountability across organizational interfaces, and make response routines more executable under time pressure. Value is created and amplified because these governance and coordination changes reduce downside exposure, preserve service continuity, and strengthen the credibility of the platform's service promise that sustains participation and network effects.

Several directions follow from this governance-based view of platform supplier integration, but they become clearer when stated as extensions of the same underlying design problem rather than as disconnected topics. A central step is to characterize ecosystem spillovers more precisely, because supplier failures and security incidents rarely remain confined to a single relationship. They can propagate through shared vendors, shared infrastructures, and reputational channels, shifting how other actors interpret platform reliability and, in turn, altering sourcing decisions beyond the focal exchange. Understanding spillovers at this level requires distinguishing technical contagion through tightly coupled interfaces from informational contagion through disclosure, media attention, and regulatory scrutiny, since each pathway implies different governance responses and different consequences for participation and network effects.

This spillover lens also implies that governance and portfolio design should be modeled as co-evolving choices rather than as independent levers pulled in sequence. Incidents trigger learning, and learning often reshapes contracting templates, trust-building practices, and sourcing concentration in tandem. Platforms may tighten control rights, revise reporting and audit clauses, and redraw privileged access boundaries, while simultaneously investing in relational routines that sustain cooperation under stress, such as rapid disclosure norms, joint forensic processes, and shared recovery playbooks. The key issue is that these changes interact: stronger safeguards can improve accountability, yet crowd out voluntary information sharing if suppliers become defensive, whereas high-trust arrangements can support adaptation, yet increase exposure if formal accountability remains ambiguous. Treating governance and portfolio design as a coupled system makes it possible to explain why some platforms emerge from shocks with greater resilience and credibility, while others accumulate hidden fragilities despite apparent "hardening."

These dynamics are unlikely to be uniform across platform contexts, which makes boundary conditions part of the theory rather than an afterthought. The governance–value creation link should differ when services are modular versus tightly coupled, when suppliers are mission-critical versus peripheral, and when the institutional environment is stringent versus permissive in regulation and liability.

Tightly coupled, security-critical modules may justify higher concentration and stronger control to improve governability and response speed, whereas more modular components may benefit from multi-sourcing and looser coordination to preserve innovation and avoid excessive lock-in. Making these contingencies explicit helps specify when integration primarily amplifies value through scalable reliability and when it amplifies risk through scalable interdependence.

A further frontier emerges as platforms adopt AI-enabled monitoring, anomaly detection, and automated compliance auditing. These tools can change governability itself by improving observability and accelerating response, effectively expanding what can be monitored and enforced across organizational boundaries. At the same time, they introduce new challenges around transparency, accountability, and the allocation of responsibility between platforms and suppliers, especially when automated systems are opaque, generate false positives, or trigger actions that suppliers dispute. The deeper question is therefore how algorithmic governance reshapes the balance between cooperative flexibility and credible control, and how that balance determines whether platform supplier integration serves as a durable capability for value creation under uncertainty.

References

Allen, F. (1984). Reputation and product quality[J]. *The RAND Journal of Economics*, 311–327.

Andrade-Rojas, M. G., Kathuria, A., & Lee, H.-H. (2024). Multilevel synergy of information technology for operational integration: Competition networks and operating performance. *Production and Operations Management, 33*(5), 1116–1141.

Bakshi, N., & Kleindorfer, P. (2009). Co-opetition and investment for supply-chain resilience. *Production and Operations Management, 18*(6), 583–603.

Bapna, R., Gupta, A., & Ray, G. et al. (2016). Research note—IT outsourcing and the impact of advisors on clients and vendors[J]. *Information Systems Research, 27*(3): 636–647.

Beer, R., Ahn, H.-S., & Leider, S. (2018). Can trustworthiness in a supply chain be signaled? *Management Science, 64*(9), 3974–3994.

Benaroch, M., & Chernobai, A. (2017). Operational IT failures, IT value destruction, and board-level IT governance changes. *MIS Quarterly, 41*(3), 729–A726.

Cao, Z., & Lumineau, F. (2015). Revisiting the interplay between contractual and relational governance: A qualitative and meta-analytic investigation. *Journal of Operations Management, 33*, 15–42.

Carson, S. J., Madhok, A., & Wu, T. (2006). Uncertainty, opportunism, and governance: The effects of volatility and ambiguity on formal and relational contracting. *Academy of Management Journal, 49*(5), 1058–1077.

Chai, J., & Ngai, E. W. (2020). Decision-making techniques in supplier selection: Recent accomplishments and what lies ahead. *Expert Systems with Applications, 140*, 112903.

Chen, J., Zhao, X., Lewis, M., & Squire, B. (2016). A multi-method investigation of buyer power and supplier motivation to share knowledge. *Production and Operations Management, 25*(3), 417–431.

Crossan, M. M., & Berdrow, I. (2003). Organizational learning and strategic renewal. *Strategic Management Journal, 24*(11), 1087–1105.

Dahlin, K. B., Chuang, Y.-T., & Roulet, T. J. (2018). Opportunity, motivation, and ability to learn from failures and errors: Review, synthesis, and ways to move forward. *Academy of Management Annals, 12*(1), 252–277.

Das, T. K., & Teng, B.-S. (1998). Between trust and control: Developing confidence in partner cooperation in alliances. *Academy of Management Review, 23*(3), 491–512.

Davies, J., & Joglekar, N. (2013). Supply chain integration, product modularity, and market valuation: Evidence from the solar energy industry. *Production and Operations Management, 22*(6), 1494–1508.

Dhillon, G., Syed, R., & Pedron, C. (2016). Interpreting information security culture: An organizational transformation case study. *Computers & Security, 56*, 63–69.

Fahn, M., & Zanarone, G. (2022). Transparency in relational contracts. *Strategic Management Journal, 43*(5), 1046–1071.

Feng, B., Yao, T., & Jiang, B. (2013). Analysis of the market-based adjustable outsourcing contract under uncertainties. *Production and Operations Management, 22*(1), 178–188.

Fernández-Gámez, M. A., Gil-Corral, A. M., & Galán-Valdivieso, F. (2016). Corporate reputation and market value: Evidence with generalized regression neural networks. *Expert Systems with Applications, 46*, 69–76.

Ghadge, A., Weiß, M., Caldwell, N. D., & Wilding, R. (2020). Managing cyber risk in supply chains: A review and research agenda. *Supply Chain Management: An International Journal, 25*(2), 223–240.

Gomulya, D., & Mishina, Y. (2017). Signaler credibility, signal susceptibility, and relative reliance on signals: How stakeholders change their evaluative processes after violation of expectations and rehabilitative efforts. *Academy of Management Journal, 60*(2), 554–583.

Handley, S., Skowronski, K., & Thakar, D. (2022). The single-sourcing versus multisourcing decision in information technology outsourcing. *Journal of Operations Management, 68*(6–7), 702–727.

Kannan, V. R., & Tan, K. C. (2002). Supplier selection and assessment: Their impact on business performance. *Journal of Supply Chain Management, 38*(3), 11–21.

Kim, T.-Y., Oh, H., & Swaminathan, A. (2006). Framing interorganizational network change: A network inertia perspective. *Academy of Management Review, 31*(3), 704–720.

Levina, N., & Su, N. (2008). Global multisourcing strategy: The emergence of a supplier portfolio in services offshoring. *Decision Sciences, 39*(3), 541–570.

Li, C. (2013). Sourcing for supplier effort and competition: Design of the supply base and pricing mechanism. *Management Science, 59*(6), 1389–1406.

Liu, Y., Luo, Y., & Liu, T. (2009). Governing buyer–supplier relationships through transactional and relational mechanisms: Evidence from China. *Journal of Operations Management, 27*(4), 294–309.

Lumineau, F. (2017). How contracts influence trust and distrust. *Journal of Management, 43*(5), 1553–1577.

Malhotra, D. (2004). Trust and reciprocity decisions: The differing perspectives of trustors and trusted parties. *Organizational Behavior and Human Decision Processes, 94*(2), 61–73.

Malhotra, D., & Murnighan, J. K. (2002). The effects of contracts on interpersonal trust. *Administrative Science Quarterly, 47*(3), 534–559.

Mooi, E. A., & Ghosh, M. (2010). Contract specificity and its performance implications. *Journal of Marketing, 74*(2), 105–120.

Moshtari, M. (2016). Inter-organizational fit, relationship management capability, and collaborative performance within a humanitarian setting. *Production and Operations Management, 25*(9), 1542–1557.

Nikkhah, H. R., & Grover, V. (2022). An empirical investigation of company response to data breaches. *MIS Quarterly, 46*(4), 2163–2196.

Ocasio, W. (1997). Towards an attention-based view of the firm. *Strategic Management Journal, 18*(S1), 187–206.

Oliveira, N., Schilke, O., Lumineau, F., & Huo, B. (2025). The influence of power on trust in Buyer–supplier relationships: An actor—partner interdependence approach. *Production and Operations Management*. 10591478251371270.

Poppo, L., Zhou, K. Z., & Ryu, S. (2008). Alternative origins to interorganizational trust: An interdependence perspective on the shadow of the past and the shadow of the future. *Organization Science, 19*(1), 39–55.

Schepker, D. J., Oh, W.-Y., Martynov, A., & Poppo, L. (2014). The many futures of contracts: Moving beyond structure and safeguarding to coordination and adaptation. *Journal of Management, 40*(1), 193–225.

Sosna, M., Trevinyo-Rodríguez, R. N., & Velamuri, S. R. (2010). Business model innovation through trial-and-error learning: The Naturhouse case. *Long Range Planning, 43*(2–3), 383–407.

Sullivan, B. N. (2010). Competition and beyond: Problems and attention allocation in the organizational rulemaking process. *Organization Science, 21*(2), 432–450.

Verma, R., & Pullman, M. E. (1998). An analysis of the supplier selection process. *Omega, 26*(6), 739–750.

Weber, L., & Mayer, K. J. (2011). Designing effective contracts: Exploring the influence of framing and expectations. *Academy of Management Review, 36*(1), 53–75.

Williamson, O. E. (1985). The economic institutions of capitalism. Firms, markets, relational contracting. In *Das Summa Summarum des Management: Die 25 wichtigsten Werke für Strategie, Führung und Veränderung* (pp. 61–75). Springer.

Chapter 4
Platform Customer Integration

4.1 Overview of Platform Customer Integration

4.1.1 Definition and Scope

Platform customer integration refers to the strategic coupling of a digital platform's governance architecture and operational capabilities with the multifaceted activities of its customer base—encompassing both individual end-users and organizational buyers. This coupling is not a static state but a dynamic process of mutual adaptation, enabled by data infrastructures, incentive schemes, and rule-based coordination. Its defining characteristic, which distinguishes it from traditional supply chain integration, is its operation within a multi-sided market context. Here, the platform does not merely serve a downstream customer; it must simultaneously manage cross-side externalities, align incentives across heterogeneous groups, and ensure that the actions of one participant group (e.g., trial users) generate positive, rather than negative, spillovers for others (e.g., paying customers, complementors).

The objects of integration are therefore inherently plural and interdependent. First, platforms integrate customer information, which constitutes the lifeblood of the ecosystem. This includes not only explicit data (e.g., demographics, purchase history) but, more critically, implicit behavioral signals generated through platform interaction—search queries, clickstream data, dwell time, review sentiment, and participation in community forums. Second, platforms integrate customer decisions, embedding choices about product adoption, service usage, and engagement level into their core algorithmic systems. Pricing engines, recommendation algorithms, and content curation feeds are all calibrated in real-time based on aggregated and individualized decision patterns. Third, platforms integrate customer processes, synchronizing their own operational workflows with key customer journey stages such as onboarding, experimentation, post-purchase support, and co-creation. This process integration often extends beyond the platform's boundaries, linking with sellers' inventory systems or logistics providers to create a seamless

B. Huo et al., *Platform Supply Chains 4*, Platform Supply Chains in the AI Era,
https://doi.org/10.1007/978-981-92-0133-4_4

end-to-end experience. Finally, at the most strategic level, platforms integrate customers as value co-creators, whose active participation becomes a direct input into product development, brand equity, and ecosystem learning.

The scope of this integration spans three analytically distinct but practically intertwined layers. At the micro-interaction layer, integration is manifested in the design of user interfaces and incentive structures (e.g., loyalty points, free trials), and community norms that shape individual behavior. At the meso-coordination layer, integration demands internal alignment across the platform's own functional silos, marketing, operations, data science, product management, and legal/compliance, to ensure that customer-facing initiatives are executed coherently and without internal friction. A free trial campaign, for instance, is not merely a marketing tactic; it requires synchronized action from inventory management (to allocate units), fraud detection (to filter speculators), customer support (to handle inquiries), and R&D (to process feedback). At the macro-ecosystem layer, customer integration influences the platform's broader governance strategy, affecting how it manages relationships with complementors, regulates competition among sellers, and sustains the health of its network over time. Effective integration at this layer ensures that customer participation reinforces, rather than undermines, the platform's long-term viability.

Despite its centrality, achieving deep and effective customer integration presents profound challenges. The primary challenge is participant heterogeneity. Platforms serve diverse constituencies with conflicting needs, risk preferences, and levels of sophistication—from tech-savvy early adopters to price-sensitive bargain hunters, from global brands to micro-entrepreneurs. Designing integration mechanisms that are both scalable and sensitive to this diversity is a constant tension. A second, related challenge is information asymmetry and signal noise. While platforms possess unprecedented data access, this data is often incomplete, strategically manipulated, or contextually ambiguous, making it difficult to infer true intent or future value. A third challenge is the coordination complexity inherent in managing a distributed ecosystem without hierarchical control. The platform cannot command its participants; it can only influence them through a delicate mix of carrots (incentives) and sticks (rules), a task that becomes exponentially harder as the ecosystem scales. Finally, platforms face a critical governance dilemma: the very openness that fuels network growth also invites opportunism and negative externalities. Free trials, for example, can attract genuine advocates who generate valuable social proof, but they can just as easily attract speculators seeking free goods or detractors who amplify negative sentiment. Managing this dual-edged nature of participation is perhaps the most acute challenge of platform customer integration.

To navigate these challenges, platforms rely on a sophisticated portfolio of governance and coordination mechanisms. These are not ad hoc tools but constitute the core of the platform's operational logic. Data and algorithmic infrastructure serves as the central nervous system, processing vast streams of information to enable real-time personalization and decision-making. Modular interface design allows for selective integration, providing different levels of access and functionality to different user segments based on their role and trustworthiness. Economic incentive schemes, such as freemium models, referral bonuses, and the strategic use of free trials, are used to align participant behavior with platform objectives. Crucially, these are underpinned by formal and informal governance rules that define acceptable conduct, establish dispute resolution procedures, and enforce quality standards. Together, these mechanisms form a coherent system that allows the platform to "manage" its customer relationships not through command, but through structured influence and co-evolution.

4.1.2 How Platform Customer Integration Creates Value

This section defines platform customer integration in platforms and explains why it matters for value. The ultimate purpose of overcoming the formidable challenges of integration is to unlock a unique and powerful set of value creation pathways that are unavailable to firms operating in linear value chains. Critically, this value is not created in a single step; it follows a two-stage logic that mirrors the chapter's overall structure. First, the platform must establish robust relationship governance and coordination capabilities, the "management" foundation. Only then can it leverage these capabilities to execute specific strategies that generate measurable economic value. This sequential logic—manage first, create value second—is fundamental to understanding the platform's economic engine.

The first stage, establishing governance and coordination, is itself a source of foundational value. By building the internal cross-functional alignment and external rule-based systems described above, the platform creates a stable, predictable, and trustworthy environment. This reduces the pervasive uncertainty that characterizes multi-sided markets, where participants are wary of engaging with unknown counterparts. Trust, once established, lowers participation barriers, increases user stickiness, and forms the bedrock upon which all subsequent value creation rests. A platform that cannot reliably manage its relationships will fail to attract or retain high-quality participants, regardless of its other features.

Building on this governance foundation, the platform can then pursue four primary channels of economic value creation:

1. Operational Efficiency and Liquidity Value. Deep integration streamlines the entire transaction lifecycle, from discovery to fulfillment. Real-time data sharing between the platform, sellers, and logistics partners minimizes stockouts, optimizes inventory placement, and accelerates delivery. For customers, this translates into a reliable, frictionless experience; for sellers, it means lower operational costs and higher sales conversion. This enhanced marketplace liquidity is a direct economic benefit, stabilizing cash flows and reducing the cost of doing business within the ecosystem.
2. Learning and Innovation Value. An integrated platform becomes a powerful engine for collective learning. By systematically capturing and analyzing customer feedback, usage patterns, and trial results, the platform and its ecosys-

tem partners gain unparalleled insights into market needs and product performance. This transforms the traditional, capital-intensive R&D process into a more agile, data-driven, and customer-centric one. New features and products can be validated in-market with minimal upfront investment, significantly de-risking innovation. The platform, by curating this learning loop, positions itself as an indispensable partner in its ecosystem's evolutionary trajectory.

3. Risk-Mitigated and Resilient Value. Perhaps the most distinctive form of value in platform markets is its risk-adjusted nature. Platforms operate under extreme uncertainty, particularly when launching new services or features. Customer integration mechanisms like free trials are not simply promotional giveaways; they are sophisticated risk reallocation and screening tools. By inviting self-selected users to experiment, the platform shifts the burden of initial uncertainty away from the mass market. When combined with precise identification capabilities—distinguishing between valuable advocates and opportunistic speculators—the platform can further refine this process. As empirical evidence demonstrates, this targeted approach lowers the expected costs associated with failure: poor adoption, negative reviews, reputational damage, and legal disputes. The resulting reduction in downside exposure and stabilization of revenue streams constitute a powerful, yet often overlooked, form of value creation that directly supports long-term platform health and investor confidence.
4. Amplified and Sustainable Network Value. Ultimately, the platform's core asset is its network. Customer integration is the primary lever for not just growing this network, but for enhancing its quality and sustainability. Well-integrated customers are not just numerous; they are active, engaged, and generative. They produce high-quality data, provide authentic social proof, and contribute to a positive feedback loop that attracts more high-value participants. Crucially, effective integration also involves managing the dark side of network effects. By governing participation and filtering out sources of negativity or opportunism, the platform prevents the rapid contagion of harmful sentiment that can quickly unravel trust. This curation ensures that network effects remain a source of strength rather than fragility, creating a virtuous cycle of value creation that is resilient to shocks and difficult for competitors to replicate.

In summary, platform customer integration is the linchpin of the platform business model. It is the process by which the platform transforms the chaotic potential of a multi-sided market into a structured, governable, and highly valuable ecosystem. The value created is multi-dimensional, systemic, and self-reinforcing, flowing from a foundation of sound relationship governance to the execution of sophisticated value-capture strategies. This multi-stage, systemic process, encompassing what is integrated, how it is governed, and the value it generates, is captured in the conceptual framework of platform customer integration presented in Fig. 4.1.

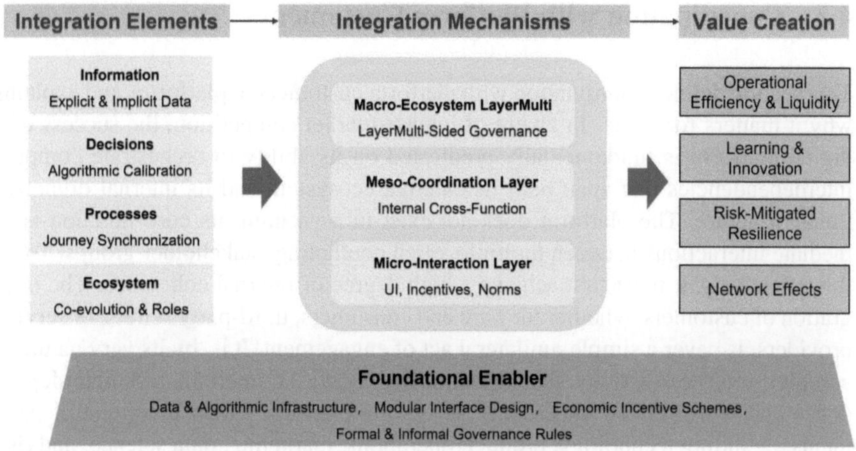

Fig. 4.1 Platform supply chain customer integration conceptual framework

4.1.3 Chapter Framework

This chapter is structured to unpack the two-stage logic of platform customer integration and value creation outlined above. It moves deliberately from the foundational question of how platforms manage and coordinate with their customers to the applied question of how this coordination is leveraged to create concrete economic value.

Section 4.2, Coordination with Platform Customers, addresses the first stage. It develops a theoretical framework grounded in the information processing view to explain how platforms build the internal cross-functional coordination capabilities necessary to manage the complexity of their customer relationships. This section defines the core objects of integration (information, decisions, processes) and analyzes the governance mechanisms, spanning systems, processes, and teams—that platforms deploy to achieve alignment. By establishing this "management" foundation, Section 4.2 sets the stage for understanding how platforms can successfully execute more advanced customer engagement strategies.

Section 4.3, Value Creation: Free Trials under Network Effects, addresses the second stage. It takes a specific, high-stakes integration mechanism, and demonstrates how its success is contingent upon the coordination capabilities developed in Sect. 4.2. Using a formal analytical model that incorporates both positive and negative non-linear network effects, and validating its predictions with rich empirical data from a major electronics platform, this section shows precisely how reallocating trial access from risky to reliable customers creates value. It quantifies the risk-mitigated gains in terms of higher prices, increased demand, and greater profit, thereby providing a concrete, evidence-based illustration of the value creation logic in action.

Finally, Section 4.4 will synthesize these insights and discuss their broader implications for platform strategy and governance, arguing that the future of platform competition will be defined not by who has the most users, but by who integrates them most effectively.

4.2 Coordination with Platform Customers

This section defines coordination with platform customers in platforms and explains why it matters for value. In an era of intense market competition, the success of a digital platform is fundamentally predicated on its ability to orchestrate complex interdependencies that span both its external ecosystem and its internal organizational structure. The platform does not exist in a vacuum; its core function is to mediate interactions between multiple, often conflicting, stakeholder groups. To do this effectively, it must first achieve a high degree of internal coherence. The integration of customers, whether they are end consumers, third-party sellers, or service providers, is never a simple, unilateral act of engagement. It is, by its very nature, a complex interfirm activity that dramatically increases interunit task interdependence and work-related uncertainty across the platform's own functional departments, including technology, product, operations, marketing, data science, and risk management. This self-imposed complexity generates substantial information processing demands that can only be met by developing a robust and multi-faceted internal coordination capability. Following the foundational principles of Information Processing Theory (IPT), this section posits that cross-functional coordination is the critical internal mechanism through which a platform builds the necessary information processing capabilities (IPCs) to manage the uncertainty inherent in deep customer relationships (Galbraith, 1974; Tushman & Nadler, 1978; Huang et al., 2014; Srinivasan & Swink, 2015). This internal governance infrastructure is the indispensable prerequisite for translating customer interaction into superior operational performance and, ultimately, sustainable economic value.

4.2.1 The Role of Cross-Functional Coordination

Cross-functional coordination is formally defined as "the extent to which a firm organizes the activities and behaviors of various intraorganizational departments into coordinated and synchronized procedures (Bendoly et al., 2012; Tsai & Hsu, 2014)." In the specific context of a platform supply chain, this definition takes on profound strategic significance. Unlike a traditional linear firm that might manage a relatively stable dyadic relationship with a supplier or customer, a platform operates in a dynamic, multi-sided environment where every action has cascading effects. A decision to modify a search algorithm, launch a promotional campaign, or adjust a fee structure simultaneously impacts user experience, seller economics, and the overall health of the network. Consequently, the platform's internal departments are inextricably linked through their shared interface with the external world. Marketing cannot design a customer acquisition strategy without understanding the operational capacity of the fulfillment network. Product and engineering cannot build new features without input from data science on user behavior and from risk on potential policy violations. This dense web of interdependence means that the platform's ability to present a unified, coherent face to its ecosystem is entirely dependent on its success in managing its own internal complexity.

The objects of this internal coordination are the platform's functional silos themselves, and the integration must occur across four critical dimensions: information and data, processes and routines, capabilities and expertise, and incentives and priorities (Turkulainen & Ketokivi, 2012; Pellathy et al., 2019). First, at the level of information, different functions hold disparate pieces of the customer puzzle. Operations possess granular data on delivery failures and service bottlenecks; product and engineering understand how features are actually used; marketing monitors campaign performance and user cohorts; and risk and compliance track fraud patterns and policy disputes. Cross-functional system coordination integrates these fragmented data streams by creating shared information systems and standardized data definitions, establishing a single source of truth that can be leveraged by all. Second, at the level of process, customer-facing activities like onboarding a new seller, handling a complex customer complaint, or executing a large-scale free trial program are not the domain of a single team but run across functional boundaries. Cross-functional process coordination integrates these routines through shared procedures, joint plans, and standardized workflows, ensuring that handoffs are smooth and responsibilities are clear. Third, each function brings specialized knowledge: engineers possess technical depth, operations understand logistics and capacity, marketing deciphers customer segments, and risk navigates regulatory and fraud landscapes. Cross-functional team coordination integrates these diverse capabilities by creating dedicated teams that can bring multiple perspectives to bear on a single problem. Finally, and perhaps most critically, true coordination requires aligning incentives. If functions are rewarded for conflicting local outcomes, engineering for system stability, marketing for user growth, risk for loss avoidance, their responses to the same customer issue will be incoherent, producing a fragmented and frustrating experience that erodes trust.

The challenges to achieving this level of coordination are formidable. Customer coordination in a platform setting is inherently demanding because it is a complex interfirm activity that increases interunit task interdependence and work-related uncertainty. Two additional features of the platform context deepen this challenge (Mohiuddin Babu, 2017; Kang et al., 2020). First is multi-sided interdependence: customer-related decisions often affect multiple sides of the platform simultaneously. A policy to amplify negative reviews may protect buyers but threaten seller retention and short-term revenue. A free trial program may boost awareness for a new device but cannibalize sales of existing models. Coordinating around such trade-offs requires an integrated view that cuts across internal silos. Second is the issue of speed and volume: platforms operate at immense scale, where small changes can affect millions of users within hours. Customer issues often arise suddenly and require rapid, coherent responses. Without strong cross-functional coordination, internal response times lag behind external pressure, and value is lost.

To navigate these challenges, platforms must implement three complementary forms of cross-functional coordination, each corresponding directly to a core mechanism for enhancing IPCs as outlined in the IPT literature.

Cross-functional system coordination refers to the use of shared information systems that connect internal functions and allow real-time access to customer-related data (Rai et al., 2006; Carr et al., 2008). As formalized in the source literature, this form of coordination "formalizes internal information-sharing languages, decreasing information processing costs, and increasing information processing capabilities. In a platform, this translates into the deployment of enterprise-wide technological infrastructure: unified data warehouses that integrate events from customers, sellers, and internal operations; shared dashboards that provide a common view of key metrics like customer satisfaction, trial participation rates, or network health; and standardized taxonomies for products, issues, and user types. These systems enable customer operational coordination, in particular by supporting day-to-day synchronization, such as routing support tickets with full context, updating users consistently on order status, or identifying operational problems early through shared service metrics. Empirical evidence from the foundational study demonstrates a clear pattern: cross-functional system coordination is positively associated with customer operational coordination (COC) defined as the joint participation in interfirm procedures and activities such as operations and new product development, but has no significant direct effect on customer strategic coordination (CSC) (Li et al., 2019). This finding is intuitive: integrated systems excel at handling the codified, high-volume information required for execution but are less suited to the ambiguous, unstructured data that informs long-term strategic planning.

Cross-functional process coordination captures formal lateral relationships such as shared procedures, joint planning, and standardized routines across functions (Sinkula et al., 1997; Srinivasan & Swink, 2015). This dimension "reflects formal lateral relationships such as shared procedures, joint planning, and standardized operating routines." On a platform, this manifests as structured workflows that govern complex initiatives. For example, a standard "customer issue escalation" process might link customer service, engineering, and risk into a defined sequence of actions. A "merchant trial setup" workflow could link the free trial operations team, product managers, and legal into a checklist for launching a new campaign. These formalized processes serve multiple purposes: they reduce redundant work, align internal timetables and responsibilities, and ensure that customer-facing activities are not ad hoc but repeatable and scalable. Critically, and in direct alignment with the empirical findings, cross-functional processes are shown to increase both COC and CSC (Li et al., 2019). This dual impact makes it the essential bridge between operational execution and strategic alignment, as it provides the procedural backbone for both routine tasks and long-term planning.

Cross-functional team coordination refers to teams, meetings, and informal networks that bring together individuals from different functions to work on customer-related decisions (Chen, 2007; Dussart et al., 2021). These teams provide multiple aspects, information, and skills for decision-making in customer strategic coordination, thus improving its quality (Ghobadi, 2015; Pakarinen & Virtanen, 2017). In the fast-paced world of platforms, such teams are often the primary vehicle for innovation and crisis management. They include dedicated "category teams" for key verticals like electronics or fashion, "incident response teams" assembled to manage sudden crises, or "strategic partner teams" for deep collaboration with top merchants. These teams foster rich, interpersonal communication that is essential for interpreting ambiguous signals and solving novel problems. The empirical pattern is again clear: cross-functional team coordination promotes CSC, the joint development of interfirm plans for production, delivery, and long-term collaboration but has no significant impact on COC (Li et al., 2019). This is because teams are optimized for strategic, non-routine work rather than the systematic execution of routine tasks.

Having established these internal mechanisms, the platform can then engage in two distinct but synergistic forms of external customer coordination, which serve as the direct conduit to value creation. Customer operational coordination (COC) involves the joint participation of the platform and its customers in routine interfirm procedures, such as monitoring business processes, co-developing specific features, or managing service-level agreements (Narasimhan & Kim, 2002; Li et al., 2019). Customer strategic coordination (CSC), by contrast, reflects the degree to which the platform collaborates with customers in high-level planning activities, such as jointly forecasting demand, co-designing long-term roadmaps, or developing strategic replenishment plans (Narasimhan & Kim, 2002, Li et al., 2019). Both are vital, but they are enabled by different internal levers, as the empirical model confirms. This nuanced mapping provides a powerful blueprint for platform managers: to improve daily operational reliability, they should invest in integrated systems and standardized processes; to enhance long-term strategic positioning, they must focus on building cross-functional teams and collaborative planning routines.

4.2.2 *Information Processing View in Platform Settings*

The entire logic of this coordination framework is anchored in Information Processing Theory (IPT), which provides a causal and coherent explanation for why these internal structures are so critical. IPT starts from a simple yet powerful premise: organizations face information processing demands created by environmental uncertainty and interdependence, and they can respond either by reducing their need for information processing or by enhancing their information processing capabilities. Performance is optimized when these capabilities match the demands (Galbraith, 1974; Tushman & Nadler, 1978).

In a platform supply chain, the decision to integrate deeply with customers is a deliberate choice to embrace high levels of environmental uncertainty. This integration generates information processing demands from at least four sources (Sepulveda Rojas & Frein, 2008; Wong et al., 2015). First, there is **complex interdependence**: a customer's action affects the platform, sellers, and other customers in a recursive loop. Trial feedback influences product design, which affects marketing campaigns, which in turn impacts seller status and inventory decisions. Managing these interdependencies requires constant information exchange. Second, there is **high variability and volatility**: customer needs and preferences change rapidly, and platform policies can trigger swift shifts in sentiment and participation, increasing uncertainty. Third, platforms are characterized by **dense and asymmetric network effects**: customers influence each other through reviews and social sharing, and negative experiences often propagate more strongly than positive ones, creating complex, system-level feedback loops that must be monitored and interpreted. Fourth, platform decisions are under constant **regulatory and reputational scrutiny**, adding another layer of complexity and uncertainty.

From an IPT perspective, these features mean that platform customer integration creates high and multi-dimensional information processing demands. The platform must collect, interpret, and act on a vast amount of information from diverse sources in a timely way. Simple, siloed structures are incapable of handling this demand. The three forms of cross-functional coordination provide the necessary IPCs to meet these demands (Tushman & Nadler, 1978; Ståhle et al., 2019).

System coordination, as vertical information systems, raises the throughput and precision of information processing. It allows the platform to cope with the high-volume, codified data flows from routine customer interactions. Process coordination, as formal lateral relationships, serves a dual role: it reduces information processing demand by making routine decisions automatic through standardized procedures, and it increases processing capability by clarifying how to handle exceptional cases through defined workflows. Team coordination, as informal lateral relationships, enhances situational understanding and problem-solving capacity under conditions of high ambiguity and novelty, which is essential for strategic decision-making.

When this matching between demands and capabilities is successful, the platform can transform uncertainty from a liability into a strategic asset. It can detect emerging risks earlier, respond to customer needs with greater agility, and design customer integration mechanisms that build trust and amplify positive network effects. The ultimate outcome of this entire internal coordination effort is enhanced operational performance. The empirical evidence is definitive on this point: both COC and CSC have a positive and significant impact on operational performance, with CSC exerting a more substantial direct effect (Thomas & McDaniel, 1990; Flynn et al., 2010; Wong et al., 2011; Ataseven & Nair, 2017). Furthermore, the interaction between COC and CSC also promotes operational performance, suggesting a powerful synergy between them (Li et al., 2019). In essence, the platform's internal governance architecture, its system, process, and team coordination, is not an administrative overhead but the very engine of its external value creation. It is the foundational capability that allows the platform to move from being a passive intermediary to an active orchestrator of a thriving, value-generating ecosystem. This internal mastery of coordination is the essential first step that enables the specific, high-leverage value creation strategies explored in the following section to succeed.

4.3 Value Creation: Free Trials Under Network Effects

4.3.1 Introduction

This section defines customer integration in digital platforms and explains why it matters for value. Specifically, it investigates how platforms integrate end customers through experiential mechanisms, namely free trials, and how such integration generates economic value in markets characterized by strong consumer network effects. The object of integration is the platform user: potential buyers whose purchasing decisions are influenced not only by product attributes but also by social signals generated by other users who have experienced the product firsthand. The primary challenge lies in the dual nature of free trials: while they reduce consumer uncertainty and amplify product visibility through peer networks, they simultaneously risk cannibalizing paid demand and triggering negative sentiment cascades if poorly targeted. Governance occurs through algorithmic identification of high-value consumers and dynamic calibration of trial scale, processes that determine whether the integration effort yields net-positive returns. Value is created when free trials successfully expand market reach, increase willingness-to-pay, and stabilize long-term profitability through enhanced trust and reduced information asymmetry.

The time characterized by digitization, intelligence and networking has arrived with the rapid development and widespread application of the new generation information technology such as big data, cloud computing, 5G, artificial intelligence (AI) and Internet of Things (IoT) (Qiu & Whinston, 2017; Kumar et al., 2018; Lee et al., 2018; Hu et al., 2019; Mallipeddi et al., 2022). The new generation of information technology has not only facilitated innovation in the traditional business model and even created the new business model and the new industry (Kanatlı & Karaer, 2022) but has also fundamentally changed the character of business operations and the competitive and operational landscape of the industry (Huang et al., 2021; Qiu et al., 2021). In the current competitive market, business models are becoming increasingly important, as the competition among modern firms is no longer limited to competition between the product and the service, but between business models, especially the new business model (Badunenko et al., 2021). In recent years, the emergence and development of new business models has changed the way that products and services are promoted (Libai et al., 2013). In the meantime, it is also changing the way firms derive value from their operational activities (Cui et al., 2018). In addition, a competitive advantage could be provided to firms by the new business model, especially when they are in a period of pursuing breakthrough growth or resisting industry disruption (Libai et al., 2013; Kanatlı & Karaer, 2022). Currently, the free business model, as one of the new business models, is being developed and applied by major e-commerce enterprises (Vidgen et al., 2020).

Over the past three decades, the free trial service has been utilized by many firms to market a variety of products, including books, CDs, magazines and software, in the free business model (Bawa & Shoemaker, 2004; Cheng & Tang, 2010; Cheng & Liu, 2012; Dou et al., 2013; Liu et al., 2014; Cheng et al., 2015; Li & Yi, 2016; Nan et al., 2016; Yang et al., 2018). In recent years, a growing number of firms have been adopting and developing the free trial as a new business model, such as JD.com, Suning, Alibaba Cloud Computing and Lenovo. The free trials of JD.com and Suning are aimed at products manufactured by other merchants, such as L'Oreal, Estee Lauder etc. The free trial of Alibaba Cloud Computing is in response to the office software products developed for its own firms. Differently, the free trial of Lenovo is offered to the new electronic products produced by its own firms. Meanwhile, after trialing the product, consumers who are lucky enough to be chosen for the free trial are required to provide Lenovo with trial feedback reports, which are utilized in the conception, design and development of new products. Meanwhile, feedback reports and reviews from lucky consumers could be captured by other consumers who are active in the mall and community to increase their purchases, searches and concerns about the product. It enables the supply chain of Lenovo to have a closed-loop structure with positive feedback, which is shown in Fig. 4.2.

However, various merchants are still in the exploratory stage of the free trial and have not developed a sound operational plan (Yang et al., 2018). There are still many problems with the free trial, and one of the most critical problems is how many lucky consumers should be available for the free trial. For example, when the number of lucky consumers for the free trial is set low, the effect of the free trial is weak, e.g. the exposure of the product decreases and the potential value of the product is reduced (Cheng & Tang, 2010; Cheng & Liu, 2012). Conversely, the free trial has a significant cannibalization effect on the original demand for the product when the number of lucky consumers is high, which directly reduces the profit of the merchant (Bawa & Shoemaker, 2004). Therefore, the problem of setting the number

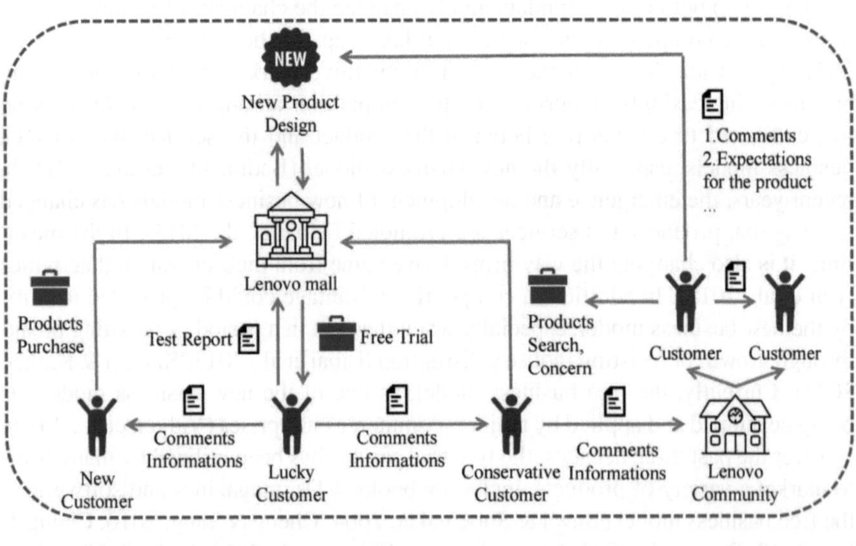

Fig. 4.2 The sketch of Lenovo Mall free trial

of lucky customers and the free trial operation scheme properly needs to be solved urgently, which has gradually attracted the attention of academia and industry.

With the gradual emergence and development of the free trial, there has been an upsurge of scholars' attention on the research of operational problems of the free trial. The free trial has been widely employed by software companies to accelerate product diffusion (Cheng & Liu, 2012; Ho et al., 2012; Dou et al., 2013; Cheng et al., 2015; Li & Yi, 2016; Yang et al., 2018). For digital experience products like software, providing free trial can remove the consumer uncertainty about the functionality of the product (Cheng & Tang, 2010; Cheng & Liu, 2012; Dou et al., 2013; Liu et al., 2014; Cheng et al., 2015; Sriram et al., 2015; Li & Yi, 2016; Nan et al., 2016; Wu et al., 2018). Currently, most of the studies focus on the following two aspects. The first aspect is investigating the impact of the free trial on the purchase intention of the consumer. Wang et al. demonstrated that experiences of consumers with the mobile newspaper software were different after the free trial than before (Wang et al., 2013). Zhu and Chang explored the intention of the consumer toward the free trial based on technical services and found that perceived usefulness, perceived usability, perceived risk and social impact were critical determinants (Zhu & Chang, 2014). Halbheer et al. indicated that strategies of the free trial could influence consumers' expectations of the product quality and ultimately influence consumers' purchasing decisions, which are closely associated with consumers' demands (Halbheer et al., 2014). Foubert and Gijsbrechts discovered that the free trial was more effective than advertising in communicating messages since the practical usage of the free trial reduce consumer uncertainty more quickly (Foubert & Gijsbrechts, 2016). Sun et al. found that there was low propensity to purchase because most consumers knew relatively little about the new service (Sun et al., 2017). However, the free trial is one of the effective marketing methods to promote consumer belief in the service. The above research has indicated that the free trial could enhance consumers' experience of the service and further influence their purchase decisions. The second aspect is researching on when and how the firm should adopt the free trial strategy. Cheng and Tang found that it would be wise for the company to provide the free trial rather than segment the market through charging for the lower quality product with strong network effects (Cheng & Tang, 2010). Cheng and Liu investigated both time-limited and function-limited free trial strategies and found that the trial period should be shorter as the network effect increased and as consumers' beforehand evaluation of the software's functionality improved (Cheng & Liu, 2012). Moreover, when the strength of the network effect is less than a certain threshold, the time-constrained strategy is better than the function-constrained strategy. Cheng et al. discussed the optimal conditions for the finite feature free trial, time-locked free trial and hybrid free trial strategies, respectively (Cheng et al., 2015). It was concluded that the finite feature free trial strategy was the most favorable due to the strong network strength, while the time-locked free trial strategy performed best when the positive network effects were weak. Meanwhile, the hybrid free trial strategy outperformed the other two strategies when the network strength was medium range. Niu et al. noted that the priori belief of customers played a vital role and the company only should adopt the free trial when the initial belief of the consumer was below a certain threshold (Niu et al., 2019). These research have revealed the conditions under which the company should implement the free trial and how to conduct it.

Previous studies have significantly advanced the understanding of free trial operations from various perspectives and provide a valuable foundation for this analysis. However, several research gaps remain, which this section seeks to address. (1) Most existing studies focus on free trials of non-physical products exhibiting network externalities, particularly software, while research on free trials for physical products remains limited. A growing body of empirical evidence indicates that free trials also significantly impact physical products (Liu et al., 2014; Sun et al., 2017; Yi et al., 2019), not only by reducing consumer uncertainty but also by enhancing product promotion and firm value. Notably, some studies suggest that the cannibalization effect of free trials may be more pronounced for physical goods than for digital ones (Bawa & Shoemaker, 2004; Srinivasan & Swink, 2015; Qiu & Whinston, 2017; Sun et al., 2017). Therefore, this section examines the optimal free trial policy for electronic products, aiming to complement existing research with theoretical and practical insights specific to tangible goods. (2) In modeling network externalities, the majority of prior work assumes a linear network effect function to simplify model construction and solution. However, recent empirical analyses of real-world data increasingly reveal that network effects are often non-linear (Bhargava, 2022; Bhargava et al., 2022). Accordingly, this section introduces a non-linear network effect function, drawing on the utility framework of Prospect Theory (Kahneman & Tversky, 1979; Tversky & Kahneman, 1992), thereby enriching the theoretical treatment of network effects in free trial research. (3) Much of the literature on software free trials considers only positive network effects, neglecting negative ones—an oversight that limits analytical realism. Empirical studies of peer-to-peer networks, for instance, have documented both positive and negative network effects (Asvanund et al., 2004; Wu et al., 2018). Furthermore, analysis of the real operational data from Lenovo presented in this chapter reveals measurable negative consumer sentiment during both the free trial application and feedback stages. Thus, this section explicitly incorporates both positive and negative network effects to assess their combined influence on electronic product free trials. Given the non-linear nature of these effects, investigating free trial operations under this more comprehensive assumption is essential and constitutes a key motivation for the present analysis.

This section aims to develop a framework for optimizing free trial policies for electronic products. By modeling consumer network effect utility, demand, and profit under three governance scenarios: (1) No free trial, (2) Free trial with precise identification, and (3) Free trial with imprecise identification while accounting for positive and negative non-linear network effects, we derive equilibrium outcomes. Comparative analysis of these results yields managerial insights and testable hypotheses. To validate the analytical framework, numerical simulations and empirical tests are conducted using real operational data from Lenovo Mall.

The structure of this section is as follows. First, the basic assumptions and the formulation of the consumer network effect function are presented, followed by a formal description of the three policy scenarios. Next, the optimal equilibrium results for each scenario are derived, analyzed, and summarized in a series of propositions. Finally, real-world data is employed for empirical validation and numerical experimentation to substantiate the theoretical conclusions. The section concludes with a summary of findings and their implications.

4.3.2 Model and Methodology

The problem of the appropriate number of lucky customers and the free trial operation scheme for a monopoly merchant selling electronic products is studied in this part. In addition, this section is divided into two parts. The first part covers the basic assumptions and the consumer network effect function. Based on the first part, different scenarios of the free trial are described in the second part.

Stage 1 Basic Assumption and Consumer Network Effect Function

Based on the reality and previous studies (Conner, 1995; Cheng & Tang, 2010; Cheng & Liu, 2012; Liu et al., 2014; Cheng et al., 2015), the basic assumptions and the consumer network effect function of the free trial physical product are provided in this part.

Basic Assumptions

Assumption 1. Both the overall size of the market and the number of consumers in this market remain stable. Meanwhile, some consumers seem to have a good impression of the free trial products in this market.

Assumption 2. Both the operational costs of the free trial and the search costs for consumers are not negligible. In other words, unlike information products or commercial and free trial software, the marginal production cost of electronic products is supposed to be considered. In addition, when participating in the free trial or purchasing a product, additional costs for consumers are incurred, including time and effort spent searching for a certain product, perusing product literature and other related product reviews, etc.

Assumption 3. It is considered as the rational expectation equilibrium, i.e. consumers do not switch between products and repeat purchases. Furthermore, there are three options available to each consumer in this market: no purchase, become the lucky consumer to receive the free trial product, or purchase the product.

Assumption 4. Consumers are not completely heterogeneous. For instance, consumer heterogeneity is manifested in the fact that the expected valuation or the priori perception of the product is different for each consumer through searching for information, comparing other products, etc. Additionally, the consumer homogeneity is reflected in the same network effect function of each consumer for the free trial.

Assumption 5. The quality of each product is qualified, which means that the product obtained by the consumer through the free trial or purchase is available. In the meantime, the return or exchange of products by the consumer is not considered.

Consumer Network Effect

Based on the utility theory, the network effect and the advertising effect, the consumer network effect function of the free trial is established in this part. Subsequently, we derived the network effect of the free trial with the number of consumers as a curve by fitting the free trial operational data provided by Lenovo Mall. In summary, the consumer network effect function is expressed by the quantity of consumers who are lucky to try the products for free. The relationship between the consumer network effect (A) and the number of lucky consumers (Q) is shown in Fig. 4.3, and the consumer network effect function of free trial is presented as follows.

$$A = \begin{cases} \gamma\sqrt{Q}, & \text{when positive} \\ -\beta\sqrt{Q}, & \text{when negative} \end{cases}$$

where γ and β refer to the network effect coefficients of the free trial, representing the sensitivity of consumers to updating their previous perceptions of the product through the free trial, similar to the sensitivity of consumers to advertising campaigns. Besides, these coefficients are constants. γ is the network effect coefficient where customers have a positive perception through the free trial, and β is the network effect coefficient where customers have a negative perception through the free trial. The values of these coefficients need to be determined by fitting the consumer purchase behavior data, including consumer browsing data, purchase data, posted information data, etc. Q is the number of consumers who are lucky enough to be chosen to try the product for free in the free trial.

In the real operational scenario, the consumer network structure is extremely complex. For instance, a portion of the consumer network structure is illustrated in Fig. 4.4, where the cartoon people represent consumers, and the edge represents the association between consumers, including kinship, friendship, consumer alliances, etc. In this part of the consumer network structure, it is obvious to observe that Consumer 1 has the highest number of associations with other consumers. Consequently, after the free trial product is chosen to be distributed to Consumer 1

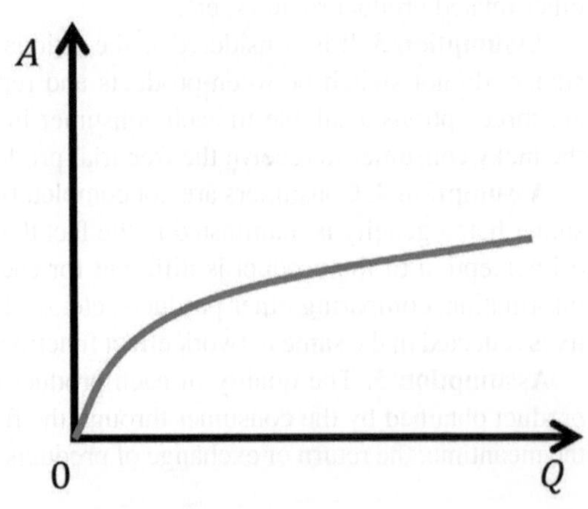

Fig. 4.3 Consumer network effect function

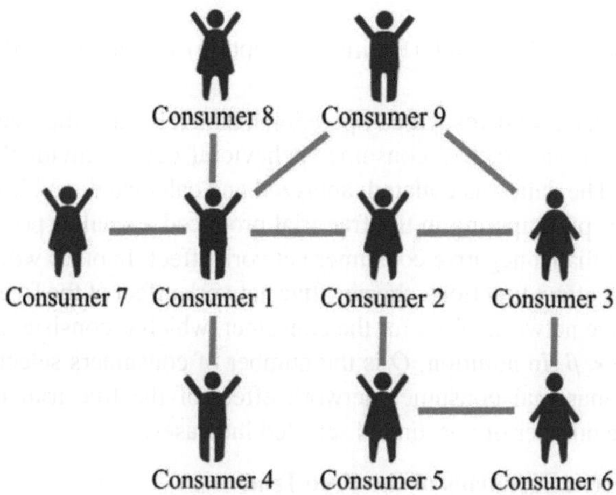

Fig. 4.4 Consumer network structure

by the merchant and the consumer is willing to promote this product to other consumers associated with him directly, it could be observed that six additional consumers received some relevant information and learned about the product. Subsequently, the merchant could choose either Consumer 2 or Consumer 3 for the free trial, since only two more new consumers could be introduced to learn about the product and relevant information, regardless of whether choosing Consumer 2 or Consumer 3 on the basis of selecting Consumer 1 first. In addition, as the number of consumers selected by the merchant for the free trial within this consumer network structure increases, the number of new consumers added through the free trial is progressively decreasing. It is similar to the law of diminishing marginal utility. In summary, the increase in the number of consumers resulting from the free trial is a non-linear increase rather than simply a linear increase. Hence, the consumer network effect resulting from the free trial should also be non-linear, similar to the diffusion effect in the advertising effect, which has been mentioned and empirically proven by many previous studies.

In the free trial, the knowledge of the potential value, demand and reviews of the new product for the merchant is vague and uncertain. Similarly, consumers selected for the free trial have little knowledge of the quality and use experience of the product. Both the merchant and the consumer are making decisions based on incomplete information and irrationality, which is comparable to the conditions of the Prospect Theory (Kahneman & Tversky, 1979; Tversky & Kahneman, 1992). Therefore, the consumer network effect functions constructed in this paper refer to the value functions of the Prospect Theory, which was proposed by Kahneman and Tversky. In the Prospect Theory, the value functions are $v(x) = x^{\alpha'}$ (Revenue Status) and $v(x) = -\lambda(-x)^{\beta'}$ (Loss Status), where $\alpha' = \beta' = 0.88$ and $\lambda = 2.25$. To facilitate the model calculating and solving, the consumer network effect functions constructed in this paper are $A(Q) = \gamma\sqrt{Q}$ (Positive Perception) and $A(Q) = -\beta\sqrt{Q}$ (Negative Perception).

Simultaneously, we investigated operational data related to the free trial provided by Lenovo Mall and tracked consumer behavioral data (individual consumer) in Lenovo Mall. The data was collated, analyzed and calculated, and it was found that each consumer participating in the free trial produced a smaller positive consumer network effect than a negative consumer network effect. In other words, in the consumer network effect functions, the negative network effect of the free trial is greater than the positive network effect for the consumer, which is consistent with Prospect Theory, i.e., $\gamma < \beta$. In addition, Q is the number of consumers selected by the free trial and the marginal consumer network effect of the free trial is non-linearly reduced as the number of consumers selected increases.

Stage 2 Different Scenarios of the Free Trial

In this section, there is only one merchant in the market. In other words, the merchant is in a monopoly position, and the scenario where the merchant competes or collaborates with other merchants on the free trial is not considered. Furthermore, only the electronic product is considered for the free trial in this study. The electronic product is the physical product consisting of electronic components and circuits that perform a specific function or provide a specific service. These products can include electronic devices such as mobile phones, televisions and computers. Unlike other physical products, such as food, clothing and daily necessities, electronic products are more expensive and updated rapidly, resulting in longer lead times for consumers to make purchasing decisions. Moreover, owing to the overlapping functions of the same or similar electronic products, most consumers do not make repeat purchases within a short period of time. Meanwhile, according to Assumption 3, consumers who are not selected for the free trial could purchase the product at its original price or give up using the product. To better analyze the impact of the free trial on the electronic product demand, pricing and profitability under different conditions, three different scenarios are considered. The first scenario is no free trial for the electronic product in the market. The second scenario is that the merchant not only provides a free trial of electronic products, but can also accurately identify valuable consumers in the market. The third scenario is that although the merchant offers the free trial of electronic products, there are some mistakes in identifying valuable consumers in the market. Meanwhile, this section constructs the consumer network utility model for different scenarios. Subsequently, the different consumer demand models and product profit models are built up. These equilibrium results of different scenarios would be displayed in the next section, and the differences of these equilibrium results would be discussed.

Scenario 1: No Free Trial

In this scenario, the merchant does not provide the free trial of the electronic product. Therefore, the consumer is left with the choice of purchasing the product or giving up using it. It should be pointed out that each consumer has an expected valuation of the electronic product, $\theta_1(i)$ (i represents consumers, i.e., $i = 1$ represents consumer 1), which is generated while consumers are searching for information about the electronic product or comparing it with other electronic products. The expected valuation, $\theta_1(i)$, follows a uniform distribution, $[-(a-1), 1]$, where the negative value means that the total cost to the consumer of using the electronic product is higher than the total benefit. Let θ_0 denote the "marginal" consumer who has zero utility from knowing and purchasing the product. Consumers with a higher expected valuation of the product than the marginal consumer will purchase the product. Conversely, consumers with lower expected valuation than the marginal consumer will give up purchasing the product. Since the expected valuations are uniformly distributed in the interval $[-(a-1), 1]$, the sub-interval $[\theta_0, 1]$ corresponds to buyers of the product. Consequently, the consumer demand of the electronic product for Scenario 1 is shown as Fig. 4.5.

The cost and quality of the electronic product, c and s, as well as the cost incurred by consumers searching for the electronic product, b, are determined values in the market. Under the above conditions, the total consumers are also uniformly distributed at $[-(a-1), 1]$ and $1 - \theta_0$ can be regarded as consumer demand for the product. Moreover, the profit of the merchant is actually per unit demanded. Since the consumer has only two choices in Scenario 1, the consumer network utility model, the demand model and the product profit model are shown as follows.

$$\theta_0 \cdot s - p_1 - b = 0,$$
$$D_1 = 1 - \theta_0,$$
$$\pi_1 = D_1 \cdot (p_1 - c),$$

where p_1 and D_1 are the pricing and demand of the electronic product in Scenario 1, respectively. π_1 is the total profit for the merchant in Scenario 1.

Scenario 2: Free Trial with Precise Identification

In this scenario, the merchant not only provides the free trial of the electronic product, but also identifies the most valuable consumers accurately. In particular, the merchant can accurately identify consumers who are motivated by the free trial and spread the positive sentiment, rather than the speculator who takes advantage through the free trial and mistrustful people who spread the negative sentiment. Similar to Scenario 1, each consumer also has an expected valuation of the electronic product, $\theta_2(i)$ (i represents consumers, i.e., $i = 1$ represents consumer 1).

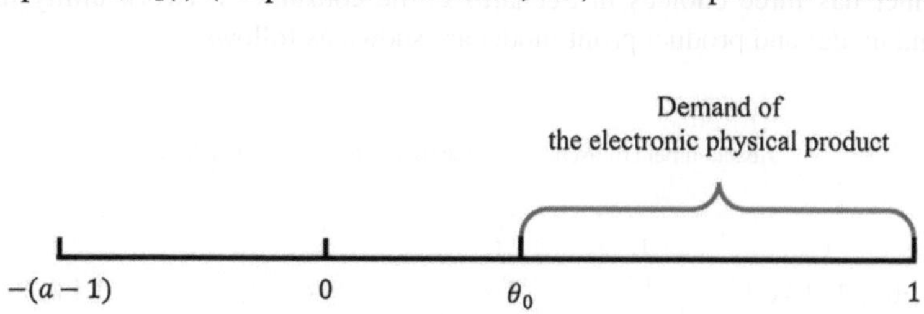

Fig. 4.5 The consumer demand of the electronic product for Scenario 1

Different from Scenario 1, according to Assumption 2, the consumer has three choices in this scenario: purchasing the product at full price, obtaining a free product with the free trial, and giving up buying the product. Let θ_{2L} denote the "low-marginal" consumer who has zero utility from knowing the product. Let θ_{2H} denote the "high-marginal" consumer who has zero utility from knowing and purchasing the product. Consumers could take an interest in the electronic product when their expected valuation is higher than θ_{2L}, i.e., $\theta_2(i) \geq \theta_{2L}$. As the consumers' expected valuation is higher than θ_{2H}, consumers could purchase the electronic product at the full price, i.e., $\theta_2(i) \geq \theta_{2H}$. Owing to the consumer network effect, the distribution of consumers' expected valuations is shifted rightwards to the interval $\left[-(a-1)+\gamma\sqrt{Q_2}, 1+\gamma\sqrt{Q_2}\right]$, implying that the potential market size has been expanded to $1+\gamma\sqrt{Q_2}$. In summary, the expected valuations are uniformly distributed in the interval $\left[-(a-1)+\gamma\sqrt{Q_2}, 1+\gamma\sqrt{Q_2}\right]$ and the sub-interval $\left[\theta_{2H}, 1+\gamma\sqrt{Q_2}\right]$ corresponds to buyers of the product. Therefore, the consumer demand of the electronic product for Scenario 2 is shown as Fig. 4.6.

Similar to Scenario 1, the cost and quality of the electronic product, c and s, as well as the cost incurred by consumers searching for the electronic product, b, are determined values in the market. Under the above conditions, the total consumers are also uniformly distributed at $\left[-(a-1)+\gamma\sqrt{Q_2}, 1+\gamma\sqrt{Q_2}\right]$ and $1-\theta_{H2}+\gamma\sqrt{Q_2}$ can be regarded as consumer demand for the product. Moreover, the profit of the merchant is actually per unit demanded. Unlike Scenario 1, the merchant provides a portion of the electronic product and selects a certain number of consumers for the free trial. The electronic product is not as easy to expend as household products such as food, clothing and cosmetics, or as susceptible to updates and widely varying functions as digital products such as software and games. Thus, once the lucky consumer has received the electronic product through the free trial, they could hardly ever purchase this product again. In other words, the free trial can cannibalize the original consumer demand for the electronic product. However, these consumers could bring more exposure, browsing, and even potential demand for this product. In summary, in Scenario 2, the optimal number of consumers is determined to participate in the free trial to maximize the electronic product pricing, demand and profit, while balancing the benefits and drawbacks of the free trial. Since the consumer has three choices in Scenario 2, the consumer network utility model, demand model and product profit model are shown as follows.

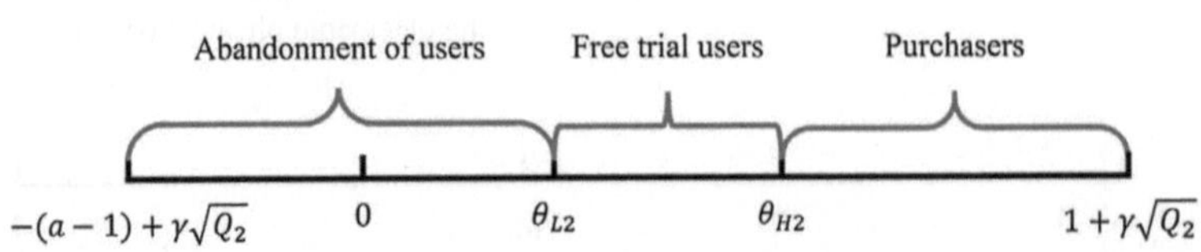

Fig. 4.6 The consumer demand of the electronic product for Scenario 2

$$\theta_{H2} \cdot s - p_2 - b = 0,$$
$$\theta_{L2} \cdot s - b = 0,$$
$$D_2 = 1 - \theta_{H2} + \gamma \sqrt{Q_2},$$
$$\pi_2 = D_2 \cdot (p_2 - c) - Q_2 \cdot c,$$

where p_2 and D_2 are the pricing and demand of the electronic product in Scenario 2, respectively. π_2 is the total profit for the merchant in Scenario 2.

Scenario 3: Free Trial with Imprecise Identification

In this scenario, the merchant provides the free trial of the electronic product and identifies the most valuable consumers without complete accuracy. Similar to Scenario 2, each consumer also has an expected valuation of the electronic product, $\theta_3(i)$ (i represents consumers, i.e., $i = 1$ represents consumer 1) and has three choices in this scenario. Different from Scenario 2, the merchant is unable to accurately identify the most valuable consumers. In other words, the merchant has chosen some of the non-most valuable consumers for the free trial campaign. Non-most valuable consumers may have a negative perception of the product compared to the most valuable consumers and pass the negative emotion to other consumers. Meanwhile, non-most valuable consumers have fewer and weaker ties to other consumers in the overall consumer group, which results in not maximizing the effect of the free trial. Furthermore, non-most valuable consumers may be speculators who take advantage through the free trial. Therefore, in scenario 3, the accuracy of identifying the most valuable consumers is critical. As a merchant selects a non-most valuable consumer, there could be a significant drop in the consumer demand for the electronic product. As a result, the consumer demand of the electronic product for Scenario 3 is shown in Fig. 4.7.

Unlike Scenario 2, the merchant has mistaken in choosing the most valuable consumer in Scenario 3, which leads to the negative network effect of the free trial. Like information dissemination, the negative network effect of the free trial spreads more rapidly and widely than the positive network effect. Meanwhile, the negative network effect of the free trial could be very detrimental to the pricing and demand for the product. In Scenario 3, the optimal number of consumers is determined to participate in the free trial to maximize the electronic product pricing, demand and profit, while not only balancing the benefits and drawbacks of the free trial, but also considering the accuracy of the merchant in identifying the most valuable consumers. Hence, the consumer network utility model, demand model and product profit model of Scenario 3 are shown as follows.

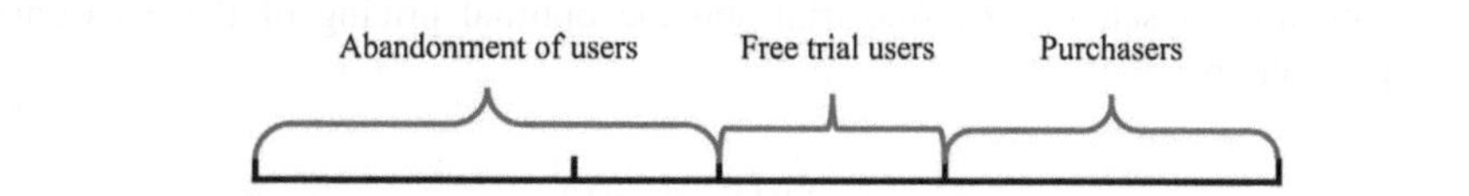

Fig. 4.7 The consumer demand of the electronic product for Scenario 3

$$\theta_{H3}\cdot s - p_3 - b = 0,$$
$$\theta_{L3}\cdot s - b = 0,$$
$$D_3 = 1 - \theta_{H3} + \alpha\cdot\gamma\sqrt{Q_3} - (1-\alpha)\cdot\beta\sqrt{Q_3},$$
$$\pi_3 = D_3\cdot(p_3 - c) - Q_3\cdot c,$$

where p_3 and D_3 are the pricing and demand of the electronic product in Scenario 3, respectively. π_3 is the total profit for the merchant in Scenario 3. α is the accuracy of the merchant in identifying the most valuable consumers.

4.3.3 *Results and Discussions*

Two parts are contained in this section. One part is the optimal results of different scenarios of the free trial, and the other part discusses the variations of the optimal results in different scenarios of the free trial.

Results

In the previous section, three different scenarios of the free trial of the electronic product are mentioned and modeled. Considering the maximization of the merchant's profit, three different scenarios of the optimal equilibrium state of the market could be obtained, including the optimal equilibrium number of consumers who are chosen for the free trial, the optimal equilibrium pricing of the electronic product, and the optimal equilibrium profit of the merchant.

(1) **Scenario 1: No free trial** Taking the derivative of Eq. (4) and making its derivative function equal to 0, it could be obtained that the optimal pricing of the electronic product is $p_1^* = \frac{1}{2}(s + c - b)$. In addition, the maximum demand of the electronic product is $D_1^* = \frac{1}{2s}(s - c - b)$ and the maximum profit of the merchant is $\pi_1^* = \frac{1}{4s}(s - c - b)^2$ in Scenario 1.

(2) **Scenario 2: Free trial with precise identification** It could be obtained the optimal state of the market for Scenario 2 by taking the derivative of Eq. (8) and making its derivative functions equal to 0. The optimal number of consumers who are chosen for the free trial and the optimal pricing of the electronic product are

$$Q_2^* = \left(\frac{\gamma(s - c - b)}{4c - s\gamma^2}\right)^2$$

and

$$p_2^* = \frac{2c(s-c-b)}{4c-s\gamma^2} + c,$$

respectively. Furthermore, in this scenario, the maximum demand of the electronic product is

$$D_2^* = 1 + \gamma\sqrt{Q_2^*} - \frac{1}{s}(p_2^* + b)$$

and the maximum profit of the merchant is

$$\pi_2^* = D_2^* \cdot (p_2^* - b) - Q_2^* \cdot c.$$

(3) **Scenario 3: Free trial with imprecise identification** Taking the derivative of Eq. (12) and making its derivative functions equal to 0, it could be obtained the optimal state of the market for Scenario 3. In Scenario 3, the optimal number of consumers who are chosen for the free trial is

$$Q_3^* = \left(\frac{(\alpha\gamma-(1-\alpha)\beta)(s-c-b)}{4c-s(\alpha\gamma-(1-\alpha)\beta)^2}\right)^2.$$

The optimal pricing of the electronic product is

$$p_3^* = \frac{2c(s-c-b)}{4c-s(\alpha\gamma-(1-\alpha)\beta)^2} + c.$$

In addition, in this scenario, the maximum demand of the electronic product is

$$D_3^* = 1 + \alpha\gamma\sqrt{Q_3^*} - (1-\alpha)\beta\sqrt{Q_3^*} - \frac{1}{s}(p_3^* + b)$$

and the maximum profit of the merchant is

$$\pi_3^* = D_3^* \cdot (p_3^* - b) - Q_3^* \cdot c.$$

Discussions of the Results for Different Scenarios

In order to compare and analyze the equilibrium optimal results in different scenarios more clearly and visually, the optimal equilibrium results are summarized in Table 4.1.

Table 4.1 The equilibrium results of three scenarios

	Scenario 1	Scenario 2	Scenario 3
The optimal pricing of the electronic product	$\frac{1}{2}(s+c-b)$	$\frac{2c(s-c-b)}{4c-s\gamma^2}+c$	$\frac{2c(s-c-b)}{4c-s(\alpha\gamma-(1-\alpha)\beta)^2}+c$
The optimal demand of the electronic product	$\frac{1}{2s}(s-c-b)$	$1+\gamma\sqrt{Q_2^*}-\frac{1}{s}(p_2^*+b)$	$1+\alpha\gamma\sqrt{Q_3^*}-(1-\alpha)\beta\sqrt{Q_3^*}-\frac{1}{s}(p_3^*+b)$
The optimal number of lucky consumers	0	$\left(\frac{\gamma(s-c-b)}{4c-s\gamma^2}\right)^2$	$\left(\frac{(\alpha\gamma-(1-\alpha)\beta)(s-c-b)}{4c-s(\alpha\gamma-(1-\alpha)\beta)^2}\right)^2$
The optimal profit of the electronic product	$\frac{1}{4s}(s-c-b)^2$	$D_2^*(p_2^*-b)-Q_2^*c$	$D_3^*(p_3^*-b)-Q_3^*c$

It can be visualized from Table 4.1 that equilibrium results are significantly different in three scenarios. And it would bring certain beneficial improvements to the market and merchants after conducting the free trial under certain circumstances. In addition, the maximum demand of the electronic product and the maximum profit of the merchant can be seen in Scenario 2. Hence, after conducting the free trial, the more accurately the merchant identifies its most valuable customers, the greater the profitability and demand for the merchant's electronic products.

Comparing the optimal results of Scenario 1 and Scenario 2, the following lemmas and propositions could be summarized.

The free trial of the electronic product should only be adopted when the quality of the product satisfies the certain condition, i.e. $b+c<s<\frac{4c}{\gamma^2}$.

It follows from Lemma 1 that not all products are appropriate for the free trial. First, the merchant should never apply fake and inferior products for the free trial. Otherwise, consumers could get negative publicity about the product, quickly become distrustful of the merchant, and abandon purchasing other products from the merchant in the future. Second, in quality management, the cost of the general product increases non-linearly with the quality. The merchant may suffer from increased operating costs and reduced profits, resulting from the free trial of the high-cost but high-quality product. Hence, it is cautious for the merchant to select products for the free trial.

With the same electronic product quality, the pricing of the electronic product is increased significantly by the free trial which is conducted by merchant measure compared to the no free trial measure, and the increase in value is

$\Delta p_1 = \frac{s\gamma^2(s-c-b)}{2(4c-s\gamma^2)}$. Meanwhile, the increment increases as the effect of the free trial, γ, increases.

For the same electronic product quality, the demand of the electronic product is increased significantly by the free trial which is conducted by merchant measure compared to the no free trial measure, and the increase in value is $\Delta D_1 = \frac{1}{2}\gamma\sqrt{Q_2^*}$. Moreover, the increment increases as the effect of the free trial, γ, increases.

Further conclusions could be drawn from Propositions 1 and 2. It is obvious that after the free trial, there is a significant increase in the pricing and demand for the electronic product. Hence, when merchants can accurately identify the most valuable consumers in their consumer group, the free trial should be adopted to increase the consumer demand for the electronic product and its price.

In case of the same electronic product quality, even if the free trial through the merchant increases the operating costs of the business, the total profit for the merchant increases significantly in the long term, compared to measures without the free trial, and the increasing value to $\Delta\pi_1 = \frac{\gamma^2(s\gamma-4c)(s-c-b)^2}{4(4c-s\gamma^2)}$. Furthermore, the increment increases as the effect of the free trial, γ, increases.

With Proposition 3, it is clear that when the merchant can accurately identify their most valuable consumers, although it makes operating costs increase after adopting the free trial, the total profit is higher than the no free trial scenario. Consequently, when the merchant can accurately identify the most valuable consumers, the merchant is supposed to apply the free trial to further increase its profit.

Comparing the equilibrium results of Scenario 2 and Scenario 3 and analyzing the difference between the two, the propositions are summarized as follows.

The free trial should only be conducted when the merchant's accuracy, $\frac{\beta}{\beta+\gamma} \leq \alpha \leq 1$, in identifying the most valuable consumers.

Further conclusions can be drawn from Proposition 4. As the accuracy of the merchant in identifying the most valuable consumer is less than $\frac{\beta}{\beta+\gamma}$, the number of optimal consumers selected by the free trial can be solved for as a negative number. Therefore, the free trial should not be applied when the merchant's accuracy in identifying the most valuable customers is low. Otherwise, the free trial could not only increase the merchant's operating costs for nothing, but also reduce the consumer demand and pricing for the electronic product. In summary, the success of the free trial depends on whether the merchant can correctly identify the consumer group. In addition, according to Lemma 1 and Proposition 4, the merchant needs to consider the quality of the product as well as the accuracy of identifying consumers to determine whether they conduct the free trial for the product. The decision on whether the merchant should conduct the free trial is shown in Fig. 4.8.

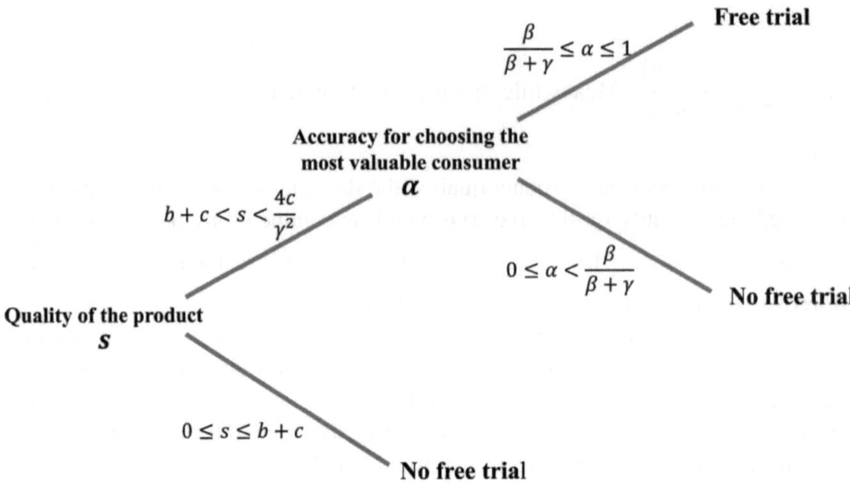

Fig. 4.8 Free trial or not free trial?

Comparing the merchant identifies its most valuable consumers without any mistakes, the price of the product decreases when the merchant identifies its most valuable consumers with some mistakes, and the decrease in value is $\Delta p_2 = \frac{2c(s-c-b)\left(\gamma^2 - (\alpha\gamma - (1-\alpha)\beta)^2\right)}{(4c - s\gamma^2)\left(4c - s(\alpha\gamma - (1-\alpha)\beta)^2\right)}$. In addition, the reduction decreases as the accuracy, α, increases. Nevertheless, comparing the no free trial, the price of the product increases when the merchant identifies its most valuable consumers with some mistakes, and the increase in value is $\Delta p_3 = \frac{s\left(\gamma^2 - (\alpha\gamma - (1-\alpha)\beta)^2\right)(s-c-b)}{2\left(4c - s(\alpha\gamma - (1-\alpha)\beta)^2\right)}$. Meanwhile, the increment increases as the accuracy, α, increases.

Comparing the merchant identifies its most valuable consumers without any mistakes, the demand of the product decreases when the merchant identifies its most valuable consumers with some mistakes, and the decrease in value is $\Delta D_2 = \frac{\left(4c - s\gamma(\alpha\gamma - (1-\alpha)\beta)\right)(s-c-b)(1-\alpha)(\gamma+\beta)}{(4c - s\gamma^2)\left(4c - s(\alpha\gamma - (1-\alpha)\beta)^2\right)}$, which decreases as the accuracy, α, increases. Nevertheless, comparing the no free trial, the demand of the product increases when the merchant identifies its most valuable consumers with some mistakes, and the increase in value is $\Delta D_3 = \frac{1}{2}(\alpha\gamma - (1-\alpha)\beta)\sqrt{Q_3^*}$. Meanwhile, the increment increases as the accuracy, α, increases.

It follows from Propositions 5 and 6 that the price and demand of the electronic product can be reduced by misidentifying the most valuable consumers in the free trial. However, compared to Scenario 1: no free trial, the free trial significantly increases the price and demand for the product, regardless of the fact that the merchant makes some mistakes in identifying the most valuable consumers in free trials. Consequently, as far as possible, the merchant should try to identify speculators who take advantage of the product or mistrustful people who generate and spread negative emotions, etc. and then select other more appropriate consumers for the free trial.

Comparing the merchant identifies its most valuable consumers without any mistakes, the number of consumers who are lucky enough to participate in the free trial decreases when the merchant identifies its most valuable consumers with some mistakes, and the decrease in value is

$$\Delta Q=\frac{\left(4c+s\gamma\left(\alpha\gamma-(1-\alpha)\beta\right)\right)\left(4c-s\gamma\left(\alpha\gamma-(1-\alpha)\beta\right)\right)\left(\gamma+\left(\alpha\gamma-(1-\alpha)\beta\right)\right)\left(\gamma-\left(\alpha\gamma-(1-\alpha)\beta\right)\right)(s-c-b)^2}{\left(4c-s\gamma^2\right)^2\left(4c-s\left(\alpha\gamma-(1-\alpha)\beta\right)^2\right)^2},$$

which decreases as the accuracy, α, increases.

Further conclusions can be drawn from Proposition 7. When the merchant identifies its most valuable consumers with some mistakes, it is wise for the merchant to reduce the number of consumers participating in the free trial to prevent negative effects, similar to the Chinese proverb, talks much errs much.

Comparing the merchant identifies its most valuable consumers without any mistakes, the profit of the merchant decreases when identifying its most valuable consumers with some mistakes, and

$$\Delta\pi_2=\frac{(s-c-b)^2\left(4cs\left(\gamma^3-\left(\alpha\gamma-(1-\alpha)\beta\right)^3\right)-s^2\gamma^2\left(\alpha\gamma-(1-\alpha)\beta\right)^2(1-\alpha)(\gamma+\beta)-16c^2\left(\gamma^2-\left(\alpha\gamma-(1-\alpha)\beta\right)^2\right)\right)}{4\left(4c-s\gamma^2\right)\left(4c-s\left(\alpha\gamma-(1-\alpha)\beta\right)^2\right)},$$

which decreases as the accuracy, α, increases. However, comparing the no free trial, the profit of the merchant increases when identifying its most valuable consumers with some mistakes, and the increase in value is $\Delta\pi_3=\dfrac{\left(\alpha\gamma-(1-\alpha)\beta\right)^2\left(s\left(\alpha\gamma-(1-\alpha)\beta\right)-4c\right)(s-c-b)^2}{4\left(4c-s\left(\alpha\gamma-(1-\alpha)\beta\right)^2\right)}$. Furthermore, the increment increases as the accuracy, α, increases.

It follows from Proposition 8 that the profit of the merchant can be reduced by misidentifying the most valuable consumers in the free trial. However, compared to Scenario 1: no free trial, the free trial significantly increases the profit for the merchant, regardless of the fact that the merchant makes some mistakes in identifying the most valuable consumers in free trials. Consequently, the more accurately the merchant identifies the consumer, the more significant the positive effect of the free trial. In other words, the merchant should focus on identifying consumers and removing the speculators and mistrustful consumers to enhance the effectiveness of the free trial.

The above analysis, combined with Propositions 1–8, leads to the following hypotheses from the model:

The effectiveness of the free trial increases with the merchant's accuracy in selecting the most valuable consumers increases (H1).
The pricing of the product increases with the merchant's accuracy in selecting the most valuable consumers increases (H2).
The demand of the product increases with the merchant's accuracy in selecting the most valuable consumers increases (H3).
The network effect generated by the free trial strengthens the positive impact of the accuracy on the effectiveness of the free trial (H4).
The network effect generated by the free trial strengthens the positive impact of the accuracy on the pricing of the product (H5).
The network effect generated by the free trial strengthens the positive impact of the accuracy on the demand of the product (H6).

4.3.4 Data and Analysis

Through the Lenovo Mall, all the real operational data of the free trial from Issue 50 to Issue 142 is obtained, including the total number of applicants and the lucky consumer for the free trial, the reasons for applying, the feedback reports after the free trial, the cost and the selling price of the products, etc.

First of all, after the sentiment analysis of the 338,462 reasons for applications obtained in the free trial, it is apparent that 89.16% of the application reasons have positive sentiments, 10.73% of the application reasons have neutral sentiments, and 0.11% of the application reasons have negative sentiments toward the free trial. Among the positive sentiments, the consumer mostly wished to be the lucky consumers in the free trial, while the consumer also expressed their expectations and preferences for the product in the free trial. In addition, in the negative sentiment, the consumers feel mostly frustrated by the fact that they had participated in the free trial several times but had not become the lucky consumer, and some consumers had a negative attitude toward the free trial products and raised their own doubts about the products. It supports the validity of Assumption 1 in the model construction, that some consumers have a good impression of the free trial product.

Secondly, after the textual analysis of the content of all the application reasons in the free trial conducted, it is known that the words "referred by friends", "through other channels" and "access to information" appeared more frequently. According to the tracking survey, nearly 40% of consumers were indirectly introduced to the free trial for Lenovo through sharing with friends, searching through other channels, etc. It not only supports the obvious network externality of the free trial for the physical product, but also supports Assumption 2 that consumers could be exposed to the free trial by searching for products, channel information, etc. Meanwhile, we investigated the relevant data provided by Lenovo Mall, including data on the cost of free trial products, consumer behavior data on participation in the free trial. It was found that the total cost of the products in almost every free trial issue was about 5000–20,000 dollars. It was also discovered that a number of consumers did not click to participate in the free trial as soon as they clicked through to the free trial page. Subsequently, most consumers first clicked to view the free trial product information, including: product content information, the number of lucky consumers who can try the product, free trial application end time, etc. This time spent can be accounted for as an additional cost to the consumer incurred when participating in the free trial. Therefore, Assumption 2 is valid.

Finally, after performing textual and sentiment analysis on all feedback reports in the free trial, it is discovered that the feedback and reviews for the consumer of the free trial products are different, where 91.32% of the feedback reports have positive sentiments, 8.13% of the feedback reports have neutral sentiments, and 0.55% of the feedback reports have negative sentiments towards the free trial products. It confirms the validity of Assumption 4. Additionally, no consumers were found to have reacted to the product abnormally during the free trial. Meanwhile, the merchant also provides after-sales and repair services for the free trial products to ensure that the products can be tried properly, which confirms the effectiveness of Assumption 5.

Empirical Analysis

One of the largest online platforms for selling electronic products in the world, Lenovo Mall, which was launched in 2010, is our context. The free trial, one of the emerging business models on the Lenovo Mall, was developed in 2018 and has conducted 167 campaigns with more than one million consumers participating. The free trial of Lenovo Mall is to test and promote the electronic products produced by Lenovo itself, which is the fundamental difference between it and the majority of e-commerce platforms. In addition, the free trial of Lenovo Mall focuses more on consumer feedback reports and delivers consumer feedback to product manufacturers to guide new product design and production.

Our data is provided directly by the Lenovo Mall. Considering the change of the free trial policy due to the change in the department head and excluding the enterprise purchased products, portfolio crowdsourced products, the real operation data of 83 consecutive issues during the free trial period were finally selected from Issue 50 to Issue 142.

In order to test H1–H6, the effectiveness of the free trial, the incremental pricing of the product and the incremental demand for the product are selected as dependent variables. In these dependent variables, the effectiveness of the free trial is measured by the difference in the number of participants between the current free trial and the next free trial. The pricing increment of a product is the change in pricing of the product before the free trial and after the free trial. The demand increment for the product is the change in sales volume of the product in the 3 months prior to the free trial versus the 3 months after the free trial. The number of consumers who are lucky enough to try the product in the free trial was the independent variable. The participating trial consumers are divided into appropriate and inappropriate persons so as to better measure the accuracy of the merchant's selection of the most valuable consumer. TextCNN is used to analyze the feedback reports of trial consumers and trial consumers with positive sentiment are considered as the appropriate persons,

Table 4.2 The summary statistics of main variables

Variable name	Description	Min	Max	Mean	Std.dev.
Effectiveness of free trial	Change in the number of consumers participating in	−13,380	8666	−32.71	3499.11
Pricing increments	Change in pricing before and after the free trial	−361	423	35.52	201.85
Demand increments	Change in demand before and after the free trial	−3542	4843	277.11	2022.17
Appropriate persons	The most valuable consumer for the free trial	0	17	2.13	3.99
Inappropriate persons	The least valuable consumer for the free trial	0	8	1.16	1.60
Network effect	The network effect generated by the free trial	0.01	0.85	0.17	0.22
Duration	Duration of the free trial	9	46	17.95	6.73
Month	The month in which the free trial was conducted	1	12	5.53	3.74
Interval time	Interval time between free trials	0	56	14.21	10.81

and those with negative sentiment are considered inappropriate persons. In addition, the network effect generated by the free trial is the moderating variable. The month in which the free trial was conducted, the duration and the interval time between free trials are the control variables. The summary statistics and description of our main variables are presented in Table 4.2.

Based on the propositions obtained and the hypotheses constructed in the previous section, our main estimation models are as follows:

$$\text{Effectiveness of Free Trial}_i = \lambda_0 + \lambda_1 \text{AppropriatePersons}_i$$
$$+\lambda_2 \text{InappropriatePersons}_i + \lambda_3 \text{Duration}_i + \lambda_4 \text{Month}_i + \lambda_5 \text{IntervalTime}_i + \xi_i.$$

$$\text{PricingIncrements}_i = \lambda_0 + \lambda_1 \text{AppropriatePersons}_i + \lambda_2 \text{InappropriatePersons}_i$$
$$+\lambda_3 \text{Duration}_i + \lambda_4 \text{Month}_i + \lambda_5 \text{IntervalTime}_i + \xi_i.$$

$$\text{DemandIncrements}_i = \lambda_0 + \lambda_1 \text{AppropriatePersons}_i + \lambda_2 \text{InappropriatePersons}_i$$
$$+\lambda_3 \text{Duration}_i + \lambda_4 \text{Month}_i + \lambda_5 \text{IntervalTime}_i + \xi_i.$$

Next, two interaction terms are added, AppropriatePersons×NetworkEffect and InappropriatePersons×NetworkEffect (Eq. (16)–(18)), into the models to test the moderating effect of the network effect generated by the free trial.

$$\text{Effectiveness of FreeTrial}_i = \lambda_0 + \lambda_1 (\text{AppropriatePersons} \times \text{NetworkEffect})_i + \lambda_2 (\text{InappropriatePersons} \times \text{NetworkEffect})_i + \lambda_3 \text{Duration}_i + \lambda_4 \text{Month}_i + \lambda_5 \text{IntervalTime}_i + \xi_i,$$

$$\text{PricingIncrements}_i = \lambda_0 + \lambda_1 (\text{AppropriatePersons} \times \text{NetworkEffect})_i + \lambda_2 (\text{InappropriatePersons} \times \text{NetworkEffect})_i + \lambda_3 \text{Duration}_i + \lambda_4 \text{Month}_i + \lambda_5 \text{IntervalTime}_i + \xi_i,$$

$$\text{DemandIncrements}_i = \lambda_0 + \lambda_1 (\text{AppropriatePersons} \times \text{NetworkEffect})_i + \lambda_2 (\text{InappropriatePersons} \times \text{NetworkEffect})_i + \lambda_3 \text{Duration}_i + \lambda_4 \text{Month}_i + \lambda_5 \text{IntervalTime}_i + \xi_i.$$

where the NetworkEffect_i represents the network effect generated by the free trial of issue i, which is derived by fitting and comparing the historical operational data of the free trial.

Table 4.3 presents the main results. The results with and without the control variables are fairly consistent, as can be visualized between Column (1–1) and (1–2), Column (2–1) and (2–2) as well as Column (3–1) and (3–2). Column (1–2), Column (2–2) and Column (3–2) presents the estimation of Eq. (13), Eqs. (14) and (15), respectively. Column (3–1), Column (3–2) and Column (3–3) exhibit the results for the moderating effect of the network effect (Eqs. (16)–(18)). From Column (1–2), Column (2–2) and Column (3–2), it could be shown that the coefficients of $\text{AppropriatePersons}$ are positive and significant, and the coefficients $\text{InappropriatePersons}$ are negative and significant, suggesting that the appropriate person is beneficial for the free trial, i.e. the more accurate the merchant is in selecting the most valuable consumers, the better the free trial could be and the pricing and demand for the product could increase, which supports H1–H3. In Column (1–3), Column (2–3) and Column (3–3), the coefficients of $\text{AppropriatePersons} \times \text{NetworkEffect}$ are positive and significant and the coefficients $\text{InappropriatePersons} \times \text{NetworkEffect}$ are negative and significant. These results suggest that the network effect strengthens the positive impact of the accuracy on the effect of the free trial, the pricing of the product and the demand for the product, which support H4–H6. Furthermore, the absolute value of the coefficient of $\text{InappropriatePersons}$ is greater than that of $\text{AppropriatePersons}$, which empirically tests the reliability and reasonableness of the network effect function for the free trial of electronic products proposed in this paper.

Numerical Experiments Analysis

Numerical experiments are conducted using real operational data to further analyze and confirm all of the proportions and results in this section. Through analyzing and fitting the real operational data of the free trial in Lenovo Mall, the free trial for

Table 4.3 The results of the empirical analysis

Variables	Effectiveness of free trial			Pricing increments			Demand increments		
	(1–1)	(1–2)	(1–3)	(2–1)	(2–2)	(2–3)	(3–1)	(3–2)	(3–3)
Appropriate persons	0.406***	0.467***	0.281**	0.374***	0.634***	0.674***			
	(98.541)	(110.555)	(6.387)	(6.926)	(46.147)	(50.985)			
Inappropriate persons	−0.716***	−0.709***	−0.670***	−0.661***	−0.690***	−0.694***			
	(245.577)	(254.573)	(15.918)	(15.948)	(115.004)	(117.402)			
Appropriate persons*network effect			0.280***			0.240**			0.403***
			(1661.04)			(112.740)			(955.531)
Inappropriate persons*network effect			−0.745***			−0.699***			−0.645***
			(1677.628)			(113.868)			(965.089)
Network effect			0.206**			0.186*			0.083
			(1706.729)			(115.843)			(981.830)
Duration		−0.154	−0.047		−0.255*	−0.170		−0.118	0.037
		(63.715)	(46.085)		(3.992)	(3.128)		(29.383)	(26.511)
Month		−0.071	−0.056		−0.106	0.091		−0.122	−0.093
		(111.555)	(87.731)		(6.989)	(5.955)		(51.446)	(50.469)
Interval time		−0.137	−0.018		−0.198	−0.109		−0.119	0.066
		(41.218)	(28.191)		(2.582)	(1.913)		(19.009)	(16.218)
Observations	83	83	83	83	83	83	83	83	83
R_squared	0.572	0.600	0.786	0.459	0.528	0.704	0.719	0.745	0.788
adj_R2	0.547	0.537	0.745	0.429	0.454	0.647	0.703	0.705	0.747
F	23.374	9.592	19.002	14.874	7.159	12.291	44.747	18.713	19.224

different issues of the product cost, the product quality and the consumer cost of searching for information could be obtained. Simultaneously, analyzing the reasons for the applications of the consumer and the feedback reports of the consumer who is lucky to be selected for the free trial, the existence of a significant network effect for the free trial of electronic products, particularly the positive network effect, also known as the network externality, is captured. Next, from Proportions 1 to 8 could be verified with the mean value of real data. Based on Proportions 1 to 3, line charts of sensitivity analysis under different values of γ are shown in Fig. 4.9.

According to Fig. 4.9, it could be clearly observed that the price and demand of the electronic product as well as the profit of the merchant obviously increase after the free trial, compared to Scenario 1: No free trial. Due to the design of the model, consumer demand for the product is evenly distributed at [0,1], which can be regarded as the percentage of consumer demand for the product. From Fig. 4.9, it can be noted that when the consumer network effect is at the maximum, Lenovo can increase the demand of products through the free trial by approximately 38% of consumers in the market. Moreover, as the coefficient of the consumer network effect, γ, increases, the price and the demand of the electronic product as well as the profit of the merchant increase non-linearly and rapidly. It is consistent with Propositions 1–3.

Notably, the real operational data shows that the free trial selection mechanism of Lenovo is efficient in selecting valuable consumers and removing low-value consumers, such as speculators and negative consumers. Therefore, it was decided to simulate the real operational data to verify that when the merchant makes mistakes in identifying their consumers, the effect of the original free trial is diminished. In addition, it is determined to apply the mean of γ and β through analyzing and simulating real data, i.e. $\gamma = 0.6$ and $\beta = 0.8$. According to Proposition 4, the accuracy of

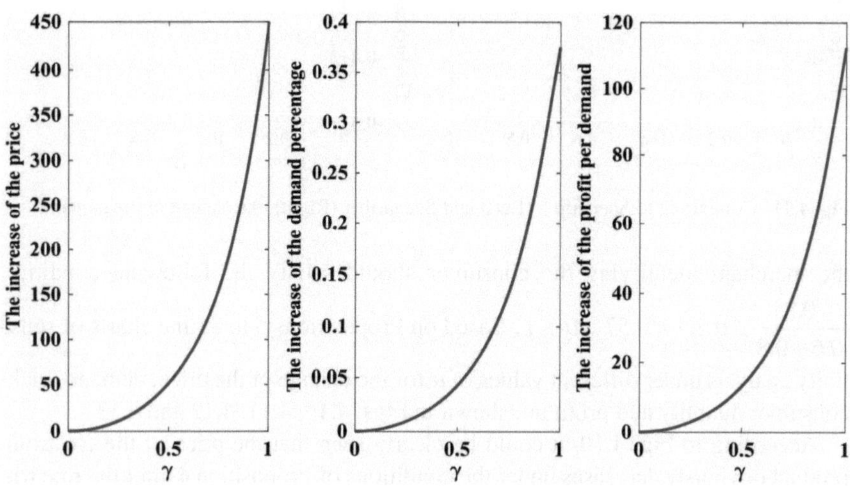

Fig. 4.9 The increase of the price (Left), demand (Middle) and profit (Right) after free trial with precise identification

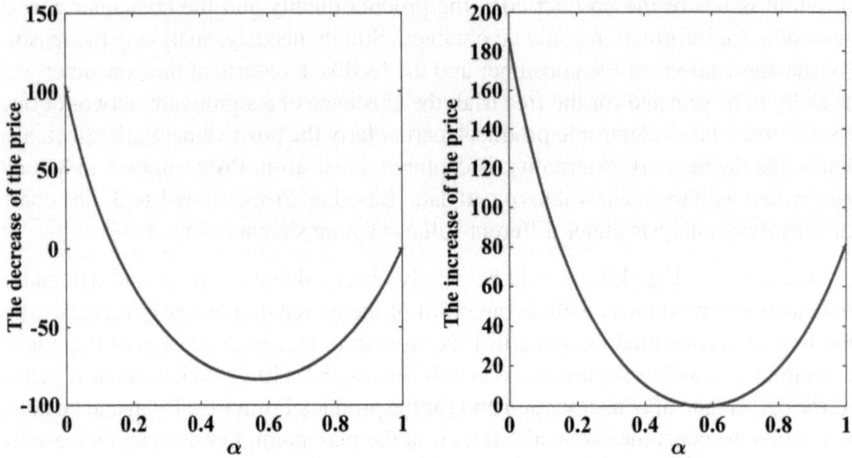

Fig. 4.10 Comparing Scenario 2 (Left) and Scenario 1 (Right), the change of the price

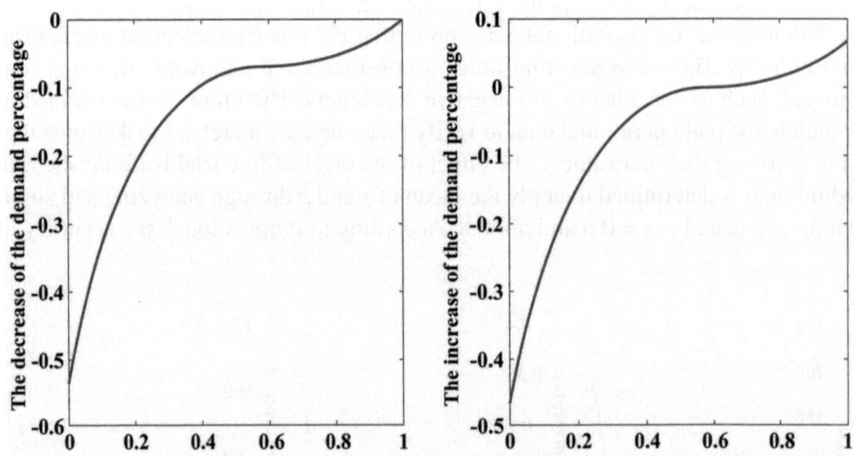

Fig. 4.11 Comparing to Scenario 2 (Left) and Scenario 1 (Right), the change of the demand

the merchant identifying the consumer should satisfy the following condition, $\frac{0.8}{0.6+0.8} \le \alpha \le 1 \approx 0.57 \le \alpha \le 1$. Based on Propositions 5 to 8, line charts of sensitivity analysis under different values of α for the change of the price, demand, lucky consumer quantity and profit are shown in Figs. 4.10, 4.11, 4.12 and 4.13.

According to Fig. 4.10, it could be clearly seen that the price of the electronic product obviously decreases under the conditions of Proposition 4 after the free trial with mistakes, compared to the free trial without mistakes. Similarly, the price of the electronic product obviously increases, yet under the conditions of Proposition 4

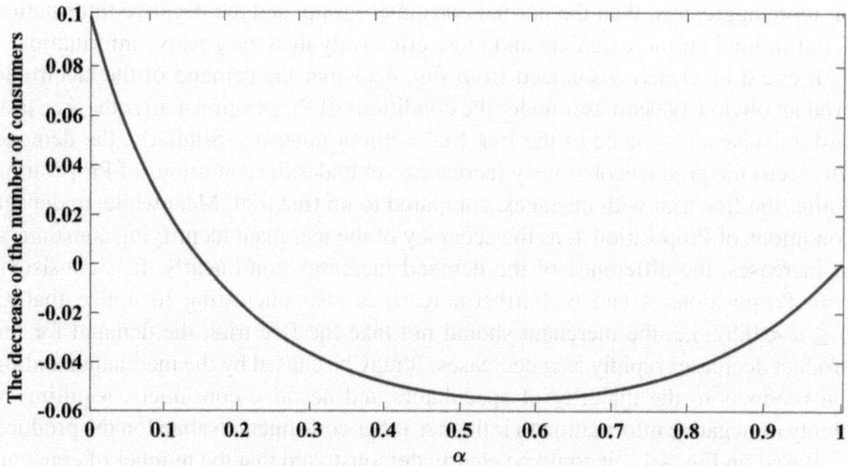

Fig. 4.12 The decrease in the number of consumers after free trial with mistakes

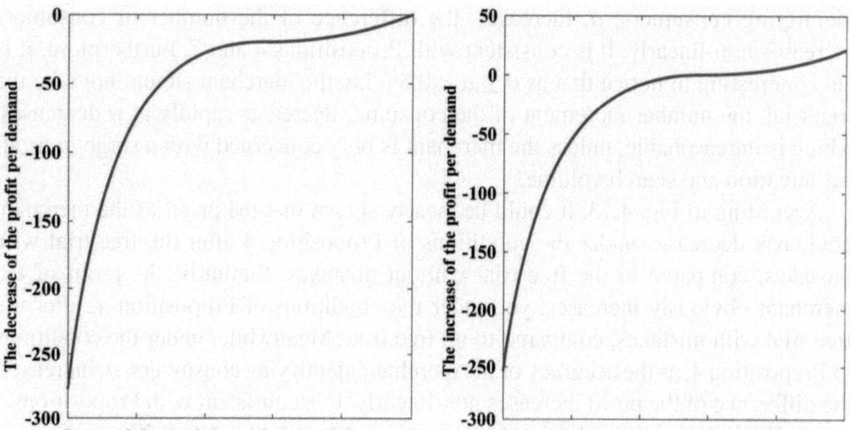

Fig. 4.13 Comparing Scenario 2 (Left) and Scenario 1 (Right), the change of the profit

after the free trial with mistakes, compared to no free trial. Meanwhile, under the conditions of Proposition 4, as the accuracy of the merchant identifying consumers, α, increases, the difference of the price increase non-linearly. It is consistent with Propositions 4 and 5. Furthermore, it is interesting to notice that as $0 \leq \alpha < 0.57$, i.e. the merchant should not take the free trial, the price increment of the product decreases rapidly as α increases. It may be caused by the merchant handing out products to speculators and negative consumers in pursuit of the surge in attention and search volume which comes with the free trial. It is well known that speculators are far more aggregated than the normal consumer group, and the negative information is transmitted far more quickly and more effectively than the positive information.

It could be clearly visualized from Fig. 4.11 that the demand of the electronic product obviously decreases under the conditions of Proposition 4 after the free trial with mistakes, compared to the free trial without mistakes. Similarly, the demand for electronic products obviously increases, yet under the conditions of Proposition 4 after the free trial with mistakes, compared to no free trial. Meanwhile, under the conditions of Proposition 4, as the accuracy of the merchant identifying consumers, α, increases, the difference of the demand increases non-linearly. It is consistent with Propositions 4 and 6. Furthermore, it is also interesting to notice that as $0 \leq \alpha < 0.57$, i.e. the merchant should not take the free trial, the demand for the product decreases rapidly as α decreases. It may be caused by the merchant handing out products to the majority of speculators and negative consumers, resulting in plenty of negative information to influence other consumers to abandon the product.

Based on Fig. 4.12, it could be clearly demonstrated that the number of consumers who participate in the free trial decreases under the conditions of Proposition 4 after the free trial with mistakes, compared to the free trial without mistakes. Meanwhile, under the conditions of Proposition 4, as the accuracy of the merchant identifying consumers, α, increases, the difference of the number of consumers increases non-linearly. It is consistent with Propositions 4 and 7. Furthermore, it is also interesting to notice that as $0 \leq \alpha < 0.57$, i.e. the merchant should not take the free trial, the number increment of the consumer decreases rapidly as α decreases, which is unreasonable, unless the merchant is only concerned with a surge in product attention and search volume.

According to Fig. 4.13, it could be clearly shown that the profit of the merchant obviously decreases under the conditions of Proposition 4 after the free trial with mistakes, compared to the free trial without mistakes. Similarly, the profit of the merchant obviously increases, yet under the conditions of Proposition 4, after the free trial with mistakes, compared to no free trial. Meanwhile, under the conditions of Proposition 4, as the accuracy of the merchant identifying consumers, α, increases, the difference of the profit increases non-linearly. It is consistent with Propositions 4 and 8. Furthermore, it is also interesting to notice that as $0 \leq \alpha < 0.57$, i.e. the merchant should not take the free trial, the profit of the merchant decreases rapidly as α decreases. Hence, it is not appropriate for the merchant to conduct the free trials at this point. In summary, not all merchants are suitable for conducting the free trial. When merchants are unable to accurately identify the most valuable consumers in the free trial, the free trial may become a burden to the merchant. Even when the merchant tries to make speculators and negative consumers help expand the publicity of the product or change their attitudes toward it by letting them have a free trial, it can result in greater loss of profit. In addition, the free trial brings an increase in the merchant's profit when the accuracy of identifying the most valuable customers for the merchant is higher than a certain value, i.e., $\frac{\beta}{\beta+\gamma} \leq \alpha$, compared to no free trial.

4.3.5 *Implications for Platform Customer Management*

This analysis demonstrates that free trials, while a potent tool for platform customer integration, are effective only under specific conditions. Their value lies in transforming users into co-creators of market intelligence and social proof, thereby reducing uncertainty, stimulating demand, and enabling premium pricing. This value, however, is fragile and can collapse if the platform fails to govern the integration process effectively.

The findings yield several critical managerial implications. First, the depth of integration achievable through trials depends fundamentally on a platform's discriminative capability. Success requires investment in sophisticated, AI-driven user segmentation that moves beyond basic demographics to predict a user's potential for advocacy. Lenovo's case highlights this precisely: by proactively filtering out speculators and detractors, the platform converted trial participants into brand assets rather than liabilities.

Furthermore, the analysis underscores the asymmetric and potentially dangerous nature of network effects in this context. While positive externalities justify the investment in trials, negative externalities, often amplified by behavioral biases, can dominate if user targeting fails. This necessitates continuous monitoring of real-time sentiment and the dynamic adjustment of trial eligibility to safeguard the ecosystem. Ultimately, value creation is not an automatic outcome of offering free trials. It is earned only when three conditions converge: sufficient product quality, the genuine presence of network effects, and targeting accuracy that surpasses a critical threshold. In the absence of these conditions, trials risk wasting resources and eroding brand equity.

In sum, this research reframes free trials as a governance-intensive form of customer integration. When precisely designed and executed, they close the feedback loop between product, user, and platform, transforming a cost center into a source of co-created value and converting market uncertainty into durable trust. This captures the essential logic of value creation within platform ecosystems.

4.4 Chapter Conclusions and Future Directions

Synthesis of Core Arguments

This chapter has advanced a central thesis regarding the operation and competitiveness of digital platform supply chains. It posits that the fundamental source of sustainable advantage in platform-mediated markets is not merely the possession of a large network, but rather the capability to deeply and intelligently integrate that network of customers into the platform's operational and strategic fabric. This process, termed platform customer integration, is conceptualized as the strategic coupling of a multi-sided customer base—encompassing end-users, buyers, and often complementors—with the platform's governance architecture and core operational workflows. It transcends traditional, linear supply chain integration by operating in a context defined by cross-side externalities, participant heterogeneity, and the simultaneous management of demand and supply-side actors.

The analysis unfolds through a deliberate, two-stage logic that structures the chapter and clarifies the causal pathway to value creation. The first stage, detailed in Sect. 4.2, addresses the foundational imperative: governance and coordination must be established before value can be reliably captured. In platform supply chains, the decision to integrate deeply with customers dramatically increases task interdependence and information processing demands across internal functions such as marketing, product development, operations, and data science. Drawing upon Information Processing Theory, the chapter demonstrates that platforms must cultivate robust cross-functional coordination mechanisms—spanning integrated systems, formalized processes, and dedicated teams—to build the necessary internal capacity. This internal alignment enables effective external customer coordination, both at an operational level (e.g., synchronized workflows, joint problem-solving) and a strategic level (e.g., co-planning, joint innovation). This governance infrastructure is non-negotiable; it transforms the platform from a passive intermediary into an active orchestrator capable of managing ecosystem complexity.

The second stage, explored in Sect. 4.3, examines how this established governance foundation enables specific value creation strategies. Using the high-stakes mechanism of free trials as an empirical lens, the chapter models how precise customer integration converts uncertainty and network potential into measurable economic gains. The analysis reveals that free trials, when governed by accurate identification of high-value users, function as sophisticated risk-reallocation and market-screening tools. They mitigate the platform's downside exposure by shifting initial validation to self-selected users, while simultaneously amplifying positive network effects through authentic social proof. The resultant value is multi-faceted: enhanced operational liquidity through expanded and stabilized demand, premiums on pricing derived from reduced information asymmetry, de-risked innovation through real-world feedback loops, and the cultivation of a more resilient and generative network. Crucially, this value is contingent upon the precision of the integration mechanism, underscoring that value creation is not an automatic byproduct of customer access but a direct outcome of governed, discriminative integration.

Theoretical Contributions and Refinements

This research contributes to the intersecting literatures on platform strategy, supply chain management, and organizational design by providing a more nuanced and actionable framework. First, it recontextualizes supply chain integration for the platform era. Traditional integration paradigms, focused on linear alignment with upstream suppliers for cost efficiency and reliability, are insufficient. Platform supply chain integration must be multi-directional, simultaneously encompassing the logistical and informational integration with sellers/suppliers and the experiential and behavioral integration with end-customers. The platform sits at the nexus, and its core function is to orchestrate these flows to maximize total ecosystem value, not just its own transactional margin. The objects of integration thus expand from physical goods and forecast data to include customer attention, behavioral signals, social influence, and co-creative input.

Second, the chapter reinserts the importance of internal organization into platform theory. While much scholarship rightly emphasizes network effects and ecosystem architecture, it often treats the platform firm as a unitary actor. This analysis delineates how the platform's internal structure—its ability to coordinate across functional silos—is a critical mediator between external market opportunities and realized performance. The effectiveness of any customer-facing integration strategy (e.g., a free trial, a loyalty program, a developer API) is predicated on the platform's internal information processing capabilities. This bridges macro-level platform economics with micro-organizational behavior, offering a more complete explanation of why seemingly similar platform models yield divergent outcomes.

Third, the formal model in Sect. 4.3 provides a quantifiable link between governance precision and economic value in a network context. It moves beyond qualitative assertions about the importance of "trust" or "quality control" by modeling how the accuracy of participant identification (α) directly determines the sign and magnitude of network utility, thereby influencing optimal pricing, demand, and profit. This granularity allows for the testing of specific hypotheses and offers managers a diagnostic framework to assess the potential return on investment in advanced analytics and segmentation capabilities. It also formally captures the asymmetric and non-linear nature of network effects within integration mechanisms, highlighting how negative sentiment can outweigh positive sentiment, a critical consideration for risk management in platform supply chains.

Managerial and Strategic Implications

The findings translate into several imperative strategic actions for platform leaders and supply chain managers operating within platform ecosystems.

Architect Internal Coordination as a Core Strategic Capability. Platform leadership must recognize that the design of internal organization is a first-order strategic issue. Investing in cross-functional coordination mechanisms, unified data systems, clear lateral processes, and empowered cross-functional teams, is not an administrative overhead but the essential engine for external ecosystem orchestration. The goal is to create an organization agile enough to respond coherently to the volatile signals emanating from an integrated customer base.

Pursue Discriminative, Not Just Broad, Customer Integration. The strategy of "growth at all costs" is perilous. Value-creating integration requires discriminative capability: the use of data analytics and algorithmic governance to distinguish between high-value co-creators, neutral participants, and value-destroying opportunists (speculators, detractors). Platforms must invest in the predictive tools and governance rules that allow them to target integration efforts strategically, offering deeper access and incentives to those users whose participation generates positive spillovers for the entire network.

Reframe Customer Integration Mechanisms as Supply Chain Risk Mitigation Tools. Tactics like free trials should be elevated from the marketing department to the core operational and strategic planning process. They are instruments for demand discovery, product validation, and inventory risk reduction. By integrating a curated set of customers early in a product lifecycle, the platform can generate more accurate demand forecasts, identify product flaws before full-scale launch, and adjust supplier orders and logistics plans accordingly. This turns customer integration into a powerful lever for upstream supply chain resilience and efficiency.

Manage the Entire Platform Supply Chain as an Integrated Value Network. The ultimate implication is the need for holistic management of the triadic relationship between platform, suppliers/sellers, and customers. Decisions regarding customer integration must be made with explicit consideration of their impact on supplier performance and vice versa. For instance, a free trial that successfully stimulates demand must be coupled with supplier readiness and flexible logistics to fulfill that nascent demand without stockouts. Similarly, data from integrated customers about desired features must flow seamlessly to supplier R&D processes. The platform's role is to synchronize these flows, ensuring that value co-created with customers is effectively translated into value delivered by the supply chain.

Future Research Trajectories

This chapter opens several productive avenues for future scholarly inquiry that can further refine our understanding of platform supply chains.

The Integration of Upstream Supply Chain Partners. While this chapter focused on downstream customer integration, future research should symmetrically investigate the integration of suppliers and sellers into the platform's governance and operational systems. How do data-sharing agreements, co-inventory management, and integrated logistics workflows between platforms and their suppliers create value? How do these upstream integration dynamics interact with downstream customer integration strategies? A unified theory of multi-sided platform supply chain integration is needed.

Dynamics of Integration Across the Platform Lifecycle. The challenges and optimal mechanisms for customer integration likely evolve as a platform scales from launch to maturity to renewal. Early-stage platforms may prioritize integration for learning and liquidity, while mature platforms may focus on integration for innovation and defensive moats. Longitudinal studies tracing how integration strategies, internal coordination structures, and value outcomes co-evolve over time would yield rich insights into platform endurance.

Ethical and Operational Tensions in Algorithmic Governance. The reliance on algorithms for discriminative integration (e.g., selecting trial users, curating content) raises significant questions about fairness, transparency, and bias. Future research must explore the operational trade-offs between algorithmic efficiency and ethical governance. How can platforms design integration mechanisms that are both economically effective and socially equitable? What are the reputational and regulatory risks of opaque algorithmic integration, and how can they be mitigated within the supply chain?

Sustainability and Circularity Through Platform Integration. Platform customer integration offers a unique potential to advance circular economy goals. Research could explore how platforms can use integration mechanisms—such as take-back programs, product-as-a-service models, or peer-to-peer resale markets—to incentivize sustainable consumer behavior and close material loops. This involves designing integration points that collect products at end-of-life, provide data on product condition, and connect users to refurbishment or recycling channels, thereby integrating reverse logistics deeply into the customer experience.

In conclusion, platform customer integration represents the critical nexus where strategy, operations, and technology converge in the digital economy. It is the disciplined process through which the latent value of a network is harvested, structured, and amplified. This chapter has argued that this process follows an indispensable sequence: robust internal and external coordination must first be established to govern the inherent complexities of multi-sided interaction. Only atop this foundation can platforms reliably deploy specific mechanisms to create and capture economic value. The future of platform competition, and indeed the evolution of global supply chains, will be shaped by those enterprises that master this logic, moving beyond merely accumulating users to architecting deeply integrated, intelligently governed, and mutually valuable ecosystem supply chains.

References

Asvanund, A., Clay, K., Krishnan, R., & Smith, M. D. (2004). An empirical analysis of network externalities in peer-to-peer music-sharing networks. *Information Systems Research, 15*(2), 155–174. https://doi.org/10.1287/isre.1040.0020

Ataseven, C., & Nair, A. (2017). Assessment of supply chain integration and performance relationships: A meta-analytic investigation of the literature. *International Journal of Production Economics, 185*, 252–265. https://doi.org/10.1016/j.ijpe.2017.01.007

Badunenko, O., Kumbhakar, S. C., & Lozano-Vivas, A. (2021). Achieving a sustainable cost-efficient business model in banking: The case of European commercial banks. *European Journal of Operational Research, 293*(2), 773–785. https://doi.org/10.1016/j.ejor.2020.12.039

Bawa, K., & Shoemaker, R. (2004). The effects of free sample promotions on incremental brand sales. *Marketing Science, 23*(3), 345–363. https://doi.org/10.1287/mksc.1030.0052

Bendoly, E., Bharadwaj, A., & Bharadwaj, S. (2012). Complementary drivers of new product development performance: Cross-functional coordination, information system capability, and intelligence quality. *Production and Operations Management, 21*(4), 653–667. https://doi.org/10.1111/j.1937-5956.2011.01299.x

Bhargava, H. K. (2022). The creator economy: Managing ecosystem supply, revenue sharing, and platform design. *Management Science, 68*(7), 5233–5251. https://doi.org/10.1287/mnsc.2021.4126

Bhargava, H. K., Wang, K., & Zhang, X. (2022). Fending off critics of platform power with differential revenue sharing: Doing well by doing good? *Management Science, 68*(11), 8249–8260. https://doi.org/10.1287/mnsc.2022.4545

Carr, A. S., Kaynak, H., & Muthusamy, S. (2008). The cross-functional coordination between operations, marketing, purchasing and engineering and the impact on performance. *International Journal of Manufacturing Technology and Management, 13*(1), 55. https://doi.org/10.1504/ijmtm.2008.015973

Chen, C. J. (2007). Information technology, organizational structure, and new product development-the mediating effect of cross–functional team interaction. *IEEE Transactions on Engineering Management, 54*(4), 687–698. https://doi.org/10.1109/Tem.2007.906831

Cheng, H. K., Li, S., & Liu, Y. (2015). Optimal software free trial strategy: Limited version, time-locked, or hybrid? *Production and Operations Management, 24*(3), 504–517. https://doi.org/10.1111/poms.12248

Cheng, H. K., & Liu, Y. P. (2012). Optimal software free trial strategy: The impact of network externalities and consumer uncertainty. *Information Systems Research, 23*(2), 488–504. https://doi.org/10.1287/isre.1110.0348

Cheng, H. K., & Tang, Q. C. (2010). Free trial or no free trial: Optimal software product design with network effects. *European Journal of Operational Research, 205*(2), 437–447. https://doi.org/10.1016/j.ejor.2010.01.014

Conner, K. R. (1995). Obtaining strategic advantage from being imitated: When can encouraging "clones" pay? *Management Science, 41*(2), 209–225. https://doi.org/10.1287/mnsc.41.2.209

Cui, R. M., Gallino, S., Moreno, A., & Zhang, D. J. (2018). The operational value of social media information. *Production and Operations Management, 27*(10), 1749–1769. https://doi.org/10.1111/poms.12707

Dou, Y. F., Niculescu, M. F., & Wu, D. J. (2013). Engineering optimal network effects via social media features and seeding in Markets for Digital Goods and Services. *Information Systems Research, 24*(1), 164–185. https://doi.org/10.1287/isre.1120.0463

Dussart, P., van Oortmerssen, L. A., & Albronda, B. (2021). Perspectives on knowledge integration in cross-functional teams in information systems development. *Team Performance Management, 27*(3–4), 316–331. https://doi.org/10.1108/Tpm-11-2020-0096

Flynn, B. B., Huo, B. F., & Zhao, X. D. (2010). The impact of supply chain integration on performance: A contingency and configuration approach. *Journal of Operations Management, 28*(1), 58–71. https://doi.org/10.1016/j.jom.2009.06.001

Foubert, B., & Gijsbrechts, E. (2016). Try it, you'll like it-or will you? The perils of early free-trial promotions for high-tech service adoption. *Marketing Science, 35*(5), 810–826. https://doi.org/10.1287/mksc.2015.0973

Galbraith, J. R. (1974). Organization design: An information processing view. *Interfaces, 4*(3), 28–36. https://doi.org/10.1287/inte.4.3.28

Ghobadi, S. (2015). What drives knowledge sharing in software development teams: A literature review and classification framework. *Information & Management, 52*(1), 82–97. https://doi.org/10.1016/j.im.2014.10.008

Halbheer, D., Stahl, F., Koenigsberg, O., & Lehmann, D. R. (2014). Choosing a digital content strategy: How much should be free? *International Journal of Research in Marketing, 31*(2), 192–206. https://doi.org/10.1016/j.ijresmar.2013.10.004

Ho, T. H., Li, S., Park, S. E., & Shen, Z. J. M. (2012). Customer influence value and purchase acceleration in new product diffusion. *Marketing Science, 31*(2), 236–256. https://doi.org/10.1287/mksc.1110.0701

Hu, Y. H., Xu, A. B., Hong, Y. L., Gal, D., Sinha, V., & Akkiraju, R. (2019). Generating business intelligence through social media analytics: Measuring brand personality with consumer-, employee-, and firm-generated content. *Journal of Management Information Systems, 36*(3), 893–930. https://doi.org/10.1080/07421222.2019.1628908

Huang, N., Yan, Z. J., & Yin, H. N. (2021). Effects of online-offline service integration on e-healthcare providers: A quasi-natural experiment. *Production and Operations Management, 30*(8), 2359–2378. https://doi.org/10.1111/poms.13381

Huang, P. Y., Pan, S. L., & Ouyang, T. H. (2014). Developing information processing capability for operational agility: Implications from a Chinese manufacturer. *European Journal of Information Systems, 23*(4), 462–480. https://doi.org/10.1057/ejis.2014.4

Kahneman, D., & Tversky, A. (1979). Prospect theory: An analysis of decision under risk. *Econometrica, 47*(2), 263. https://doi.org/10.2307/1914185

Kanatlı, M. A., & Karaer, Ö. (2022). Servitization as an alternative business model and its implications on product durability, profitability & environmental impact. *European Journal of Operational Research, 301*(2), 546–560. https://doi.org/10.1016/j.ejor.2021.10.052

Kang, M., Lee, G., Hwang, D. W., Wei, J., & Huo, B. (2020). Effects of cross-functional integration on NPD success: Mediating roles of customer and supplier involvement. *Total Quality Management & Business Excellence, 32*(13–14), 1515–1531. https://doi.org/10.1080/14783363.2020.1736543

Kumar, N., Qiu, L. F., & Kumar, S. (2018). Exit, voice, and response on digital platforms: An empirical investigation of online management response strategies. *Information Systems Research, 29*(4), 849–870. https://doi.org/10.1287/isre.2017.0749

Lee, S. Y., Qiu, L. F., & Whinston, A. (2018). Sentiment manipulation in online platforms: An analysis of movie tweets. *Production and Operations Management, 27*(3), 393–416. https://doi.org/10.1111/poms.12805

Li, F., & Yi, Z. (2016). Trial or no trial: Supplying costly signals to improve profits*. *Decision Sciences, 48*(4), 795–827. https://doi.org/10.1111/deci.12233

Li, S. Y., Cui, X. L., Huo, B. F., & Zhao, X. D. (2019). Information sharing, coordination and supply chain performance the moderating effect of demand uncertainty. *Industrial Management & Data Systems, 119*(5), 1046–1071. https://doi.org/10.1108/Imds-10-2018-0453

Libai, B., Muller, E., & Peres, R. (2013). Decomposing the value of word-of-mouth seeding programs: Acceleration versus expansion. *Journal of Marketing Research, 50*(2), 161–176. https://doi.org/10.1509/jmr.11.0305

Liu, C. Z. C., Au, Y. A., & Choi, H. S. (2014). Effects of freemium strategy in the Mobile app market: An empirical study of Google play. *Journal of Management Information Systems, 31*(3), 326–354. https://doi.org/10.1080/07421222.2014.995564

Mallipeddi, R. R., Kumar, S., Sriskandarajah, C., & Zhu, Y. (2022). A framework for analyzing influencer Marketing in Social Networks: Selection and scheduling of influencers. *Management Science, 68*(1), 75–104. https://doi.org/10.1287/mnsc.2020.3899

Mohiuddin Babu, M. (2017). Impact of firm's customer orientation on performance: The moderating role of interfunctional coordination and employee commitment. *Journal of Strategic Marketing, 26*(8), 702–722. https://doi.org/10.1080/0965254x.2017.1384037

Nan, G. F., Shi, F. H., Dou, R. L., & Li, M. Q. (2016). Duopoly pricing of software products under free strategy: Limited-feature vs. seeding. *Computers & Industrial Engineering, 100*, 13–23. https://doi.org/10.1016/j.cie.2016.07.026

Narasimhan, R., & Kim, S. W. (2002). Effect of supply chain integration on the relationship between diversification and performance: Evidence from Japanese and Korean firms. *Journal of Operations Management., 20*(3), 303–323. https://doi.org/10.1016/S0272-6963(02)00008-6

Niu, B., Yue, H., Luo, H., & Shang, W. (2019). Pricing for newly-launched experience products: Free trial or not? *Transportation Research Part E: Logistics and Transportation Review, 126*, 149–176. https://doi.org/10.1016/j.tre.2019.04.001

Pakarinen, M., & Virtanen, P. J. (2017). Matrix organizations and cross-functional teams in the public sector: A systematic review. *International Journal of Public Sector Management, 30*(3), 210–226. https://doi.org/10.1108/ijpsm-04-2016-0065

Pellathy, D. A., Mollenkopf, D. A., Stank, T. P., & Autry, C. W. (2019). Cross-functional integration: Concept clarification and scale development. *Journal of Business Logistics, 40*(2), 81–104. https://doi.org/10.1111/jbl.12206

Qiu, L. F., Chhikara, A., & Vakharia, A. (2021). Multidimensional observational learning in social networks: Theory and experimental evidence. *Information Systems Research, 32*(3), 876–894. https://doi.org/10.1287/isre.2021.0993

Qiu, L. F., & Whinston, A. B. (2017). Pricing strategies under behavioral observational learning in social networks. *Production and Operations Management, 26*(7), 1249–1267. https://doi.org/10.1111/poms.12693

Rai, A., Patnayakuni, R., & Seth, N. (2006). Firm performance impacts of digitally enabled supply chain integration Capabilities1. *MIS Quarterly, 30*(2), 225–246. https://doi.org/10.2307/25148729

Sepulveda Rojas, J. P., & Frein, Y. (2008). Coordination and demand uncertainty in supply chains. *Production Planning & Control, 19*(7), 712–721. https://doi.org/10.1080/09537280802573965

Sinkula, J. M., Baker, W. E., & Noordewier, T. (1997). A framework for market-based organizational learning: Linking values, knowledge, and behavior. *Journal of the Academy of Marketing Science, 25*(4), 305–318. https://doi.org/10.1177/0092070397254003

Srinivasan, R., & Swink, M. (2015). Leveraging supply chain integration through planning comprehensiveness: An organizational information processing theory perspective. *Decision Sciences, 46*(5), 823–861. https://doi.org/10.1111/deci.12166

Sriram, S., Chintagunta, P. K., & Manchanda, P. (2015). Service quality variability and termination behavior. *Management Science, 61*(11), 2739–2759. https://doi.org/10.1287/mnsc.2014.2105

Ståhle, M., Ahola, T., & Martinsuo, M. (2019). Cross-functional integration for managing customer information flows in a project-based firm. *International Journal of Project Management, 37*(1), 145–160. https://doi.org/10.1016/j.ijproman.2018.11.002

Sun, K., Zuo, M., & Kong, D. (2017). What can product trial offer? *International Journal of Asian Business and Information Management, 8*(1), 24–37. https://doi.org/10.4018/ijabim.2017010102

Thomas, J. A., & McDaniel, R. R. (1990). Interpreting strategic issues: Effects of strategy and the information-processing structure of top management teams. *Academy of Management Journal, 33*(2), 286–306. https://doi.org/10.2307/256326

Tsai, K. H., & Hsu, T. T. (2014). Cross-functional collaboration, competitive intensity, knowledge integration mechanisms, and new product performance: A mediated moderation model. *Industrial Marketing Management, 43*(2), 293–303. https://doi.org/10.1016/j.indmarman.2013.08.012

Turkulainen, V., & Ketokivi, M. (2012). Cross-functional integration and performance: What are the real benefits? *International Journal of Operations & Production Management, 32*(4), 447–467. https://doi.org/10.1108/01443571211223095

Tushman, M. L., & Nadler, D. A. (1978). Information processing as an integrating concept in organizational design. *The Academy of Management Review, 3*(3), 613. https://doi.org/10.2307/257550

Tversky, A., & Kahneman, D. (1992). Advances in prospect theory: Cumulative representation of uncertainty. *Journal of Risk and Uncertainty, 5*(4), 297–323. https://doi.org/10.1007/bf00122574

Vidgen, R., Hindle, G., & Randolph, I. (2020). Exploring the ethical implications of business analytics with a business ethics canvas. *European Journal of Operational Research, 281*(3), 491–501. https://doi.org/10.1016/j.ejor.2019.04.036

Wang, T., Oh, L. B., Wang, K. L., & Yuan, Y. F. (2013). User adoption and purchasing intention after free trial: An empirical study of mobile newspapers. *Information Systems and e-Business Management, 11*(2), 189–210. https://doi.org/10.1007/s10257-012-0197-5

Wong, C. W. V., Lai, K. H., Cheng, T. C. E., & Lun, Y. H. V. (2015). The role of IT-enabled collaborative decision making in inter-organizational information integration to improve customer service performance. *International Journal of Production Economics, 159*, 56–65. https://doi.org/10.1016/j.ijpe.2014.02.019

Wong, C. Y., Boon-itt, S., & Wong, C. W. Y. (2011). The contingency effects of environmental uncertainty on the relationship between supply chain integration and operational performance. *Journal of Operations Management, 29*(6), 604–615. https://doi.org/10.1016/j.jom.2011.01.003

Wu, L. L., Deng, S. M., & Jiang, X. (2018). Sampling and pricing strategy under competition. *Omega-International Journal of Management Science, 80*, 192–208. https://doi.org/10.1016/j.omega.2018.01.002

Yang, X., Tan, C. H., Li, Y., & Teo, H. H. (2018). Psychological paradox of game software trial. *Information & Management, 55*(5), 608–620. https://doi.org/10.1016/j.im.2018.01.002

Yi, Z. L., Li, F., & Ma, L. J. (2019). The impact of distribution channels on trial-version provision with a positive network effect. *Omega-International Journal of Management Science, 85*, 115–133. https://doi.org/10.1016/j.omega.2018.06.002

Zhu, D. H., & Chang, Y. P. (2014). Investigating consumer attitude and intention toward free trials of technology-based services. *Computers in Human Behavior, 30*, 328–334. https://doi.org/10.1016/j.chb.2013.09.008

Chapter 5
Platform Supply Chain Technology Integration

5.1 Overview of Platform Supply Chain Technology Integration

5.1.1 Definition and Scope

With the rapid development of disruptive technologies such as the Internet of Things (IoT), Artificial Intelligence (AI), cloud computing, blockchain, and big data analytics, technology-driven digital intelligence capabilities have become a critical driver of value creation in supply chains (Frank et al., 2019; Ivanov et al., 2019). At the policy level, governments and international institutions alike have emphasized the strategic importance of digital infrastructure, highlighting how these technologies are reshaping production models and organizational coordination (Adner, 2017; Jackson et al., 2024). Previous studies found that digitalization can substantially improve supply chain performance by reducing design and engineering costs, shortening time-to-market, lowering management expenses, and optimizing inventory holdings (Autry et al., 2010; de Oliveira-Dias et al., 2023). These benefits underscore why technology has emerged as a core theme in contemporary operations and supply chain management.

Besides, as discussed in the above sections, value creation in platform supply chains largely depends on effective supplier integration and customer integration, with technological infrastructures playing a supporting role by enabling coordination and information sharing across supply chain participants. However, despite its potential to support and reinforce supplier integration and customer integration, technology adoption in supply chains often faces challenges related to compatibility, interoperability, and uneven implementation across different supply chain partners (Stornelli et al., 2021). In particular, fragmented adoption generates inefficiencies, creates barriers to collaboration, and hinders the realization of economies of scale. These challenges are especially evident in platform supply chains,

B. Huo et al., *Platform Supply Chains 4*, Platform Supply Chains in the AI Era,
https://doi.org/10.1007/978-981-92-0133-4_5

where the coordination of multiple suppliers and customers relies on shared technical standards and information exchange. Thus, strengthening technology integration therefore becomes a necessity. It allows firms to bridge heterogeneous systems, transform isolated data repositories into shared knowledge resources, and coordinate decision-making across organizational boundaries (Wong et al., 2015). Without such integration, the benefits of digitalization remain partial and localized, whereas integration enables collective performance gains, ecosystem resilience, and long-term competitive advantage.

Technology integration in platform supply chains acquires several distinctive features. First, integration must emphasize real-time connectivity and responsiveness, since value creation in platforms relies on the ability to sense, process, and react to dynamic market signals instantly (Yin et al., 2019). This requires not only technical infrastructures such as IoT-enabled sensors and cloud-based analytics, but also governance mechanisms that facilitate rapid coordination among actors. Second, integration emphasizes multi-actor interoperability, whereby manufacturers, logistics providers, retailers, and consumers operate within shared digital infrastructures that necessitate seamless data exchange and functional compatibility (Pagell & Shevchenko, 2014). This interoperability is essential for minimizing transaction costs, reducing duplication, and enabling efficient collaboration across organizational boundaries. Third, integration accentuates ecosystem scalability and resilience, meaning that technologies must be designed to support both the expansion of platform participants and the robustness of operations under conditions of uncertainty or disruption (Ivanov et al., 2019). Such scalability is achieved by embedding modular architectures and adaptive processes that allow platforms to evolve without compromising stability. Finally, given that the effectiveness of digital ecosystems depends on the accuracy, security, and accountability of information flows, integration increasingly involves data governance and trust-building mechanisms (Tallon et al., 2013; Hanisch et al., 2023). Platforms must address issues of privacy, data ownership, and ethical use to maintain legitimacy and ensure sustained cooperation among stakeholders. Along these lines, technology integration in platform supply chains necessitates a system-level orchestration of multiple digital technologies that jointly enable real-time coordination, cross-actor interoperability, scalable expansion, and credible data governance.

Consistent with these integration imperatives, leading digital platforms such as Alibaba and JD.com have pursued strategies that deliberately combine AI, big data, cloud infrastructures, and IoT devices into integrated architectures (Li et al., 2020). This transition highlights that integration is not merely a technical alignment, but also a strategic response to the complexity of platform ecosystems. In practice, integration manifests in multiple scenarios, ranging from end-to-end supply chain visibility to predictive demand management and decentralized trust mechanisms. Table 5.1 provides a structured overview of key technologies, their primary functions, and illustrative applications within supply chains, drawing on prior studies such as de Oliveira-Dias et al. (2023) and Frank et al. (2019).

In light of these developments, it is important to clarify the meaning of technology integration in the supply chain context. Platform supply chain technology

Table 5.1 Trending technologies in operations and supply chain management

Technology	Key Functions in Supply Chain	Illustrative Applications
ERP	Cross-functional coordination	Streamlined procurement and production planning
RFID / IoT	Real-time visibility	Tracking shipments, monitoring cold chains
AI / ML	Predictive analytics	Demand forecasting, dynamic pricing
Cloud computing	Scalability and data sharing	Multi-partner platforms, flexible IT resources
Big data	Data-driven decision-making	Inventory optimization, risk assessment
Blockchain	Decentralized trust and traceability	Provenance tracking, smart contracts

integration refers to the coordinated deployment of digital and intelligent technologies on a shared platform to connect supply chain partners and enable joint coordination of information flows, systems, and operational processes across organizational boundaries (Subramani, 2004; Rai et al., 2006). Through platform-based infrastructures, such integration facilitates real-time data exchange, system interoperability, and process alignment among suppliers, customers, and other supply chain partners, thereby supporting collective decision-making and coordinated action (Benitez et al., 2018). In terms of scope, platform supply chain technology integration is defined at the platform level and involves the coordinated use of digital technologies across multiple supply chain partners (Rai et al., 2006; Jacobides et al., 2018; Kretschmer et al., 2022). Rather than treating digital technologies as isolated instruments, integration emphasizes the development of interconnected systems that enable data exchange, collaborative innovation, and ecosystem-wide responsiveness. This interpretation is particularly salient in platform supply chains, where the ability to orchestrate multiple actors through shared technological architectures constitutes the foundation of sustainable value creation.

5.1.2 How Platform Supply Chain Technology Integration Creates Value

Platform supply chain technology integration has undergone significant evolution, transitioning from traditional IT-driven systems to intelligent, platform-oriented, and decentralized architectures (Dubey et al., 2021). Rather than merely connecting disparate digital tools, platform supply chain technology integration enables platforms to transform dispersed data, heterogeneous actors, and fragmented processes into coordinated value-generating systems (Lin et al., 2021; de Oliveira-Dias et al., 2023). For instance, platforms such as Alibaba show how integration across merchant systems, logistics providers, and payment infrastructures enables dispersed transactional data to be recombined into coordinated fulfillment and demand-sensing processes, instead of being confined to firm-level IT systems. Prior research indicates that platform supply chain technology integration creates value by enabling systematic coordination of information, activities, and innovations across organizational boundaries (Subramani, 2004; Rai et al., 2006). Evidence from logistics supply chain relationships demonstrates that value emerges when firms move beyond transaction-level information exchange and adopt integration mechanisms that support the sharing of strategic information (Klein & Rai, 2009). Such integration allows customers and suppliers to align operational decisions, coordinate asset deployment, and respond jointly to uncertainty, generating relationship-specific performance gains. Besides, the effectiveness of strategic information integration depends on relationship-specific technological investments, such as customized IT systems, as well as relational conditions that mitigate opportunism. In this sense, platform supply chain technology integration functions as an infrastructure that transforms bilateral supply chain relationships from arm's-length exchanges into coordinated systems capable of generating relational rents (Klein & Rai, 2009).

Furthermore, the value of platform supply chain technology integration depends on where coordination frictions arise along the activity chain and which side's constraints most strongly limit system-level performance (Adner & Kapoor, 2010). Prior research distinguishes between upstream interdependent activities coordinated by the focal firm and downstream complementary activities that shape customers' ability to realize value, and shows that constraints at different locations along the activity chain have asymmetric effects on value creation (Adner & Kapoor, 2010). In platform supply chains, technology integration creates value by reducing these location-specific frictions. On the upstream side, platform supply chain technology integration facilitates the coordination of interdependent activities required to deliver a reliable platform-level offering. On the downstream side, they enable complements to align with the platform in ways that allow customers to fully utilize the core offering. By standardizing interfaces and supporting predictable coordination across interdependent actors, platform supply chain technology integration prevents bottlenecks that would otherwise stall value creation. These benefits become increasingly salient as technologies evolve, because integration mechanisms interact with boundary choices such as vertical integration to mitigate contractual and coordination hazards over the technology life cycle (Klein & Rai, 2009). Thus, platform supply chain technology integration creates value by expanding high-quality participation while ensuring that coordination constraints at specific locations do not undermine relationship-specific or system-level performance. As shown in Fig. 5.1, platform supply chain technology integration facilitates value creation by transforming dispersed actors, data, and processes into coordinated upstream and downstream activities.

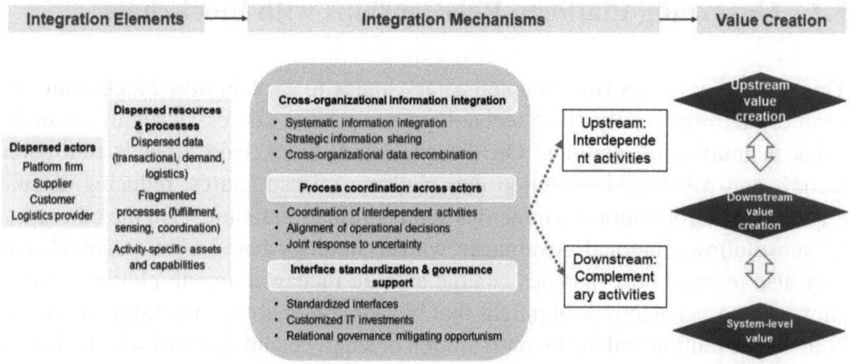

Fig. 5.1 Framework for platform supply chain technology integration and value creation

5.1.3 Chapter Framework

Effective platform supply chain technology integration ensures that heterogeneous technologies and participants are not merely connected but work synergistically to generate adaptive, resilient, and innovation-driven supply chain ecosystems. It also highlights that integration is both a technological and organizational endeavor, requiring alignment of infrastructures, processes, and governance structures to fully capture the benefits of digitalization (Treiblmaier, 2018; Casino et al., 2019). In this context, digital technologies play a critical role, with blockchain being particularly salient because it directly addresses key challenges related to interoperability, transparency, and trust (Awasthy et al., 2025). In addition, blockchain and related decentralized technologies introduce a new layer of integration emphasizing trust, transparency, and automated governance (Bai & Sarkis, 2020; Wamba et al., 2020). Furthermore, blockchain enables immutable transaction records, end-to-end provenance tracking, and execution of smart contracts, enhancing the verification and enforcement of agreements among supply chain participants (Treiblmaier, 2018, Casino et al., 2019). Beyond operational coordination, blockchain integration addresses two critical dimensions of modern supply chain complexity, namely network complexity, which stems from multiple interconnected actors and multi-level processes, and relational complexity, which arises from trust, governance, and collaboration challenges in multi-party interactions. These features allow blockchain-based integration to support value creation in complex supply chain settings characterized by high network complexity and relational complexity. This discussion sets the stage for the following section, which develops two complementary perspectives to further explain how governance and value creation mechanisms operate through technology integration in platform supply chains.

5.2 Governing Platform Relationships with Blockchain

This section develops two complementary logics to explain how blockchain, as a form of platform supply chain technology integration, addresses supply chain disputes in multi-actor settings. On the one hand, blockchain embeds transparent records and rule-based execution into platform infrastructures, reducing disputes arising from information asymmetries and coordination failures. On the other hand, by substituting relational governance with technology-based controls, blockchain may also reshape how disputes emerge and are managed among platform participants. These perspectives highlight that blockchain-enabled integration influences both the prevention and the reconfiguration of supply chain disputes within platform supply chains.

5.2.1 Blockchain Implementation in Platforms

Platform supply chains have become a dominant organizational form in contemporary operations, reshaping how firms coordinate production, distribution, and service provision (Ak & Patatoukas, 2016; Choi et al., 2023; Xu et al., 2023). Compared with traditional supply chains, platform supply chains involve a larger number of heterogeneous participants and rely more heavily on digital infrastructures to mediate interactions and information flows (Wang, Chen, & Song, 2021a; Wang, Zheng, et al., 2021b; Yu et al., 2022). These features create both opportunities and challenges, particularly with respect to information asymmetry, data security, and coordination among platform participants (Chen et al., 2023). In this context, blockchain has increasingly been adopted as a foundational technology embedded within platform architectures. Conceptualized as a decentralized and distributed digital ledger, blockchain enables transparent, immutable, and traceable records of transactions and activities across the supply chain (Li et al., 2022). When implemented in platforms, blockchain supports shared data infrastructures and automated execution mechanisms, such as smart contracts, which facilitate coordination among multiple actors without relying on centralized control (Dolgui et al., 2020). By enhancing data credibility and transparency across organizational boundaries, blockchain implementation in platform supply chains provides a technological basis for coordinating interdependent actors operating under high complexity (Choi et al., 2023).

Blockchain is characterized by openness, tamper-resistant records, decentralization, and traceability, which together enable credible information sharing and verifiable transactions across organizational boundaries (Yin et al., 2019). When embedded within platform supply chains, these features allow governance functions such as verification, monitoring, and enforcement to be partially encoded into shared digital infrastructures, reducing reliance on bilateral trust and manual supervision. An emerging body of research examines how blockchain implementation affects inter-organizational interactions by altering governance mechanisms. Prior studies show that blockchain-based systems can mitigate opportunistic behaviors by enhancing transparency and traceability in multi-actor environments, such as preventing product counterfeiting and improving compliance along supply chains (Danese et al., 2021; Pun et al., 2021). Other studies suggest that blockchain can function as a credible signaling and verification mechanism, enabling firms to access favorable financing terms and facilitating data contribution and sharing among supply chain participants (Chod et al., 2020). These findings indicate that blockchain supports governance by standardizing information disclosure and aligning incentives among platform participants.

From a market perspective, blockchain implementation has also been interpreted as a governance-related signal that reflects firms' commitment to data security, transparency, and process integrity. Similar to other forms of digital infrastructure investment, blockchain adoption can generate positive reactions from investors and stakeholders, particularly when concerns over information asymmetry and data fraud are salient (Nishant et al., 2017; Bose & Leung, 2019; Klockner et al., 2022). Empirical evidence further suggests that blockchain announcements are associated with favorable market responses, consistent with the view that blockchain-enabled governance enhances organizational credibility and accountability (Cheng et al., 2019; Cahill et al., 2020). Despite these potential governance benefits, prior research also highlights that blockchain implementation entails substantial technical and operational challenges, including scalability constraints, privacy risks, high energy consumption, and a lack of standardization (Yin et al., 2019; Babich & Hilary, 2020). These limitations suggest that the governance effects of blockchain in platform supply chains are not automatic but depend on how technological controls interact with organizational capabilities and institutional arrangements. Existing studies, relying on analytical modeling, case studies, and qualitative investigations, provide valuable insights into these trade-offs but offer limited empirical evidence on how blockchain-based governance ultimately shapes inter-organizational outcomes in platform supply chains (Ziolkowski et al., 2020; Falcone et al., 2021; Kurpjuweit et al., 2021). In platform supply chains, coordination and control are exercised not only through formal contracts and relational governance, but also through digital infrastructures that shape information disclosure, verification, and rule enforcement among multiple actors (Babich & Hilary, 2020; Lumineau et al., 2021). Blockchain implementation, by encoding transparency, traceability, and execution logic into shared systems, has the potential to reconfigure these governance processes at the platform level (Du, Ma et al., 2017; Yin et al., 2019). Accordingly, blockchain implementation in platform supply chains should be understood not merely as a technological upgrade but as a form of technology-based governance that shapes how coordination and control are enacted across decentralized platform networks.

5.2.2 *Blockchain Implementation and Supply Chain Dispute*

Blockchain has increasingly been adopted within platform supply chains as a digital infrastructure to support coordination among multiple interdependent actors. By providing shared, immutable records and real-time visibility across transactions, blockchain applications within platforms enhance transparency, reduce information asymmetries, and support cross-firm synchronization of activities. In this sense, blockchain-enabled platform integration initially serves a coordination function by stabilizing information flows and aligning expectations among customers, suppliers, and other platform participants (Lumineau et al., 2021). Such coordination benefits are particularly salient in platform settings characterized by dispersed actors, repeated exchanges, and high interdependence. Beyond coordination, we conceptualize blockchain as a form of technology-based governance that reshapes how interfirm relationships are monitored, enforced, and held accountable.

By embedding procedural verification and compliance into immutable and traceable digital architectures, blockchain alters how obligations are specified, verified, and contested among interdependent actors (De Filippi et al., 2020; Menon & Jain, 2024). Such technology-based governance may fundamentally transform the balance between formal and relational governance mechanisms. While blockchain enhances transparency and reduces information asymmetry, it may simultaneously substitute for trust-based relational governance by shifting coordination from reciprocal interaction to algorithmic control (Gligor et al., 2021; Lumineau et al., 2021). In platform supply chains characterized by asymmetric power and uneven technological capabilities, this substitution can weaken relational foundations and increase the likelihood that disagreements are escalated into formal disputes rather than resolved through informal adjustment. From a resource dependence perspective, blockchain implementation may further reshape interdependence structures by granting initiating firms technological dominance over data access, rule design, and verification processes, particularly in private and permissioned blockchain systems (Kshetri, 2022; Li et al., 2025). Such technological control enables focal firms to reduce uncertainty and dependence on upstream partners, but may also intensify perceptions of unilateral monitoring and power imbalance, thereby heightening conflict potential within exchange relationships.

Moreover, the governance effects of blockchain are experienced asymmetrically across supply chain partners. While buyers often benefit from enhanced visibility and control, suppliers face additional compliance requirements, process codification pressures, and adjustment costs to align with blockchain-enabled transactions (Kouhizadeh et al., 2021; Lumineau et al., 2021). These adaptation challenges, combined with reduced relational flexibility, may amplify sensitivity to perceived opportunism and increase the incidence of supply chain disputes. Importantly, blockchain-enabled governance alters not only the distribution of information but also the locus of control and the mechanisms through which disagreements are surfaced and addressed. By embedding monitoring and verification into technologically enforced rules, blockchain can shift coordination away from informal negotiation toward more formalized and rule-based interactions (De Filippi et al., 2020). In platform supply chains characterized by asymmetric power and interdependence, such shifts may heighten tensions as suppliers reassess obligations, responsibilities, and acceptable boundaries of control. To this point, the emergence of supply chain disputes following blockchain implementation should not be interpreted simply as governance failure. Disputes can be understood as outcomes of governance reconfiguration, reflecting adjustments to newly instituted technological controls that reshape relational expectations, accountability structures, and enforcement processes among platform participants (Lumineau et al., 2021). As blockchain redefines how coordination is monitored and contested, disputes increasingly arise as part of the transition toward technology-based governance, rather than as simple failures of inter-firm exchange relationships.

Blockchain reshapes the governance architecture of platform supply chains by reallocating monitoring authority, codifying exchange processes, and altering the balance between technological and relational governance (Lumineau et al., 2021). In such contexts, supply chain disputes emerge not as aberrations but as relational outcomes of governance reconfiguration, reflecting how interdependent actors adjust to new forms of technological control, transparency, and accountability (Kouhizadeh et al., 2021; Kshetri, 2022). Accordingly, understanding disputes in blockchain-enabled platform supply chains requires moving beyond a failure-based interpretation and examining how technology-based governance interacts with power asymmetries, ethical orientations, and resource dependencies to shape inter-firm interactions.

5.3 Value Creation: Blockchain Implementation and Shareholder Value

The preceding discussion highlights that blockchain implementation in platform supply chains reshapes coordination and governance by reconfiguring how interdependence is monitored, enforced, and contested among participating actors. Such governance reconfiguration may give rise to disputes, not as simple signs of relational failure, but as manifestations of adjustment costs and power realignment during the transition toward technology-based governance. Beyond inter-organizational dynamics, an equally important question concerns how platform firms strategically leverage blockchain implementation to enhance market value. By adopting blockchain within platform supply chains, firms actively signal their capacity to manage complexity, coordinate dispersed activities, and reconfigure governance structures in technologically mediated environments. In this chapter, we therefore examine blockchain implementation and shareholder value by conceptualizing value creation as the market response to platform firms' deliberate use of blockchain-enabled governance to strengthen coordination, manage interdependence, and reshape supply chain relationships.

5.3.1 Introduction

Blockchain is a distributed ledger technology that uses cryptography to ensure transmission and access security (Du, Ma et al., 2017). With the characteristics of decentralization, stability, security, traceability, and immutability, blockchain has attracted the attention of the business community. According to a PwC survey, 84% of companies are dabbling in blockchain. The World Economic Forum (2015) predicts that 10% of the world's GDP will be stored on the blockchain network by 2027. Although it has great potential, blockchain implementation is still risky, with technical and operational challenges (Babich & Hilary, 2020). In platform supply chains, where coordination and governance are mediated by digital infrastructures, it remains uncertain whether blockchain implementation can be translated into economic value and shareholder value. On the one hand, blockchain has some technical problems, such as scalability, which increase storage space requirements and reduce propagation speed (Yin et al., 2019), and proof-of-work mechanisms require substantial energy consumption (Zheng et al., 2018). On the other hand, significant specific investments are required to align blockchain with firms' platform strategies and operational architectures (Durach et al., 2021). Besides, the black-box effect and lack of standardization may further hinder firms from realizing value from blockchain implementation (Babich & Hilary, 2020). Therefore, a central question is whether blockchain implementation contributes to value creation for firms embedded in platform supply chains, as reflected in shareholder value.

Blockchain can be implemented in many fields, among which supply chain management, particularly platform-enabled supply chains, represents one of the most promising application scenarios (Babich & Hilary, 2020). Platform supply chains rely on digital platforms to orchestrate interactions among heterogeneous and interdependent actors, which makes transparency, traceability, and information credibility especially salient. Blockchain enhances the credibility and immutability of information shared across platform participants, thereby offering solutions to coordination challenges in complex and multi-sided supply networks where agility, speed, and transparency are critical (Cole et al., 2019). Prior studies indicate that blockchain implementation improves supply chain traceability and coordination (Hastig & Sodhi, 2020), reduces lead time, and enhances visibility across platform-mediated transactions (Martinez, Zhao et al., 2019). Firms such as Amazon, IBM, and Maersk have explored blockchain to support platform-based logistics and data-sharing infrastructures (Babich & Hilary, 2020), while companies including JD.com and Lenovo have implemented blockchain within digital platforms to manage large-scale supplier and distributor networks in China.

Platform supply chains can be regarded as complex adaptive systems (CASs) (Choi et al., 2001; Yeoman & Santos, 2019; Zhao et al., 2019). As self-organizing systems, platform supply chains evolve through decentralized interactions among platform owners, suppliers, and complementors, while continuously adapting to environmental complexity (Choi et al., 2001). In such environments, blockchain can reshape inter-organizational relationships and governance structures on platforms

(Babich & Hilary, 2020), while supporting new platform-based business models (Lumineau et al., 2021). Compared with centralized information systems, blockchain's distributed architecture is particularly compatible with platform supply chains characterized by dispersed participants and dense interaction networks, promoting autonomy and self-organizing behavior among platform actors (Swierczek, 2022). From this perspective, blockchain represents a form of platform governance infrastructure that may influence not only coordination and disputes, as discussed in the previous section, but also how value is created and evaluated by capital markets.

Importantly, the value implications of blockchain implementation in platform supply chains are unlikely to be uniform. Business diversification reflects internal complexity that shapes how platform firms integrate blockchain across multiple business units (Su & Tsang, 2015, Tang, Tang et al., 2019). Supply chain concentration captures the structural configuration of platform ecosystems and affects the degree to which blockchain can enhance coordination among dispersed suppliers and customers (Giannoccaro et al., 2018; Fosso Wamba et al., 2020). Environmental complexity further conditions firms' ability to leverage blockchain as a platform governance mechanism and to convert technological adoption into economic returns (Azadegan et al., 2013; Lam et al., 2019).

5.3.2 Hypotheses

5.3.2.1 The Direct Effect of Blockchain Implementation on Shareholder Value

As an emerging technology, blockchain can not only bring competitive advantages by reshaping processes and promoting new business models (Babich & Hilary, 2020; Hastig & Sodhi, 2020), it can also solve the obstacles that exist in other technologies (Chanson et al., 2019). In platform supply chains, where transactions and coordination are increasingly mediated through digital infrastructures, blockchain further enhances the credibility and interoperability of information flows across multiple sides of the platform. Blockchain implementation shifts trust from interpersonal relationships to system-level mechanisms, thereby fostering mutual trust based on high-quality information (Babich & Hilary, 2020). Blockchain also enables companies to track the entire order process and improve operational visibility (Hastig & Sodhi, 2020), which is particularly valuable in platform environments characterized by dispersed and heterogeneous participants.

Besides, blockchain implementation reduces the average order time and improves operational efficiency (Martinez et al., 2019). Danese et al. (2021) claimed that blockchain applied in product counterfeiting can effectively prevent counterfeiting. Chod et al. (2020) hold that blockchain ensures the verifiability of transactions, so that small and medium-sized companies can transmit high-quality information and obtain favorable financing conditions. These benefits are likely to be capitalized more rapidly in platform supply chains, where focal firms often orchestrate transactions among a large number of upstream and downstream partners.

Previous studies have shown that the announcement of IT plans can generate stock market value (Nishant et al., 2017). Therefore, we believe that the market will react positively to blockchain implementation. Abnormal returns refer to the stock return difference between implementing blockchain or not (Lam et al., 2019). Besides, blockchain implementation can bring positive stock market returns. Cheng et al. (2019) found an overly positive investor reaction to blockchain mania. Cahill et al. (2020) suggested that the stock market reaction to blockchain correlates with Bitcoin price. Klockner et al. (2022) showed the financial performance improvement due to blockchain implementation from a case, project, and company perspective. In the context of platform-oriented supply chains, blockchain implementation may further signal a firm's capability to govern complex, multi-actor transactions through scalable digital infrastructures. We hypothesize that:

H1. The market will react positively to blockchain implementation.

5.3.2.2 The Moderating Effect of Business Diversification and Supply Chain Concentration

In order to remain competitive, companies increasingly develop differentiated products and business models (Jacobs, 2013). Companies with business diversification expand their business by entering new products, new markets, and new activities (Hendricks et al., 2009). Business diversification actively helps companies to broaden the scope of a business beyond industry-specific contexts (Salampasis & Mention, 2019). In platform supply chains, diversification is often accompanied by the integration of multiple business units and ecosystem partners onto shared digital platforms. However, when companies share resources and co-specialize to achieve economies of integration, monitoring the business processes is more complex and difficult (Su & Tsang, 2015; Tang et al., 2019), leading to a higher likelihood of opportunistic behaviors (Ljubownikow & Ang, 2020).

Previous studies have shown that business diversification increases the complexity of tasks involved in operations (Chari et al., 2008), thereby increasing the need for information processing capabilities and IT capabilities to manage internal information flows (Gomez et al., 2016). Companies with business diversification are more likely to implement blockchain to handle the information processing and coordination of complex tasks. In addition, the decentralization and sharing characteristics of blockchain technology are helpful for information transfer and resource sharing among multiple business models and reduce internal coordination costs (Babich & Hilary, 2020; Wang, Zheng, et al., 2021b). This coordinating role becomes particularly salient in platform supply chains, where diversified activities are embedded within a common digital architecture. Therefore, the value of blockchain implementation will be enhanced in companies with a higher business diversification. It will help them to better coordinate diverse business units.

H2. The stock market reaction to blockchain implementation will be more positive for companies with higher business diversification.

5.3.2.3 The Moderating Effect of Supply Chain Concentration

According to the complex adaptive systems perspective, a complex supply chain network can be understood as a self-organizing system (Choi et al., 2001; Swierczek, 2022). Compared with centralized information systems, decentralized blockchain technologies can better support decentralized supply chain partners by enhancing the autonomy and spontaneity of individual agents, thereby facilitating self-organizing behavior within the supply chain (Swierczek, 2022). In platform supply chains, such decentralized coordination is often enabled through a focal platform firm that connects multiple upstream and downstream actors.

We argue that higher supply chain concentration weakens the value of blockchain implementation. A concentrated supply chain structure indicates that the focal firm has embedded and stable connections with a limited number of supply chain partners, which may increase dependence on these partners (Saboo et al., 2017; Schwieterman et al., 2018). Customer concentration reflects the extent to which a firm's sales are derived from a small number of major customers and thus captures the degree of dispersion among downstream partners (Lanier Jr. et al., 2010; Schwieterman et al., 2018). Major customers are often better positioned to identify market trends and anticipate product demand (Wang, Chen, & Song, 2021a). When customer concentration is high, firms are more likely to maintain stable and long-term relationships with a few key customers (Crawford et al., 2020). Such concentrated relationships facilitate the development of strong relational ties, enabling effective information sharing and reducing coordination conflicts and relational risks (Schwieterman et al., 2018).

By contrast, when customer concentration is low, information exchange between firms and their customers becomes more complex and fragmented. In this context, the decentralization and traceability features of blockchain technologies can better realize their value by reducing information acquisition costs and improving the efficiency of information sharing (Wang, Zheng, et al., 2021b). This effect is particularly salient in platform supply chains, where blockchain can partially substitute for bilateral coordination mechanisms by enabling standardized and platform-wide information disclosure. Therefore, we propose:

H3a. The stock market reaction to blockchain implementation will be more positive for companies with lower customer concentration.

Supplier concentration refers to how many a company purchases from a few major suppliers. It reflects the degree of dispersion of upstream partners (Lanier Jr. et al., 2010, Schwieterman et al., 2018). Suppliers have information advantages in terms of purchased materials and products, and proper information sharing can reduce transaction costs and improve transaction efficiency (Lee et al., 1997; Wang, Chen, & Song, 2021a). Research on social networks shows that social relationships can be divided into strong and weak relationships (Kim & Zhu, 2018). Low supplier concentration means companies have weak relationships with their suppliers. They will have more alternatives and be more likely to gain mobilized resources (Borgatti & Li, 2009). However, companies have difficulties governing a less concentrated supply network. Implementing blockchain guarantees information security and improves supply visibility and traceability, and reduces transaction costs due to supply complexity (Liu et al., 2020), especially when upstream transactions are mediated through digital platforms rather than bilateral ties. Therefore, we propose:

H3b. The stock market reaction to blockchain implementation will be more positive for companies with lower supplier concentration.

5.3.2.4 The Moderating Effect of Environmental Complexity

Previous studies show that although information technology can create value, such benefits may dissipate rapidly due to competitive pressures (Ren & Dewan, 2015). For example, Lam et al. (2019) find that the benefits of implementing 3D printing are greater in less competitive environments. The deployment of blockchain requires substantial resource investments (Klockner et al., 2022), as well as the complementary use of other information technologies (Babich & Hilary, 2020). In platform-based markets, these investments are often accompanied by additional costs related to ecosystem coordination and rule setting.

In low-complexity environments, sufficient resource investments can support firms in implementing blockchain successfully. By contrast, highly complex environments are characterized by a large number of competitors (Capaldo & Giannoccaro, 2015; Xu et al., 2019), where blockchain implementation may be easily imitated and replicated by other firms, thereby eroding first-mover advantages (Lam et al., 2019). As a result, blockchain implementation is expected to generate a stronger impact on stock returns in low-complexity environments.

H4. The stock market reaction to blockchain implementation will be more positive for companies with lower environmental complexity.

From the complex adaptive systems perspective, supply chains can be characterized as complex and adaptive systems (Choi et al., 2001, Zhao, Zuo et al. 2019). Supply chain networks are complex because firms operate within interactive and dynamic networks of partners (Yeoman & Santos, 2019), and adaptive because firms must continuously reconfigure their business models and inter-firm relationships in response to environmental changes (Swierczek, 2022). Platform supply chains further intensify this adaptive process by embedding inter-firm interactions within digital infrastructures that shape coordination mechanisms and information flows.

In less complex environments, firms with complex business structures and diversified supply chain relationships are better positioned to leverage blockchain through adequate resources and financial support, thereby gaining greater competitive advantages. However, in highly complex environments, firms may face elevated risks and resource constraints that limit their ability to reconfigure diversified business activities and supply chain relationships in ways that align with blockchain characteristics (Azadegan et al., 2013; Zheng et al., 2018). Therefore, we propose:

H5a. In lower environmental complexity, the stock market reaction to blockchain implementation will be more positive for companies with higher business diversification.

H5b. In lower environmental complexity, the stock market reaction to blockchain implementation will be more positive for companies with lower customer concentration.

H5c. In lower environmental complexity, the stock market reaction to blockchain implementation will be more positive for companies with lower supplier concentration.

5.3.3 Methodology

5.3.3.1 Data and Measures

We searched for blockchain implementation announcements from the Shanghai Stock Exchange website and the Shenzhen Stock Exchange website (He et al., 2016). We also supplemented the announcements from newspapers designated by the China Securities Regulatory Commission, including China Securities News, Shanghai Securities News, Securities Daily, and Securities Times (Zhao et al., 2013). In addition, we supplemented and verified the blockchain announcement from Eastmoney Website (Yang et al., 2014) and Wind Database (Chen et al., 2022). The use of multiple sources to identify blockchain announcements can produce a more complete and accurate dataset than a single source. The sample consists of announcements from January 2015 to December 2021. We downloaded all the announcements with keywords (i.e., blockchain, bitcoin, or cryptocurrency (ies)) (Cheng et al., 2019). In addition, we collected daily stock trading data and other financial data from the China Stock Market Trading Database (CSMAR). We followed the sample selection procedure from the literature to generate the final blockchain implementation announcements (Lam et al., 2019; Arora et al., 2020).

(1) We checked the headlines and lead paragraphs of all announcements with keywords in the Shenzhen/Shanghai Stock Exchange websites during the period 2015–2021. In this step, we exclude special treatment (* ST) companies with poor financial conditions and which may be delisted. (2) Announcements should involve blockchain applications in companies' business practices. We exclude announcements that are only related to blockchain words but without specific business applications. (3) To capture the market response to the announcement, we only reserve the announcement of blockchain implementation issued by the company for the first time. However, the announcement reported different blockchain implementation types were included. (4) To avoid confounding effects, we searched the Shanghai/Shenzhen Stock Exchange websites within a three-day window (±1 trading day) around the event announcement day, companies that claimed other significant announcements during the event period were excluded.

The final sample includes 138 blockchain implementation announcements from 86 companies. Table 5.2 shows the basic information of companies that issued blockchain announcements. Panel A reports *Total Assets*, *Market value*, *Sales*, and *Net Profits*. Panel B shows that most of the announcements were announced between 2018 and 2021, indicating blockchain is gaining popularity among companies in recent years. Panel C reports that most of the companies that announced blockchain implementation are from the manufacturing and service industries.

5.3.3.2 Event Study Method

We use the event study method proposed by Brown and Warner (1985) to evaluate the impact of blockchain implementation on shareholder value. The event study method is widely used in operations management, such as SC glitches (Schmidt et al., 2020), SC strategic cooperation (Liu et al., 2020), and SC scandals (Jacobs & Singhal, 2020). To avoid the lag effect caused by the too-short estimation period and confusion of other events caused by the too-long estimation period, this study chooses a 200-day estimation period, starting on day −210 and ending on day −11 (Jacobs & Singhal, 2020; Schmidt et al., 2020).

Table 5.2 Descriptive statistics

	Mean	Median	SD	Max	Min
Panel A: Characteristics of BC implementation announcing companies					
Total assets (CNY million)	25725.47	4304.96	60402.20	617688.09	382.65
Market value (CNY million)	8538.10	5857.70	19130.80	157295.05	1804.50
Sales (CNY million)	9993.70	1824.35	22046.38	187927.76	219.30
Net profits (CNY million)	547.45	158.79	1732.72	18856.88	−2552.66
Panel B: Distribution year for announcements					
Year	Number		Percentage		
2016	3		2.17%		
2017	7		5.07%		
2018	31		22.46%		
2019	38		27.54%		
2020	44		31.88%		
2021	15		10.87%		
Total	138		100.00%		
Panel C: Sample industry description (industry 2-digit CSRC code)					
Industry	Number		Percentage		
Manufacturing	63		45.65%		
Soft and IT services	34		24.64%		
Construction and real estate	19		13.77%		
Others	22		15.94%		

We adopt the Fama-French four-factor model to calculate abnormal returns (ARs) (Jacobs & Singhal, 2020).

$$R_{it} = \alpha_i + R_{ft} + \beta_{i1}\left(\mathrm{R}_{mt} - R_{ft}\right) + \beta_{i2}SMB_t + \beta_{i3}HML_t + \beta_{i4}UMD_t + \varepsilon_{it} \tag{5.1}$$

Where R_{it} is the Day t return of stock i ; R_{mt} is the Day t return of market return; R_{ft} is the risk-free return on Day t . SMB_t is the difference between rates of return. HML_t is the difference between book-to-market ratio stocks. UMD_t is the difference between stock prices. $\pm_i$, ${}^{2}{}_{i1}$, ${}^{2}{}_{i2}$, ${}^{2}{}_{i3}$, ${}^{2}{}_{i4}$ are linear regression coefficients, μ_{it} is the error term for stock i on Day t .

The abnormal return AR_{it} for company i on Day t is estimated:

$$AR_{it} = R_{it} - \left(\alpha_i + R_{ft} + \beta_{i1}\left(R_{mt} - R_{ft}\right) + \beta_{i2}SMB_t + \beta_{i3}HML_t + \beta_{i4}UMD_t\right) \tag{5.2}$$

To investigate the impact of events on the overall security pricing, it is also necessary to calculate the average abnormal return ($\overline{AR_{it}}$):

$$\overline{AR_{it}} = \frac{1}{N}\sum_{i}^{N} AR_{it} \tag{5.3}$$

where N is the number of sample companies on day t .

During the 200-day estimation period, the average abnormal return is calculated as:

$$\overset{\blacklozenge}{AR}_{it} = \frac{1}{200}\sum_{t=-210}^{t=-11} \overline{AR_{it}} \tag{5.4}$$

The standard deviation from the mean daily abnormal returns is estimated as:

$$\hat{S}\left(\overline{AR_{it}}\right) = \sqrt{\sum_{t=-210}^{t=-11}\left(\overline{AR_{it}} - \overset{\blacklozenge}{AR}_{it}\right) / 199} \tag{5.5}$$

The test statistic TS_t is estimated as:

$$TS_t = (\overline{AR_{it}} / \hat{S}\left(\overline{AR_{it}}\right) \tag{5.6}$$

For a given period [t_1, t_2], the cumulative abnormal return (CAR_{it}) is estimated:

$$CAR\left[t_1, t_2\right] = \sum_{t=t_1}^{t_2} AR_{it} \tag{5.7}$$

The test statistic for a j -day event period, TS_j is derived like that for a single day:

$$TS_j = \frac{\sum_{t=t_1}^{t_2} \overline{AR}_{it}}{\hat{S}\left(\overline{AR}_{it}\right)\sqrt{j}} \tag{5.8}$$

To ensure the accuracy of the results, this study calculates the median and percent positive abnormal returns and uses a nonparametric test to supplement t test. Wilcoxon signed-rank test is also used to determine whether the median of abnormal return is significantly different from zero. The generalized sign test is used to determine whether the percentage of positive abnormal returns is different from 50%.

5.3.3.3 Market Reaction to Blockchain Implementation

We adopt the Fama-French four-factor model to calculate the *ARs* of blockchain implementation announcements on the announcement Day 0 and conduct a t test and two nonparametric tests. Table 5.3 presents daily *ARs* and *CARs*. For 138 announcements, the *ARs* for day 0 are significantly positive at the 1% level. The Day 0 median *AR* is 0.97%, significantly greater than zero at the 1% level. The percent positive *ARs* for day 0 is 55.80%, as 55.80% of companies experience a positive abnormal stock return. For the two-day event period (−1,0), the mean *CARs* are 1.06%, significantly greater than 0 at the 1% level. And 52.17% of companies experience a positive abnormal stock return. Overall, the results indicate that the stock market reacts positively to blockchain implementation.

5.3.3.4 Moderation Effect Tests

The dependent variable is the *ARs* calculated by the event research method described in Eq. (5.7). The explanatory variables are measured as follows:

Table 5.3 Event period abnormal returns for the 138 blockchain implementation announcements

Date	Day−1	Day0	Day1	Day[−1,0]	Day[0,1]	Day[−1,1]
n	138	138	138	138	138	138
Mean abnormal return	−0.16%	0.97%***	0.09%	0.81%**	1.06%***	0.90%**
t–statistic	−0.75	4.38	0.41	2.60	3.38	2.35
Median abnormal return	−0.18%	0.47%**	−0.55%	0.14%	0.25%	−0.33%
Wilcoxon signed–rank Z–statistic	−1.21	2.21	−1.15	0.77	0.72	−0.10
Abnormal returns positive	44.20%	55.80%	40.58%	50.72%	52.17%	47.10%
Generalized sign test (Cowan)	2.69***	5.39***	1.61	4.13***	4.49***	3.23***

[a] $p < 0.1$, ** $p < 0.05$, *** $p < 0.01$

Customer Concentration (CC_ Concentration). Customer concentration is measured as the ratio of the major customer sales to the total annual sales. Specifically, we choose the proportion of the top five customers' sales in total sales to measure customer concentration (Patatoukas, 2012; Campello & Gao, 2017).

$$Customer\ concentration_{it} = \frac{\sum_{j=1}^{5} Sales_{i,j,t}}{Sales_{i,t}} \tag{5.9}$$

Where $Sales_{i,j,t}$ means the company *i's* sales to major customer j in the most recent fiscal year t. $Sales_{it}$ means the total sales of the company i in the most recent fiscal year t.

Supplier Concentration (SC_ Concentration). The measurement for supplier concentration is similar to that of customer concentration, in which sales are replaced by purchases (Patatoukas, 2012, Campello & Gao, 2017).

$$Supplier\ concentration_{it} = \frac{\sum_{j=1}^{5} Purchases_{i,j,t}}{purchases_{i,t}} \tag{5.10}$$

Customer Concentration HHI (CCHHI_ Concentration). Since the above measurements do not consider the number of major customers, we follow the method mentioned in Patatoukas (2012) and use the Herfindahl-Hirschman Index (HHI) to measure the number of major customers and their importance to the company's sales.

$$Customer\ concentration\ HHI_{it} = \sum_{j=1}^{5} \left(\frac{Sales_{i,j,t}}{Sales_{i,t}} \right)^2 \tag{5.11}$$

Supplier Concentration HHI (SCHHI_ Concentration). Similarly, we use the HHI by calculating the ratio of the volume of purchasing from the top five suppliers to the total purchase volumes.

$$Supplier\ concentration\ HHI_{it} = \sum_{j=1}^{5} \left(\frac{purchases_{i,j,t}}{purchases_{i,t}} \right)^2 \tag{5.12}$$

Business Diversification (BD_ Diversification). We use business diversification to measure business complexity based on four-digit ISIC.

$$DT = \sum_{i=1}^{m} p_i \ln(1/p_i) \tag{5.13}$$

Herfindahl Index (BDHHI_ Diversification).

$$DT = \sum pi^2 \tag{5.14}$$

Environmental Complexity (EC_Complexity). We use the mean industry competition of the past three years to measure environmental complexity (Tang & Chen, 2020).

$$EC_{it} = 1 - \sum_{i}^{N} \left(\frac{sales_{i,j,t}}{Total\ sales\ of\ firms\ in\ the\ same\ industry} \right)^2 \tag{5.15}$$

Control variables comprise ***Market-to-book (MTB)***, ***Firm Size (Firm_size)***, ***Firm Growth (Growth)***, ***Financial Leverage (Leverage)***, **Inventory turnover** ***(Inventory)***, ***R&D intensity (RD)***, **Industry size (Indus_size)** and **Bitcoin price (Bitcoin)**, which are mentioned in previous literature that may affect shareholder value (Xia et al., 2016; Jacobs & Singhal, 2020; Schmidt et al., 2020). Companies with a larger size, higher growth, higher R&D intensity, MTB_ratio, and lower financial leverage may have more financial resources and superior technological skills to support blockchain technology (Xiong et al., 2021). Inventory turnover can measure the operational efficiency of a business, which determines how reliant a business is on emerging technologies such as blockchain (Xiong et al., 2021). Industry size might affect the extent of benefits that firms can capture from new technology implementation (Shou et al., 2021). Referring to previous studies, we also use Bitcoin price as a control variable (Cheng et al., 2019; Klockner et al., 2022). In addition, we control industry (two-digit SIC codes) and time (Year) effects. We also control industry (two-digit SIC codes) and time (Year) effects. Table 5.4 presents the measurement details for hypothesized and control variables.

The regression model is:

$$\begin{aligned} AR_i = {} & \beta_0 + \beta_1 BD\_Diversification_i + \beta_2 CC\_Concentration_i \\ & + \beta_3 SC\_Concentration_i + \beta_4 EC\_Complexity_i + \beta_5 Bitcoin_i \\ & + \beta_6 \mathrm{Inventory}_i + \beta_7 MTB_i + \beta_8 RD_i + \beta_9 Firm\_size_i + \beta_{10} Growth_i \\ & + \beta_{11} leverage_i + \beta_{12} Indus\_size_i + \beta_{13} Ind_i + \beta_{14} Year_i + \varepsilon i \end{aligned} \tag{5.16}$$

Table 5.5 presents the correlations of variables used in this study.

The VIFs of all models presented in Table 5.6 are less than 3.0, indicating that there is no multicollinearity. Model 1 contains only control variables, and we add explanatory and control variables in Models 2–5. Business diversification is significantly positively related to the dependent variable, suggesting that the stock returns of blockchain implementation are more positive for companies with higher business diversification. Thus, H2 is supported. The results indicated that the customer concentration is significantly negative at the 1% level, indicating that the stock market reaction to blockchain implemented by companies with lower customer concentration is more positive than that of companies with higher customer concentration.

Table 5.4 Measurement details for hypothesized and control variables

Variable	Measurement	Data source	Reference
Cumulative abnormal return (CAR)	$CAR[t_1,t_2] = \sum_{t=t_1}^{t_2} AR_{it}$	CSMAR	(Arora et al., 2020; Jacobs & Singhal, 2020)
Customer concentration (CC_ complexity)	$Customer\ concentration_{it} = \frac{\sum_{j=1}^{5} Sales_{i,j,t}}{Sales_{i,t}}$	CSMAR	(Patatoukas, 2012, Campello & Gao, 2017)
Supplier concentration (SC complexity)	$Supplier\ concentration_{it} = \frac{\sum_{j=1}^{5} Purchases_{i,j,t}}{purchases_{i,t}}$	CSMAR	(Patatoukas, 2012, Campello & Gao, 2017)
Customer concentration HHI (robust check)	$Customer\ concentration\ HHI_{it} = \sum_{j=1}^{5} \left(\frac{Sales_{i,j,t}}{Sales_{i,t}} \right)^2$	CSMAR	(Patatoukas, 2012, Campello & Gao, 2017)
Supplier concentration HHI (robust check)	$Supplier\ concentration\ HHI_{it} = \sum_{j=1}^{5} \left(\frac{purchases_{i,j,t}}{purchases_{i,t}} \right)^2$	CSMAR	(Patatoukas, 2012, Campello & Gao, 2017)
Business diversification (BD_Complexity)	Entropy measure based on four-digit ISIC $DT = \sum_{i=1}^{m} p_i \ln(1/p_i)$	Annual report	(Hendricks et al., 2009)
Business diversification (robust check)	*Herfindahl index* $DT = \sum pi^2$	Annual report	(Tang, Tang et al., 2019)

Table 5.4 (continued)

Variable	Measurement	Data source	Reference
Environmental complexity (EC)	$EC_{it} = 1 - \sum_{i}^{N} \left(\frac{sales_{i,j,t}}{Total\ sales\ of\ firms\ in\ the\ same\ industry} \right)^2$	CSMAR	(Lam et al., 2019)
Bitcoin price	Bitcoin Price on announcement day	Investing.com	(Klockner et al., 2022)
Market-to-book (MTB)	*MTB* is measured by the ratio of market value to the book value of equity	CSMAR	(Jacobs & Singhal, 2020)
Firm size (Firm_size)	The natural logarithm of total sales in the most recent fiscal year.	CSMAR	(Lam et al., 2019)
Leverage	Total debts to total equity in the most recent fiscal year.	CSMAR	(Klockner et al., 2022)
Growth	Annual percentage change in total sales in the most recent fiscal year.	CSMAR	(Klockner et al., 2022)
Inventory turnover (inventory)	The COGS divided by average inventory in the most recent fiscal year.	CSMAR	(Xiong et al., 2021)
Industry size (Industry_Size)	The natural logarithm of the total assets of all companies in the same two-digit industry in the most recent fiscal year.	CSMAR	(Shou et al., 2021)
Industry dummies	Dummy variables for two-digit SIC codes	CSMAR	(Klockner et al., 2022)
Year dummies	Dummy variables for announcement years	Announcement	(Lam et al., 2019)

Table 5.5 Correlation matrix

	1	2	3	4	5	6	7	8	9	10	11	12	13
1. CAR	1												
2. CC_Concentration	−0.019	1											
3. SC_Concentration	−0.012	0.322***	1										
4. BD_Diversification	0.202**	0.033	0.031	1									
5. EC_Complexity	−0.020	0.067	0.051	0.040	1								
6. Bitcoin	−0.157[a]	−0.064	−0.152[a]	0.053	−0.097	1							
7. Inventory	0.036	−0.157[a]	−0.274***	−0.055	−0.200**	−0.034	1						
8. MTB_ratio	−0.126	0.0650	−0.063	0.111	−0.027	−0.018	0.168**	1					
9. RD	−0.180**	0.188**	0.171**	0.066	0.158[a]	0.031	−0.124	0.236***	1				
10. Firm_size	−0.029	0.244***	−0.030	−0.196**	−0.014	−0.011	0.080	−0.450***	−0.432***	1			
11. Leverage	−0.031	0.179**	−0.052	0.049	−0.026	−0.073	0.042	−0.114	−0.234***	0.575***	1		
12. Growth	−0.021	−0.119	−0.148[a]	0.056	0.028	−0.124	0.035	0.020	−0.061	0.074	0.100	1	
13. Industry_Size	0.170**	−0.159[a]	−0.009	0.123	0.341***	−0.0660	−0.065	−0.136	−0.252***	0.380***	0.464***	0.146[a]	1
Mean	0.010	0.261	0.307	0.572	0.864	11941.213	646.037	3.046	0.058	21.596	1.141	0.239	27.219
SD	0.037	0.159	0.171	0.474	0.110	11868.064	3707.500	2.587	0.052	1.320	1.320	0.407	1.460

[a] $p < 0.1$, ** $p < 0.05$, *** $p < 0.01$

Table 5.6 Regression analysis

	Model 1	*Model 2*	*Model 3*	*Model 4*	*Model 5*	*Model 6*	*Model 7*
CC_Concentration		−0.055**				−0.060**	−0.505**
		(−2.09)				(−2.26)	(−2.19)
SC_Concentration			0.013			0.020	−0.137
			(0.54)			(0.89)	(−0.57)
BD_Diversification				0.017**		0.017**	−0.070
				(2.23)		(2.24)	(−0.74)
EC_Complexity					−0.101**	−0.125***	−0.376**
					(−2.20)	(−2.77)	(−2.43)
EC*CC							0.503[a]
							(1.94)
EC*SC							0.178
							(0.67)
EC*BD							0.096
							(0.91)
Bitcoin	0.000	0.000	0.000	0.000	0.000	0.000	0.000
	(1.22)	(1.20)	(1.21)	(1.29)	(1.19)	(1.24)	(1.19)
Inventory	0.000	0.000	−0.000	0.000	0.000	0.000	0.000
	(0.08)	(0.73)	(−0.07)	(0.32)	(0.02)	(0.73)	(0.56)
MTB_ratio	−0.004**	−0.005***	−0.004**	−0.003**	−0.004**	−0.005***	−0.005***
	(−2.23)	(−2.79)	(−2.24)	(−2.19)	(−2.29)	(−2.92)	(−2.96)
RD	−0.210**	−0.235**	−0.198**	−0.186**	−0.213**	−0.200**	−0.195**
	(−2.26)	(−2.55)	(−2.06)	(−2.03)	(−2.34)	(−2.18)	(−2.13)
Firm_size	−0.011***	−0.015***	−0.010**	−0.009**	−0.012***	−0.014***	−0.014***
	(−2.65)	(−3.36)	(−2.57)	(−2.13)	(−2.90)	(−3.12)	(−3.07)
Leverage	−0.002	−0.001	−0.003	−0.003	−0.002	−0.003	−0.005
	(−0.49)	(−0.28)	(−0.58)	(−0.61)	(−0.52)	(−0.61)	(−1.14)
Growth	−0.001	0.001	−0.001	−0.002	−0.001	−0.001	0.000
	(−0.09)	(0.13)	(−0.16)	(−0.23)	(−0.10)	(−0.10)	(0.01)
Industry_Size	0.003	0.005	0.003	0.002	0.008[a]	0.009**	0.012***
	(0.99)	(1.39)	(1.00)	(0.65)	(1.97)	(2.34)	(2.95)
Year dummies	Included	Included	Included	Included	Included	Included	Included
Industry dummies	Included	Included	Included	Included	Included	Included	Included
_cons	0.264[a]	0.340**	0.260[a]	0.229	0.257[a]	0.297**	0.428**
	(1.80)	(2.28)	(1.76)	(1.58)	(1.78)	(2.05)	(2.50)
N	138	138	138	138	138	138	138
R^2	0.076	0.104	0.070	0.108	0.107	0.177	0.188
F	1.435	1.587[a]	1.384	1.615**	1.610**	1.983***	1.962***

[a] $p < 0.1$, ** $p < 0.05$, *** $p < 0.01$

Thus, H3a is supported. Supplier concentration is positive but not significantly different from zero. Therefore, H3b is not supported. Environmental complexity is significantly negative to ARs, suggesting that the stock market reaction to blockchain implementation is more positive for companies with lower environmental complexity. Thus, H4 is supported. We add customer concentration, supplier concentration, business diversification, and environmental complexity in Model 6, the results are the same as those in Model 2–5. In model 7, the results indicated the stock market reaction to blockchain implementation is more positive for companies with lower customer concentration in a lower complex environment. Thus, H5b is supported.

5.3.3.5 Post Hoc Analysis

To further investigate the long-term impact of blockchain implementation, we carried out a set of post-hoc analyses. Specifically, return on assets (ROA) measured by operating income/book value of total assets, return on sales (ROS) measured by operating income/sales, and sales over assets (SOA) measured by sales/total assets are chosen to represent operational performance. In addition, we also consider net operating working capital (NET), which reflects the ability to manage capital flows in the SC (Shou et al., 2021). NET is measured by (current assets—current liabilities)/total assets.

We estimate the performance impact over a total of 4 years before and after the blockchain implementation. Specifically, we regard the fiscal year of the blockchain implementation as Year 0. The last 2 years (the next 2 years) are Year −2 (Year 2). We follow the method outlined by Hendricks and Singhal (2008) to obtain abnormal operational performance by comparing the sample company with the benchmark company. In the process of matching the benchmark company, the covariates we use include previous performance (ROA), firm size (total assets), and industry (two-digit SIC code). To handle the tradeoff between the three annotations, we matched the benchmark company in three ways, including *Performance-industry-matched, Performance-industry-size-matched, and Performance-size-matched.*

Panel A of Table 5.7 presented the results of the impact of blockchain implementation on operational performance from Year −2 to Year 0. For all operational indicators, there is no significant difference between the overall median of ROA, ROS, and SOA and zero, and the binomial sign test of these performance indicators is not significant. Therefore, there is no evidence that these companies have significant abnormal operational performance before the implementation of the blockchain. Panel B in Table 5.7 shows that the operational performance of the sample companies after blockchain implementation is poor compared with the benchmark. The mean (median) change of NET is −5.65% (−4.44%), significantly different from 0 at the 1% level. The median change of ROA is −0.96%, significantly different from 0 at the 10% level. In addition, considering the global economic impact caused by the COVID-19 pandemic, we further explored whether the impact of blockchain implementation on company performance is affected by COVID-19 within Year −1

Table 5.7 Operational performance in different periods

	Panel A: From year −2 to year 0				Panel B: From year 0 to year 2				Panel C: From year −1 to year 0				Panel D: From year 0 to year 1			
	Obs.	Mean	Median	% POS.	Obs.	Mean	Median	% NEG.	Obs.	Mean	Median	% POS.	Obs.	Mean	Median	% NEG.
Performance–industry–matched																
Change in the level of NET	102	0.03%	1.52%	52.94%	62	−5.65%	−4.44%	64.53%	30	1.54%	2.68%	57.67%	30	−5.02%	−5.11%	63.33%
		0.017	0.269	0.495		−3.111***	−2.766***	2.159**		0.760	0.751	0.548		−2.768**	−2.808***	2.739***
Change in the level of ROA	102	0.24%	0.12%	51.96%	62	−0.62%	−0.96%	66.13%	30	−0.11%	−0.44%	46.67%	30	−0.48%	−1.09%	66.13%
		0.529	0.526	0.297		−0.8965	−1.812^{a}	2.413**		−0.159	0.195	−0.183		−0.466	−1.306	1.278
Change in the level of ROS	101	1.68%	0.14%	50.50%	62	−2.70%	−1.06%	61.29%	29	−0.68%	0.14%	43.33%	29	−2.74%	−1.06%	60.00%
		0.829	−0.069	0.000		−1.4413	−1.553	1.651^{a}		−0.639	−0.812	−0.548		−1.262	−1.059	0.913
Change in the level of SOA	102	3.24%	0.30%	51.96%	62	1.55%	−0.82%	54.84%	30	1.12%	−1.26%	40.00%	30	1.47%	0.27%	50.00%
		0.772	1.213	−0.297		0.4692	−0.137	0.635		0.237	−0.710	−0.913		0.268	0.483	0.000
Performance–industry–size–matched																
Change in the level of NET	100	0.31%	0.36%	51.00%	61	−4.38%	−3.22%	57.38%	28	0.39%	1.27%	53.57%	29	−4.52%	−2.94%	70.00%
		0.1357	−0.75	0.100		−2.371**	−2.187**	1.024		0.187	0.228	0.189		−2.768**	−2.714**	0.371
Change in the level of ROA	100	0.06%	0.42%	54.00%	61	−0.29%	−0.75%	62.29%	28	−0.34%	−0.51%	39.29%	29	−0.15%	−1.01%	55.17%
		0.1171	0.591	0.700		−0.411	−1.110	1.793^{a}		−0.496	−0.182	−0.945		−0.142	−0.703	1.793^{a}
Change in the level of ROS	100	0.97%	0.21%	51.00%	61	−2.43%	−1.11%	59.02%	27	−1.37%	0.21%	39.29%	28	−2.72%	−1.11%	55.17%

(continued)

Table 5.7 (continued)

	Panel A: From year −2 to year 0				Panel B: From year 0 to year 2				Panel C: From year −1 to year 0				Panel D: From year 0 to year 1			
		0.4649	−0.23	−0.100		−1.2967	−1.433	1.280		−1.141	−1.116	−0.945		−1.228	−1.114	0.371
Change in the level of SOA	100	6.14%	0.02%	50.00%	61	2.90%	2.03%	44.26%	28	1.42%	−0.56%	46.43%	29	3.32%	1.93%	37.93%
		2.229**	1.021	0.000		0.8678	0.822	−0.768		0.285	−0.250	−0.189		0.590	1.222	−1.114
Performance–size–matched																
Change in the level of NET	94	−1.16%	−0.08%	48.94%	59	−4.78%	−3.08%	62.71%	28	0.32%	0.82%	53.57%	29	−5.18%	−3.60%	65.52%
		−0.735	−0.387	−0.103		−2.502**	−2.295**	1.823[a]		0.151	−0.159	−0.189		−2.780**	−2.541**	1.486
Change in the level of ROA	94	0.26%	0.03%	50.00%	59	−0.28%	−0.28%	55.93%	28	0.76%	0.43%	53.57%	29	−0.29%	−1.13%	62.07%
		0.587	0.526	0.000		−0.398	−1.102	0.781		1.134	1.002	0.189		−0.262	−1.178	1.114
Change in the level of ROS	94	−0.94%	−0.09%	50.00%	59	−3.31%	−1.23%	57.63%	27	0.51%	−0.09%	42.86%	28	−2.26%	−1.23%	55.17%
		−1.006	−0.481	0.000		−1.813[a]	−1.766[a]	1.042		0.421	−0.023	−0.567		−0.929	−0.897	0.371
Change in the level of SOA	94	4.24%	0.64%	55.32%	59	1.99%	2.10%	42.37%	28	2.82%	−0.97%	39.29%	29	0.72%	1.33%	44.83%
		1.826[a]	1.099	−0.928		0.6477	1.011	−1.042		0.569	−0.342	−0.945		0.116	0.508	−0.371

[a] $p < 0.1$, ** $p < 0.05$, *** $p < 0.01$

to Year 1. The results presented in Panels C and D of Table 5.7 are consistent with the total sample.

The result can be explained from the following two aspects. First, blockchain is a tamper-resistant and decentralized ledger storing transactions (Beck et al., 2018), rather than acquiring data (e.g., radio-frequency identification, RFID) or utilizing data (e.g., AI) (Babich & Hilary, 2020). Therefore, additional technologies (e.g., RFID, AI) are needed in the operationalization of blockchain to ensure the accuracy and synchronization of information (Chanson et al., 2019). However, because a variety of technologies are competing, their interoperability has not yet been fully established, which may increase the complexity of the technology system. Second, given the novelty of blockchain technology, special trust mechanisms of the technology need to be established. Although blockchain can sometimes address the issue of trust, it is still based on technological concepts such as distributed systems and trust protocols, rather than specific individuals, organizations, and societies (Babich & Hilary, 2020). Companies may need to implement protection mechanisms, which will incur additional operating costs (Klockner et al., 2022).

We further explore how business diversification, SC concentration, and environmental complexity affect the relationship between blockchain implementation and operational performance. The results presented in Table 5.8 indicated that the negative effect of blockchain implementation on operational performance is more negative for companies with higher customer concentration. Contrary to the short-term stock price, customer concentration has a negative moderating effect on long-term operating performance. The coefficient of business diversification and environmental complexity is insignificant, indicating that the operational performance of blockchain implementation is not affected by business diversification and environmental complexity.

5.3.4 Implications for Platform Technology Management

This study provides an empirical assessment of how blockchain implementation can improve the market value of companies varying from business diversification, supply chain concentration, and environmental complexity based on a CASs perspective, with a particular focus on platform-oriented supply chains where coordination and information exchange are mediated through digital infrastructures. Based on 138 blockchain implementation announcements of listed companies on the Chinese stock market, we use event study methodology to evaluate the impact of blockchain implementation on shareholder value.

The results show that blockchain implementation has a positive impact on shareholder value. For the announcement day, the mean (median) ARs are 0.97% (0.47%). For the two-day event period, the mean (median) CARs are 1.06% (0.25%). We further identify how complexity factors, including business diversification, SC concentration, and environmental complexity, influence the stock market reaction in platform supply chain contexts. Specifically, companies with higher business

Table 5.8 Regression analysis with operational performance

	Model 1	*Model 2*	*Model 3*	*Model 4*	*Model 5*	*Model 6*
CC_Concentration		−0.315**				−0.334**
		(−2.28)				(−2.24)
SC_Concentration			−0.137			−0.083
			(−1.21)			(−0.73)
BD_Diversification				−0.020		−0.046
				(−0.48)		(−1.09)
EC_Complexity					0.095	0.122
					(0.35)	(0.47)
Bitcoin	0.000	0.000	0.000	0.000	0.000	−0.000
	(0.26)	(0.12)	(0.12)	(0.18)	(0.23)	(−0.19)
Inventory	0.006*	0.006	0.006*	0.006	0.006	0.005
	(1.78)	(1.66)	(1.79)	(1.66)	(1.59)	(1.23)
MTB_ratio	−0.032**	−0.036**	−0.033**	−0.032**	−0.033**	−0.037**
	(−2.11)	(−2.46)	(−2.18)	(−2.08)	(−2.11)	(−2.49)
RD_Sales	0.199	0.110	−0.002	0.181	0.186	−0.073
	(0.45)	(0.26)	(−0.00)	(0.40)	(0.42)	(−0.16)
Firm_size	−0.042*	−0.062**	−0.046*	−0.043*	−0.040	−0.066**
	(−1.84)	(−2.65)	(−2.01)	(−1.87)	(−1.68)	(−2.66)
Leverage	0.004	0.012	0.010	0.005	0.004	0.018
	(0.19)	(0.55)	(0.44)	(0.22)	(0.18)	(0.78)
Growth	0.009	0.021	0.022	0.010	0.010	0.034
	(0.23)	(0.56)	(0.54)	(0.25)	(0.26)	(0.84)
Industry_Size	−0.027	−0.023	−0.025	−0.028	−0.032	−0.029
	(−1.20)	(−1.05)	(−1.13)	(−1.21)	(−1.18)	(−1.12)
Year dummies	Included	Included	Included	Included	Included	Included
Industry dummies	Included	Included	Included	Included	Included	Included
_cons	1.594*	1.962**	1.688**	1.647*	1.609*	2.179**
	(1.97)	(2.49)	(2.09)	(2.00)	(1.96)	(2.67)
N	61	61	61	61	61	61
R^2	0.214	0.286	0.222	0.198	0.196	0.267
F	1.857**	2.203**	1.857**	1.742*	1.733*	1.951**

t statistics in parentheses
* $p < 0.1$, ** $p < 0.05$, *** $p < 0.01$

diversification can generate more significant stock returns from blockchain implementation, suggesting that blockchain facilitates coordination across diversified activities embedded within platform supply chains.

Interestingly, customer concentration and supplier concentration exhibit different moderating effects on the relationship between blockchain implementation and stock market reaction. Companies with lower customer concentration gain more benefits from blockchain implementation, consistent with the role of blockchain in supporting information aggregation and coordination across dispersed downstream participants on platforms. However, the stock market reaction to blockchain implementation is not affected by supplier concentration. In addition, from the perspective of environmental support, the implementation of blockchain in a low-complex environment has a higher positive impact on stock returns, indicating that platform-enabled value creation from blockchain is more readily capitalized by the market when external competitive pressures are limited.

However, in the post hoc analysis, two operational performance measures, ROA and NET, show that blockchain implementation is negatively associated with operational performance compared to benchmark companies within Year 0 to Year 2. This divergence between short-term market value and longer-term operational outcomes suggests that, in platform supply chains, blockchain may initially enhance perceived governance and coordination capabilities while simultaneously introducing adjustment costs and rigidity in ongoing operations. In addition, we find that, contrary to short-term stock price reactions, customer concentration has a positive moderating effect on the relationship between blockchain implementation and operational performance.

5.3.4.1 Implications for Research

This study makes several theoretical contributions to the literature on blockchain and platform supply chains. First, our research shows that the impact of blockchain implementation on stock market reaction varies with business diversification, SC concentration, and environmental complexity from a CASs perspective. Specifically, companies with higher business diversification experience more significant stock returns following blockchain implementation. One explanation is that business diversification increases the complexity of operational tasks and the demand for information-processing capabilities (Gomez et al., 2016). In platform-oriented supply chains, where diversified activities are coordinated through digital interfaces, blockchain is more likely to be adopted to support cross-unit information processing and coordination, thereby enhancing perceived value. Interestingly, customer concentration and supplier concentration exhibit different moderating effects on the relationship between blockchain implementation and stock market reaction. The stock market reaction to blockchain implementation is more positive for companies with lower customer concentration. This finding is consistent with the SC information-sharing literature (Crawford et al., 2020; Wang, Zheng, et al., 2021b). For companies facing higher downstream complexity, information sharing between focal firms and customers becomes more challenging, and the decentralization and traceability features of blockchain can better exert their value by reducing information acquisition costs and improving information-sharing efficiency (Wang, Zheng, et al., 2021b), a mechanism that is particularly salient in platform supply chains with dispersed customer participation.

However, the stock market reaction to blockchain implementation is not affected by supplier concentration. One possible explanation is that blockchain implementation can reduce operating costs through information sharing and process standardization (Ak & Patatoukas, 2016). Our findings suggest that dependence on a few major customers differs fundamentally from dependence on a few suppliers in platform supply chains, where downstream coordination and demand aggregation play a more prominent role. These results help clarify the asymmetric effects of blockchain adoption across upstream and downstream relationships and may inform managerial decisions regarding blockchain implementation in platform-mediated supply networks. In addition, our results indicate that blockchain implementation has a more positive impact on stock returns in low-complexity environments. Although blockchain can create new business models (Lumineau et al., 2021) and competitive advantages (Babich & Hilary, 2020), insufficient resources and intensified competition in highly complex environments may constrain firms' ability to fully realize the value of blockchain implementation, particularly when platform ecosystems amplify competitive imitation and coordination pressures.

Second, this study provides evidence of the differential impacts of blockchain implementation on short-term and long-term performance. Blockchain has been widely regarded as one of the most promising applications in SC management (Babich & Hilary, 2020), yet whether it improves firm performance remains debated (Cole et al., 2019; Hastig & Sodhi, 2020). Our findings indicate that blockchain implementation generates positive stock returns in the short term but is associated with weaker long-term operational performance. The short-term market response captures investors' early reactions to blockchain announcements (Olsen & Tomlin, 2020), whereas the longer-term effects reflect the evolving costs and organizational adjustments associated with blockchain adoption (Bose & Leung, 2019). In the post hoc analysis, we further extend prior research by examining how SC concentration moderates the relationship between blockchain implementation and long-term operational performance. We find that, contrary to short-term stock price reactions, customer concentration positively moderates the effect of blockchain implementation on long-term operational outcomes. This divergence suggests that, in platform supply chains, blockchain may initially be valued by markets for its governance and coordination potential, while its longer-term operational benefits depend on the stability and concentration of platform-based exchange relationships. This finding is particularly relevant for understanding blockchain implementation in complex SC networks and offers preliminary evidence for future research.

Third, our research provides a more comprehensive explanation of blockchain implementation mechanisms from a complex adaptive systems perspective. Although prior studies have conceptualized supply chain networks as complex adaptive systems (Choi et al., 2001; Yeoman & Santos, 2019; Zhao et al., 2019), technology-enabled supply chains, especially platform-based supply chains, have received limited attention in this research stream. On the one hand, this study contributes to theory by explicitly incorporating blockchain technology into the complex adaptive systems framework. Our results suggest that decentralized blockchain infrastructures can support geographically dispersed supply chain partners (Babich & Hilary, 2020), enhance agent autonomy and spontaneity (Lumineau, Wang et al. 2021), and promote self-organizing behaviors in complex supply chain networks (Swierczek, 2022). On the other hand, this study advances understanding of how complexity characteristics shape the effectiveness of blockchain implementation.

By examining business diversification, supply chain concentration, and environmental complexity, we demonstrate that the value of blockchain adoption depends on the interaction between technological architecture and network structure. These insights extend complex adaptive systems theory to platform-based supply chains and clarify how firms can leverage blockchain to create value by simultaneously managing internal operational complexity and external environmental complexity.

5.3.4.2 Implications for Practice

Although blockchain is expected to provide solutions to dilemmas in operations and supply chain management, it has not become pervasive or been implemented by the majority of companies (Babich & Hilary, 2020). This phenomenon may stem from practitioners' uncertainty regarding the consequences of blockchain implementation, particularly in complex and platform-mediated supply chain settings (Babich & Hilary, 2020; Kurpjuweit et al., 2021). Our research provides objective verification of the positive impact of blockchain implementation on firm value, which may help encourage companies to adopt blockchain technologies to obtain financial benefits. These findings can also assist managers operating platform-based supply chains in persuading shareholders or investors to support blockchain implementation initiatives. Our findings further suggest that managers are more likely to benefit from implementing blockchain technology when their businesses and supply chains are internally complex but embedded in relatively less complex external environments. First, the decentralized and shareable characteristics of blockchain facilitate information transfer and resource sharing across diversified business models, thereby reducing internal coordination costs. This advantage is particularly relevant for platform supply chains, where multiple business units, partners, and complementors interact through digital interfaces. Accordingly, we encourage companies with higher internal business complexity to leverage blockchain implementation to enhance coordination efficiency.

Second, in supply chains characterized by a large number of customers, the decentralization and traceability of blockchain can more effectively address complex information flows between firms and their customers, improve transparency, and enhance information sharing efficiency. In platform-based supply chains with dispersed downstream participants, blockchain can serve as a critical infrastructure supporting scalable coordination and data credibility. We therefore suggest that practitioners prioritize blockchain implementation in supply chains with high customer complexity. However, when external environments are highly competitive and uncertain, firms may struggle to secure sufficient resources to support effective blockchain implementation. This finding has important implications for policymakers. Governments may consider providing financial support or institutional incentives to facilitate blockchain adoption, enabling firms, particularly platform orchestrators, to gain competitive advantages through blockchain-enabled supply chain coordination.

Finally, the post hoc analysis further reveals that blockchain implementation is associated with weaker operational performance from Year 0 to Year 2. In addition, a more concentrated supply chain appears to mitigate the negative impact of blockchain implementation on long-term operational performance. Blockchain implementation is inherently a complex and resource-intensive process, requiring firms to overcome multiple obstacles, such as additional costs arising from the black box effect of blockchain technology and the need to establish new trust mechanisms (Cole et al., 2019; Hastig & Sodhi, 2020). These challenges may be amplified in platform supply chains, where blockchain adoption often necessitates alignment among heterogeneous participants. Therefore, managers should remain patient regarding the long-term value of blockchain technology and actively address technological and organizational barriers during the implementation process.

5.3.4.3 Limitation and Future Research

Our study has several limitations that also point to promising directions for future research. First, due to the availability of stock price data, our sample is limited to A-share listed companies. Future studies are therefore encouraged to extend the analysis to private firms, particularly small and medium-sized enterprises that often participate in platform supply chains as complementors or peripheral partners. Examining these firms may provide a more comprehensive understanding of how blockchain implementation creates value across different positions within platform-based supply networks.

Second, this study focuses on the moderating effects of business diversification, supply chain concentration, and environmental complexity. However, other factors may also influence the relationship between emerging technologies and stock market reactions, especially in platform supply chain contexts. For example, prior technological experience, the maturity of blockchain applications, and the degree of platform-level technical support may shape how effectively blockchain implementation is perceived and valued by investors (Nishant et al., 2017; Lam et al., 2019). Future research could therefore explore additional moderating factors from technological, organizational, and platform governance perspectives.

Finally, although we provide initial evidence that blockchain implementation is associated with weaker operational performance from Year 0 to Year 2, the underlying mechanisms driving this negative effect remain unclear. In platform supply chains, such performance implications may stem from coordination frictions, adjustment costs borne unevenly by different participants, or misalignment between technological governance and relational practices. Future research could further investigate these mechanisms from multiple angles to generate more fine-grained insights into the long-term consequences of blockchain implementation in platform-oriented supply chain systems.

5.4 Conclusions and Future Directions

5.4.1 Conclusions

This chapter has examined blockchain as a representative governance-oriented technology within platform supply chains, highlighting how certain digital technologies extend beyond operational coordination to shape inter-firm governance and strategic value creation. Unlike platform technologies such as IoT, big data analytics, or AI, which primarily support information processing, prediction, and operational optimization, governance-oriented technologies operate at a deeper level of integration. They embed rules and enforcement logic directly into shared technological infrastructures through features such as decentralization, immutability, traceability, and programmable execution. In this sense, this chapter uses blockchain to illustrate a broader category of platform technologies that reorganize how coordination and control are institutionalized across supply chain networks.

By synthesizing insights from recent empirical studies, this chapter demonstrates how the integration of such technologies reconfigures coordination, transparency, and control among heterogeneous platform participants, while also shaping how capital markets evaluate firm value. The analysis shows that technology-enabled coordination can simultaneously enhance efficiency and adaptability, while generating new forms of friction within platform relationships. These mixed outcomes reflect a fundamental reorganization of governance arrangements, as firms increasingly rely on technologically embedded mechanisms rather than purely relational or contractual tools to structure exchanges and manage interdependence in platform supply chains. From this perspective, the emergence of disputes and relational tensions should be understood as part of governance realignment during technology integration, rather than as evidence of implementation failure.

Overall, this chapter suggests that the value implications of platform supply chain technology integration are contingent on governance design, contextual conditions, and organizational capabilities. Governance-oriented digital technologies do not generate value in isolation, nor do they function merely as efficiency-enhancing tools. Their contribution to shareholder value depends on how technological features that embed coordination and control are aligned with platform governance structures and firm-level strategic objectives. Following this logic, blockchain serves not simply as a standalone innovation, but as an illustrative case of how platform technologies that institutionalize governance can act as conditional drivers of value creation in platform supply chains, distinguishing them from digital tools that operate primarily at the level of coordination and analytics.

5.4.2 Future Directions

The integration of blockchain technology into platform supply chains has generated significant implications for transparency, coordination, and value creation. However, as this chapter has illustrated, the outcomes of blockchain adoption are complex and often contradictory, simultaneously enabling efficiency gains while introducing new forms of friction, power asymmetries, and relational challenges. To deepen scholarly understanding and inform responsible practice, several important directions for future research arise. These directions underscore the need for more nuanced theoretical integration, greater methodological rigor, and deeper interdisciplinary engagement.

5.4.2.1 Bridging Governance and Strategy Perspectives through Theoretical Synthesis

A central limitation of existing research is that blockchain has been examined primarily as an isolated governance tool or a strategic signal, rather than as a core component of platform technology integration in supply chains. In platform supply chains, coordination, transparency, and value creation are jointly shaped by technological architectures, data infrastructures, and platform-level technological rules. Future research should therefore move beyond isolated perspectives and develop integrative frameworks that explain how blockchain functions as part of a broader technological system embedded in platform supply chains. Insights from complex adaptive systems theory and governance substitution frameworks can be productively combined to advance such technology-oriented models. From a CAS perspective, platform supply chains are characterized by emergent, adaptive, and nonlinear interactions among interdependent actors that are increasingly mediated by shared digital infrastructures. Governance substitution extends this perspective by highlighting how technology-enabled mechanisms embedded in platform architectures can replace, complement, or reconfigure traditional coordination mechanisms through automated verification, standardized interfaces, and rule-based execution.

An integrated technological perspective enables the examination of how blockchain contributes to platform-level adaptability while simultaneously reshaping information processing, coordination intensity, and control structures across interconnected firms. In platform supply chains, blockchain-enabled integration may enhance interoperability, data reliability, and system-wide visibility. Furthermore, it may reduce flexibility in firm-level adjustments or amplify technological dependence on platform infrastructures. Such an approach also clarifies how platform technologies allocate decision rights, configure information access, and condition the technological autonomy of participating firms. Future research is encouraged to develop multi-theoretical, technology-centered models that capture feedback effects, path dependence, and architectural lock-in associated with blockchain integration in platform supply chains, thereby advancing a more nuanced understanding of how platform technologies structure coordination and value creation over time.

5.4.2.2 Longitudinal and Multi-Level Analytical Approaches

Existing evidence on the impact of blockchain implementation largely relies on cross-sectional analyses or short-term market reactions, which may obscure the longer-term structural implications of technology integration in platform supply chains. Given the temporal gap between initial investor enthusiasm and sustained operational performance, longitudinal research designs are essential for examining how blockchain-enabled integration unfolds over time. Such approaches can help identify critical phases in the technological adoption process, including periods in which transparency and traceability benefits stabilize, technology-based control mechanisms become more salient, or adjustment frictions among platform participants intensify. Adopting a multi-level analytical perspective is equally important for advancing research on blockchain integration in platform supply chains. Platform-based systems inherently link micro-level technological interactions, such as data sharing and process alignment between suppliers and platform operators, with meso- and macro-level dynamics related to platform governance, standardization trajectories, and regulatory environments. Multi-level modeling can further illuminate how firm-level adoption choices and implementation practices aggregate into system-wide patterns, including the formation of shared digital infrastructures, the concentration of technological coordination authority, and the differentiation of competitive positions within platform-based supply chain ecosystems. Such analyses can deepen understanding of how platform technologies evolve through the interaction of actors, architectures, and institutional conditions over time.

5.4.2.3 Behavioral, Ethical, and Socio-Cultural Dimensions of Technology Adoption

Beyond technological performance and economic efficiency, the effectiveness of technology integration in platform supply chains critically depends on human and organizational responses to digitally embedded coordination mechanisms. As platform technologies increasingly automate rules, standardize transactions, and embed coordination logic into shared digital infrastructures, they inevitably reshape relational dynamics among participating firms. In particular, technology-enabled monitoring and data visibility may weaken relational capital when platform participants perceive these systems as instruments of surveillance or asymmetric control rather than as facilitative coordination mechanisms. Future research on platform supply chain technology integration should pay closer attention to the behavioral, ethical, and socio-cultural conditions that shape technology adoption and use. This includes examining how platform participants perceive fairness, transparency, and participation when coordination is mediated through shared technological infrastructures. It also involves understanding how data governance principles such as privacy protection, inclusiveness, and sustainability influence compliance and engagement in platform-based relationships, as well as how cultural norms shape interpretations of trust, accountability, and authority in globally distributed supply chains. Qualitative research approaches, including ethnographic studies, in-depth interviews, and design-oriented methodologies, are particularly well suited to capturing how actors experience, interpret, and adapt to technology-mediated coordination within platform supply chains. In addition, future research may explore how large-scale platform technology integration influences broader system-level outcomes, including participation barriers, workforce reconfiguration, and the distribution of coordination costs and benefits across supply chain actors.

References

Adner, R. (2017). Ecosystem as structure: An actionable construct for strategy. *Journal of Management, 43*(1), 39–58.

Adner, R., & Kapoor, R. (2010). Value creation in innovation ecosystems: How the structure of technological interdependence affects firm performance in new technology generations. *Strategic Management Journal, 31*(3), 306–333.

Ak, B. K., & Patatoukas, P. N. (2016). Customer-base concentration and inventory efficiencies: evidence from the manufacturing sector. *Production and Operations Management, 25*(2), 258–272.

Arora, P., Hora, M., Singhal, V., & Subramanian, R. (2020). When do appointments of corporate sustainability executives affect shareholder value? *Journal of Operations Management, 66*(4), 464–487.

Autry, C. W., Grawe, S. J., Daugherty, P. J., & Richey, R. G. (2010). The effects of technological turbulence and breadth on supply chain technology acceptance and adoption. *Journal of Operations Management, 28*(6), 522–536.

Awasthy, P., Haldar, T., & Ghosh, D. (2025). Blockchain enabled traceability—An analysis of pricing and traceability effort decisions in supply chains. *European Journal of Operational Research, 321*(3), 760–774.

Azadegan, A., Patel, P. C., Zangoueinezhad, A., & Linderman, K. (2013). The effect of environmental complexity and environmental dynamism on lean practices. *Journal of Operations Management, 31*(4), 193–212.

Babich, V., & Hilary, G. (2020). Distributed ledgers and operations: what operations management researchers should know about blockchain technology. *M&Som-Manufacturing & Service Operations Management, 22*(2), 223–240.

Bai, C. G., & Sarkis, J. (2020). A supply chain transparency and sustainability technology appraisal model for blockchain technology. *International Journal of Production Research, 58*(7), 2142–2162.

Beck, R., Muller-Bloch, C., & King, J. L. (2018). Governance in the blockchain Economy: a framework and research agenda. *Journal of the Association for Information Systems, 19*(10), 1020–1034.

Benitez, J., Ray, G., & Henseler, J. (2018). Impact Of Information Technology Infrastructure Flexibility On Mergers And Acquisitions. *Mis Quarterly, 42*(1), 25.

Borgatti, S. P., & Li, X. (2009). On social network analysis in a supply chain context. *Journal of Supply Chain Management, 45*(2), 5–22.

Bose, I., & Leung, A. C. M. (2019). Adoption of identity theft countermeasures and its short- and long-term impact on firm value. *Mis Quarterly, 43*(1), 313–327.

Brown, S. J., & Warner, J. B. (1985). Using daily stock returns: The case of event studies. *Journal of Financial Economics, 14*(1), 3–31.

Cahill, D., Baur, D. G., Liu, Z. X., & Yang, J. W. (2020). I am a blockchain too: how does the market respond to companies' interest in blockchain? *Journal of Banking & Finance, 113.*

Campello, M., & Gao, J. (2017). Customer concentration and loan contract terms. *Journal of Financial Economics, 123*(1), 108–136.

Capaldo, A., & Giannoccaro, I. (2015). How does trust affect performance in the supply chain? The moderating role of interdependence. *International Journal of Production Economics, 166*, 36–49.

Casino, F., Dasaklis, T. K., & Patsakis, C. (2019). A systematic literature review of blockchain-based applications: Current status, classification and open issues. *Telematics and Informatics, 36*, 55–81.

Chanson, M., Bogner, A., Bilgeri, D., Fleisch, E., & Wortmann, F. (2019). Blockchain for the IoT: privacy-preserving protection of sensor data. *Journal of the Association for Information Systems, 20*(9), 1274–1309.

Chari, M. D. R., Devaraj, S., & David, P. (2008). The impact of information technology investments and diversification strategies on firm performance. *Management Science, 54*(1), 224–234.

Chen, J., Pun, H., & Zhang, Q. (2023). Eliminate demand information disadvantage in a supplier encroachment supply chain with information acquisition. *European Journal of Operational Research, 305*(2), 659–673.

Chen, L., Li, T., Jia, F., & Schoenherr, T. (2022). The impact of governmental COVID-19 measures on manufacturers' stock market valuations: The role of labor intensity and operational slack. *Journal of Operations Management.*

Cheng, S. F., De Franco, G., Jiang, H., & Lin, P. (2019). Riding the blockchain mania: public firms' speculative 8-K disclosures. *Management Science, 65*(12), 5901–5913.

Chod, J., Trichakis, N., Tsoukalas, G., Aspegren, H., & Weber, M. (2020). On the financing benefits of supply chain transparency and blockchain adoption. *Management Science, 66*(10), 4378–4396.

Choi, T. M., Chen, J., Li, G., & Yue, X. H. (2023). Platform supply chain innovations in the blockchain era: the ABCDE framework. *International Journal of Production Research, 61*(11), 3505–3511.

Choi, T. Y., Dooley, K. J., & Rungtusanatham, M. (2001). Supply networks and complex adaptive systems: control versus emergence. *Journal of Operations Management, 19*(3), 351–366.

Cole, R., Stevenson, M., & Aitken, J. (2019). Blockchain technology: implications for operations and supply chain management. *Supply Chain Management, 24*(4), 469–483.

Crawford, S., Huang, Y., Li, N., & Yang, Z. (2020). Customer concentration and public disclosure: evidence from management earnings and sales forecasts. *Contemporary Accounting Research, 37*(1), 131–159.

Danese, P., Mocellin, R., & Romano, P. (2021). Designing blockchain systems to prevent counterfeiting in wine supply chains: a multiple-case study. *International Journal of Operations & Production Management, 41*(13), 1–33.

De Filippi, P., Mannan, M., & Reijers, W. (2020). Blockchain as a confidence machine: The problem of trust & challenges of governance. *Technology in Society, 62.*

de Oliveira-Dias, D., Maqueira-Marin, J. M., Moyano-Fuetes, J., & Carvalho, H. (2023). Implications of using Industry 4.0 base technologies for lean and agile supply chains and performance. *International Journal of Production Economics, 262.*

Dolgui, A., Ivanov, D., Potryasaev, S., Sokolov, B., Ivanova, M., & Werner, F. (2020). Blockchain-oriented dynamic modelling of smart contract design and execution in the supply chain. *International Journal of Production Research, 58*(7), 2184–2199.

Du, M., Ma, X., Zhang, Z., Wang, X., Chen, Q. & Ieee 2017. *A review on consensus algorithm of blockchain*. Paper presented at IEEE International Conference on Systems, Man, and Cybernetics (SMC). OCT 05–08, 2017.

Dubey, R., Bryde, D. J., Foropon, C., Tiwari, M., Dwivedi, Y., & Schiffling, S. (2021). An investigation of information alignment and collaboration as complements to supply chain agility in humanitarian supply chain. *International Journal of Production Research, 59*(5), 1586–1605.

Durach, C. F., Blesik, T., von Düring, M., & Bick, M. (2021). Blockchain Applications in Supply Chain Transactions. *Journal of Business Logistics, 42*(1), 7–24.

Falcone, E. C., Steelman, Z. R., & Aloysius, J. A. (2021). Understanding managers' reactions to blockchain technologies in the supply chain: The reliable and unbiased software agent. *Journal of Business Logistics, 42*(1), 25–45.

Fosso Wamba, S., Queiroz, M. M., & Trinchera, L. (2020). Dynamics between blockchain adoption determinants and supply chain performance: An empirical investigation. *International Journal of Production Economics, 229*.

Frank, A. G., Dalenogare, L. S., & Ayala, N. F. (2019). Industry 4.0 technologies: Implementation patterns in manufacturing companies. *International Journal of Production Economics, 210*, 15–26.

Giannoccaro, I., Nair, A., & Choi, T. (2018). The Impact of Control and Complexity on Supply Network Performance: An Empirically Informed Investigation Using NK Simulation Analysis. *Decision Sciences, 49*(4), 625–659.

Gligor, D. M., Pillai, K. G., & Golgeci, I. (2021). Theorizing the dark side of business-to-business relationships in the era of AI, big data, and blockchain. *Journal of Business Research, 133*, 79–88.

Gomez, J., Salazar, I., & Vargas, P. (2016). firm boundaries, information processing capacity, and performance in manufacturing firms. *Journal of Management Information Systems, 33*(3), 809–842.

Hanisch, M., Goldsby, C. M., Fabian, N. E., & Oehmichen, J. (2023). Digital governance: A conceptual framework and research agenda. *Journal of Business Research, 162*.

Hastig, G. M., & Sodhi, M. S. (2020). Blockchain for supply chain traceability: Business requirements and critical success factors. *Production and Operations Management, 29*(4), 935–954.

He, X., Pittman, J., & Rui, O. (2016). Reputational implications for partners after a majoraudit failure: Evidence from China: JBE. *Journal of Business Ethics, 138*(4), 703–722.

Hendricks, K. B., & Singhal, V. R. (2008). The effect of product introduction delays on operating performance. *Management Science, 54*(5), 878–892.

Hendricks, K. B., Singhal, V. R., & Zhang, R. (2009). The effect of operational slack, diversification, and vertical relatedness on the stock market reaction to supply chain disruptions. *Journal of Operations Management, 27*(3), 233–246.

Ivanov, D., Dolgui, A. & Sokolov, B. 2019. 'The impact of digital technology and Industry 4.0 on the ripple effect and supply chain risk analytics.' International Journal of Production Research, 57:3, 829–846.

Jackson, I., Ivanov, D., Dolgui, A., & Namdar, J. (2024). Generative artificial intelligence in supply chain and operations management: A capability-based framework for analysis and implementation. *International Journal of Production Research, 62*(17), 6120–6145.

Jacobides, M. G., Cennamo, C., & Gawer, A. (2018). Towards a theory of ecosystems. *Strategic Management Journal, 39*(8), 2255–2276.

Jacobs, B. W., & Singhal, V. R. (2020). Shareholder value effects of the volkswagen emissions scandal on the automotive ecosystem. *Production and Operations Management, 29*(10), 2230–2251.

Jacobs, M. A. (2013). Complexity: Toward an empirical measure. *Technovation, 33*(4–5), 111–118.

Kim, D.-Y., & Zhu, P. (2018). Supplier dependence and R&D intensity: the moderating role of network centrality and interconnectedness. *Journal of Operations Management, 64*, 7–18.

Klein, R., & Rai, A. (2009). Interfirm strategic information flows in logistics supply chain relationships. *Mis Quarterly, 33*(4), 735–762.

Klockner, M., Schmidt, C. G., & Wagner, S. M. (2022). When blockchain creates shareholder value: empirical evidence from international firm announcements. *Production and Operations Management, 31*(1), 46–64.

Kouhizadeh, M., Saberi, S., & Sarkis, J. (2021). Blockchain technology and the sustainable supply chain: Theoretically exploring adoption barriers. *International Journal of Production Economics, 231*.

Kretschmer, T., Leiponen, A., Schilling, M., & Vasudeva, G. (2022). Platform ecosystems as meta-organizations: Implications for platform strategies. *Strategic Management Journal, 43*(3), 405–424.

Kshetri, N. (2022). Blockchain systems and ethical sourcing in the mineral and metal industry: a multiple case study. *International Journal of Logistics Management, 33*(1), 1–27.

Kurpjuweit, S., Schmidt, C. G., Klockner, M., & Wagner, S. M. (2021). Blockchain in additive manufacturing and its impact on supply chains. *Journal of Business Logistics, 42*(1), 46–70.

Lam, H. K. S., Ding, L., Cheng, T. C. E., & Zhou, H. (2019). The impact of 3D printing implementation on stock returns- a contingent dynamic capabilities perspective. *International Journal of Operations & Production Management, 39*(6/7/8), 935–961.

Lanier, D., Jr., Wempe, W. F., & Zacharia, Z. G. (2010). Concentrated supply chain membership and financial performance: Chain- and firm-level perspectives. *Journal of Operations Management, 28*(1), 1–16.

Lee, H. L., Padmanabhan, V., & Whang, S. (1997). Information distortion in a supply chain: the bullwhip effect. *Management Science, 43*(4), 546–558.

Li, C. F., Liu, Q. L., Wang, W. M., Zeng, C., & Zhou, P. (2025). Customer concentration and suppliers' Blockchain technology adoption: Evidence from China. *Production and Operations Management, 34*(10), 3082–3100.

Li, G., Xue, J., Li, N., & Ivanov, D. (2022). Blockchain-supported business model design, supply chain resilience, and firm performance. *Transportation Research Part E-Logistics and Transportation Review, 163*.

Li, X., Jiang, P., Chen, T., Luo, X., & Wen, Q. (2020). A survey on the security of blockchain systems. *Future Generation Computer Systems-the International Journal of Escience, 107*, 841–853.

Lin, Y., Chen, A. L., Yin, Y. H., Li, Q., Zhu, Q. N., & Luo, J. (2021). A framework for sustainable management of the platform service supply chain: An empirical study of the logistics sector in China. *International Journal of Production Economics, 235*.

Liu, W., Wanying, W., Cheng, S., Xie, D., & Chen, L. (2020). Effect of supply chain strategic collaboration announcements on shareholder value: an empirical investigation from China. *International Journal of Operations & Production Management, 40*(4), 389–414.

Ljubownikow, G., & Ang, S. H. (2020). Competition, diversification and performance. *Journal of Business Research, 112*, 81–94.

Lumineau, F., Wang, W., & Schilke, O. (2021). Blockchain governance-a new way of organizing collaborations? *Organization Science, 32*(2), 500–521.

Martinez, V., Zhao, M., Blujdea, C., Han, X., Neely, A. & Albores, P. 2019. 'Blockchain-driven customer order management.' International Journal of Operations & Production Management, 39:6/7/8, 993–1022.

Menon, S., & Jain, K. (2024). Blockchain technology for transparency in agri-food supply chain: Use cases, limitations, and future directions. *Ieee Transactions on Engineering Management, 71*, 106–120.

Nishant, R., Teo, T. S. H., & Goh, M. (2017). Do shareholders value green information technology announcements? *Journal of the Association for Information Systems, 18*(8), 542–576.

Olsen, T. L., & Tomlin, B. (2020). 'Industry 4.0: opportunities and challenges for operations management. *M&Som-Manufacturing & Service Operations Management, 22*(1), 113–122.

Pagell, M., & Shevchenko, A. (2014). Why research in sustainable supply chain management should have no future. *Journal of Supply Chain Management, 50*(1), 44–55.

Patatoukas, P. N. (2012). Customer-base concentration: implications for firm performance and capital markets. *Accounting Review, 87*(2), 363–392.

Pun, H., Swaminathan, J. M., & Hou, P. (2021). Blockchain adoption for combating deceptive counterfeits. *Production and Operations Management, 30*(4), 864–882.

Rai, A., Patnayakuni, R., & Seth, N. (2006). Firm performance impacts of digitally enabled supply chain integration capabilities. *Mis Quarterly, 30*(2), 225–246.

Ren, F., & Dewan, S. (2015). Industry-level analysis of information technology return and risk: What explains the variation? *Journal of Management Information Systems, 32*(2), 71–103.

Saboo, A. R., Kumar, V., & Anand, A. (2017). Assessing the impact of customer concentration on initial public offering and balance sheet-based outcomes. *Journal of Marketing, 81*(6), 42–61.

Salampasis, D., & Mention, A. L. (2019). From a-value to value-multiplication: Leveraging outbound open innovation practices for unrelated diversification in the sensor industry. *Technology Analysis & Strategic Management, 31*(11), 1327–1340.

Schmidt, C. G., Wuttke, D. A., Ball, G. P., & Heese, H. S. (2020). Does social media elevate supply chain importance? An empirical examination of supply chain glitches, Twitter reactions, and stock market returns. *Journal of Operations Management, 66*(6), 646–669.

Schwieterman, M. A., Goldsby, T. J., & Croxton, K. L. (2018). Customer and supplier portfolios: Can credit risks be managed through supply chain relationships? *Journal of Business Logistics, 39*(2), 123–137.

Shou, Y., Shao, J., & Wang, W. (2021). How does reverse factoring affect operating performance? An event study of Chinese manufacturing firms. *International Journal of Operations & Production Management, 41*(4), 289–312.

Stornelli, A., Ozcan, S., & Simms, C. (2021). Advanced manufacturing technology adoption and innovation: A systematic literature review on barriers, enablers, and innovation types. *Research Policy, 50*, 6.

Su, W., & Tsang, E. W. K. (2015). Product diversification and financial performance: the moderating role of secondary stakeholders. *Academy of Management Journal, 58*(4), 1128–1148.

Subramani, M. (2004). How do suppliers benefit from information technology use in supply chain relationships? *Mis Quarterly, 28*(1), 45–73.

Swierczek, A. (2022). 'Decentralization of information and supply chain self-organization: the resulting effect on network performance in the transitive service triads. *Supply Chain Management-an International Journal.*

Tallon, P. P., Ramirez, R. V., & Short, J. E. (2013). The information artifact in IT governance: Toward a theory of information governance. *Journal of Management Information Systems, 30*(3), 141–177.

Tang, C., Tang, Y., & Su, S. (2019). R&D internationalization, product diversification and international performance for emerging market enterprises: An empirical study on Chinese enterprises. *European Management Journal, 37*(4), 529–539.

Tang, H.-W., & Chen, A. (2020). How do market power and industry competition influence the effect of corporate governance on earnings management? *Quarterly Review of Economics and Finance, 78*, 212–225.

Treiblmaier, H. (2018). The impact of the blockchain on the supply chain: A theory-based research framework and a call for action. *Supply Chain Management-an International Journal, 23*(6), 545–559.

Wamba, S. F., Queiroz, M. M., & Trinchera, L. (2020). Dynamics between blockchain adoption determinants and supply chain performance: An empirical investigation. *International Journal of Production Economics, 229*.

Wang, L. S., Chen, J. & Song, H. M. 2021a. *Marketplace or reseller? Platform strategy in the presence of customer returns*. Transportation Research Part E-Logistics and Transportation Review, 153.

Wang, Z., Zheng, Z., Jiang, W., & Tang, S. (2021b). Blockchain-enabled data sharing in supply chains: Model, operationalization, and tutorial. *Production and Operations Management, 30*(7), 1965–1985.

Wong, C. W. Y., Lai, K. H., & Bernroider, E. W. N. (2015). The performance of contingencies of supply chain information integration: The roles of product and market complexity. *International Journal of Production Economics, 165*, 1–11.

Xia, Y., Singhal, V. R., & Zhang, G. P. (2016). Product design awards and the market value of the firm. *Production and Operations Management, 25*(6), 1038–1055.

Xiong, Y., Lam, H. K. S., Kumar, A., Ngai, E. W. T., Xiu, C., & Wang, X. (2021). The mitigating role of blockchain-enabled supply chains during the COVID-19 pandemic. *International Journal of Operations & Production Management, 41*(9), 1495–1521.

Xu, D., Zhou, K. Z., & Du, F. (2019). Deviant versus aspirational risk taking: The effects of performance feedback on bribery expenditure and R&D intensity. *Academy of Management Journal, 62*(4), 1226–1251.

Xu, X. P., Yan, L. L., Choi, T. M., & Cheng, T. C. E. (2023). When is it wise to use Blockchain for platform operations with remanufacturing? *European Journal of Operational Research, 309*(3), 1073–1090.

Yang, J., Lu, W., & Zhou, C. (2014). The immediate impact of purchasing/sales contract announcements on the market value of firms: An empirical study in China. *International Journal of Production Economics, 156*, 169.

Yeoman, R., & Santos, M. M. (2019). A complex systems model for transformative supply chains in emerging markets. *International Journal of Emerging Markets, 15*(1), 50–69.

Yin, H. H. S., Langenheldt, K., Harlev, M., Mukkamala, R. R., & Vatrapu, R. (2019). Regulating cryptocurrencies: A supervised machine learning approach to de-anonymizing the Bitcoin Blockchain. *Journal of Management Information Systems, 36*(1), 37–73.

Yu, H., Huang, M., Chao, X. L., & Yue, X. H. (2022). Truthful multi-attribute multi-unit double auctions for B2B e-commerce logistics service transactions. *Transportation Research Part E-Logistics and Transportation Review, 164*.

Zhao, K., Zuo, Z. Y., & Blackhurst, J. V. (2019). Modelling supply chain adaptation for disruptions: an empirically grounded complex adaptive systems approach. *Journal of Operations Management, 65*(2), 190–212.

Zhao, X., Li, Y., & Flynn, B. B. (2013). The financial impact of product recall announcements in China. *International Journal of Production Economics, 142*(1), 5.

Zheng, Z., Xie, S., Dai, H.-N., Chen, X., & Wang, H. (2018). Blockchain challenges and opportunities: a survey. *International Journal of Web and Grid Services, 14*(4), 352–375.

Ziolkowski, R., Miscione, G., & Schwabe, G. (2020). Decision problems in blockchain governance: old wine in new bottles or walking in someone else's shoes? *Journal of Management Information Systems, 37*(2), 316–348.

Chapter 6
Platform Logistics Integration

6.1 Overview of Platform Logistics Integration

6.1.1 Challenges in Platform Logistics

In the contemporary era, the focal point of firm competition has transitioned from the business unit to the entire supply chain, encompassing suppliers, customers, and logistics service providers (Maskey et al., 2020). The evolution from traditional logistics to digital logistics has substantially propelled the development of logistics services on a global scale (Wang et al., 2020). Moreover, the market for logistics services has witnessed exponential growth, with approximately 96% of Fortune 100 firms availing themselves of these services (Zhang et al., 2022).

In practical scenarios, enterprises generally regard logistics as a management expense. The fundamental objective of logistics management is to ensure the accurate and timely delivery of appropriate products to customers at the lowest feasible cost. Nevertheless, the implications of logistics transcend mere cost related considerations. It exerts a profound influence on corporate strategic decision making (Li & Li, 2023). Logistics services have emerged as a critical factor that exerts a significant impact on enterprises' competitiveness and operational efficiency (He et al., 2022). Empirical research also indicates that the sharing of logistics services substantially improves supply chain performance (Huo et al., 2017; Hwang & Kim, 2018).

Logistics service providers, which specialize in transportation, distribution, warehousing, and other customized services, assist firms in reducing logistics costs, enhancing logistics performance, and concentrating on their core business competencies (Huo et al., 2018). Several leading third—party logistics (3PL) service providers, including Burris Logistics, C. H. Robinson, and DB Schenker, offer a wide array of support services. However, this growth has also presented challenges that mirror the core value creation bottlenecks in platform supply chains as delineated in Chap. 1, particularly those associated with coordination failures and inefficient

B. Huo et al., *Platform Supply Chains 4*, Platform Supply Chains in the AI Era,
https://doi.org/10.1007/978-981-92-0133-4_6

resource allocation across the network. Logistics services are confronted with an increasing number of adversities that disrupt logistics operations and undermine logistics efficiency (Choi, 2021). Any errors or miscalculations in information can lead to delays in product or service delivery, especially in a digitalized and omni-channel environment, which ultimately elevates the cost to consumers (Demoulin & Coussement, 2020). These challenges stem from the escalating demand for sophisticated service attributes, such as timely delivery to specified locations, monitoring of delivery status, and return provisions. The urgent need to meet these demands has spurred the emergence of innovative and collaborative business models, necessitating close cooperation between logistics service providers and e-commerce operators (Giuffrida et al., 2019).

Although information sharing activities enable logistics service providers to be regarded as valuable partners, several obstacles remain. First, both parties in the relationship of a logistics service provider need to make substantial investments to ensure the accuracy and timeliness of logistics information. These investments manifest as economic assets that are continuously procured to support specific transactions and cannot be reallocated to other uses (Liu et al., 2009; Suh & Kwon, 2006; Wu et al., 2016). For instance, warehouse and transportation management systems integrate real—time data throughout the logistics chain, which facilitates joint decision making in a dynamic market (Choi et al., 2018). Second, aligning incentives and benefits between partners in an alliance (Huang et al., 2018), which is essentially a governance dilemma. Most information sharing in logistics services primarily focuses on operational matters while overlooking strategic issues. In fact, information sharing necessitates contributions from both user and provider enterprises. In the absence of appropriate governance, this may result in prolonged negotiations and non cooperative behaviors, ultimately leading to the failure of information sharing. Third, the sensitivity of commercial information needs attention. If confidentiality agreements are inadequate, logistic service providers may disclose user information to other parties to gain a competitive edge (Klein & Rai, 2009). Furthermore, if two users in the same market utilize the same logistic platform, they may be concerned about provider opportunism, such as the leakage of information to competitors (Cheng et al., 2021). These trust and incentive problems pose threats to the stability required for positive network effects. Finally, information sharing in logistics services is process—oriented and is subject to adjustments when circumstances change, which requires the establishment of strategic agendas to leverage business value and promote logistics cooperation (Wei et al., 2012).

Moreover, we have concentrated on the challenges faced in the development of logistics park platforms. With the support of the government and large—scale enterprises, the establishment of logistics parks in China has been on the rise. Nevertheless, there are still a plethora of substantial challenges to be addressed in areas such as planning, financing, operations, and factors related to operational performance. Currently, many enterprises have established professional platforms to integrate products, warehousing, transport vehicles, and relevant infrastructure (Krysiński & Miller, 2017; Kong et al., 2017). However, achieving a balance among resource diversity, the profitability prospects of the park, and site selection has emerged as a new challenge for logistics platforms.

6.1.2 The Objects of Platform Logistics Integration

In light of the challenges encountered in information acquisition and resource equilibrium within platform logistics, we conduct an examination of platform logistics integration from two crucial perspectives: information integration and resource integration. These two aspects directly correspond to two core mechanisms for value creation in platform supply chains, namely coordination (facilitated by information integration), and allocation (enabled by resource integration.

Information integration of platform logistics services. Information integration embodies a collaborative model in which logistics users and suppliers jointly administer cross—organizational processes to forge strategic partnerships. It mainly serves as a coordination mechanism, which promotes the efficient circulation of products, services, information, capital, and decision making. This allows for the provision of maximum value to customers with higher speed and lower cost. Distinct from the basic warehousing and transportation functions of traditional logistics outsourcing, the information integration of platform logistics services emphasizes the strategic and operational collaboration between logistics providers and users, thereby promoting mutual development (Luo et al., 2015). In platform logistics services, information integration is highly emphasized. Information integration is a primary mechanism in a dyadic relationship that reflects the connection between users and their major providers. It ensures end—to—end information flow and indicates voluntary participation in logistics alliances, thus tapping into the vast potential beyond market transactions (Liu et al., 2015; Wang et al., 2020). The simplest form of platform logistics information integration is a dyad where both user firms and provider firms make investments that are valued by the other (Tanskanen, 2015) party. It can be regarded as a reciprocal social reaction to the investments of user and provider firms. Information integration is a complex activity that can be carried out at both the operational and strategic levels (Kembro et al., 2017; Klein & Rai, 2009; Lee et al., 2010).

We explore the two dimensions of information integration, namely operational information integration and strategic information integration. Operational information integration pertains to the sharing of information regarding daily operations within the dyads of logistics service users and providers, including cargo status, service schedules, and service capacities. It is demand-driven, function-centered, short-term oriented, and highly structured in standardized formats (Lee et al., 2010). Constant et al. (1994) were the first to propose that information integration pragmatically contributes to the manifestation and consistency of a firm's identity and value at the strategic level (Constant et al., 1994). Strategic information integration emphasizes shared norms and involves the sharing of sensitive and confidential information that transcends order-related data, thereby ensuring the future planning and development of the alliance (Newell et al., 2018; Samaddar et al., 2006). The information is proprietary, distinctive, unstructured, and related to resources, strategic plans, and financial status (Klein & Rai, 2009). Such an emphasis provides an open platform for sincere information integration. Therefore, both operational and strategic information integration are crucial for establishing stable and competitive logistics chains.

For the logistics providers of the platform, the integration of operational information and strategic information ought to adopt a differentiated strategy. In the process of operational information integration, user enterprises should guarantee the unimpeded flow of information regarding service schedules, capacities, and demand during their continuous interactions with logistics service providers. In the case of strategic information integration, user enterprises should enhance the frequency and flexibility of communication and promote long standing and mutually beneficial alliances instead of those based on predetermined agreements.

Resource integration of platform logistics services. Resource integration represents the core process by which enterprises allocate and optimize the utilization of their resources. It mainly serves as an allocation mechanism. The resource integration capability stems from platform logistics services and relationship building practices, such as those related to information technology (IT) and supplier—customer relationships (Wang et al., 2016). This study focuses on two types of resource integration: platform resource integration and location resource integration. Logistics platforms form the tangible infrastructure of logistics service providers, encapsulating explicit knowledge. Platform resource integration pertains to the provider led allocation of resources, including public information platforms, management platforms, technical services, and financial services. Although contemporary IT infrastructures are frequently modular and standardized, they endow a company with a valuable and non-explicable system of automatic routines shaped by past experiences and decisions, and exert influence on most organizational processes, encompassing technical, information, management, and financial processes and platforms. The efficient implementation of these distinctive platforms typically enhances the reputation of IT functions, leading to improved collaboration between IT and other functions, both within and outside the company.

Location resource integration denotes the procedure by which logistics service providers allocate and optimize resources to leverage distinctive geographical advantages. This facilitates the establishment of efficient logistics hubs that link products to diverse markets through optimal routes. Location resource integration empowers a company to more effectively integrate its products, vehicles, and other relevant facilities. Logistics location specificity pertains to access to unique supply sources, government agencies, services, labor skills, and network opportunities (Freeman & Styles, 2014). From this viewpoint, logistics location is an intangible resource encompassing more implicit knowledge. High-level regional economic development introduces sustainable technology, and the government offers favorable policies and investments to expedite the development of logistics services. These value—added advantages render high quality location resources scarce and inimitable. For example, the eastern coastal areas hold advantages in terms of logistics service providers, which can reduce business costs, such as access to a larger and more educated human resource pool.

6.1.3 How Platform Logistics Integration Creates Value

Information integration (coordination) and resource integration (allocation) are widely recognized as crucial for establishing connections between platform logistics providers and users. Nevertheless, the success of integration also hinges on specific assets and mutual trust. Therefore, we introduce governance as the third essential mechanism, thereby completing the triad of coordination, allocation, and governance that serves as the foundation for value creation in platform logistics. In conclusion, the current competitive, information-abundant, and data-driven environment significantly promotes the development of platform logistics integration, which gives rise to several issues that demand greater attention. First, platform logistics service providers and their users are increasingly establishing strategic partnerships for long term success rather than merely transactional relationships (Valashiya & Luke, 2022). This underscores the significance of strategic information integration, which places more emphasis on value—added relationships beyond order—related information and guarantees the future planning and growth of the alliance (Heide & John, 1992; Newell et al., 2018; Samaddar et al., 2006). For instance, BMW has upgraded its outsourcing relationship with TNT Logistics to a strategic partnership. Second, based on the Social Exchange Theory (SET), information integration can be regarded as a partnership formed and sustained through the provision of reciprocal benefits or penalties for non—compliance (Wei et al., 2012; Wu et al., 2014). This raises a question regarding what serves as the means of offering reciprocal benefits or penalties for violations. We suggest that specific assets (of the user firm and the provider firm) and mutual trust play distinct roles.

Relying solely on either the specific assets of providers or users is inadequate, as each type of specific asset plays a unique role in supporting information integration. A high level of providers' specific assets indicates a bilateral credible commitment that binds both parties to a long term alliance. This directly promotes strategic information integration, which yields long term rewards and benefits, and enhances mutual trust based on the credible commitment made by providers. However, both providers' and users' specific assets are essential for the implementation of operational information integration. The establishment of formal information systems in 3PL relationships necessitates an understanding of the daily transaction information of both parties (Kosmol et al., 2019). Therefore, providers' specific assets alone cannot fully realize operational information sharing without the involvement of users' specific assets.

Nevertheless, the phenomenon that users' specific assets may not directly promote mutual trust exposes a crucial problem in platform logistics resource integration. In emerging markets, platform logistics services are relatively immature, and enterprises encounter numerous challenges, including insufficient knowledge, inadequate infrastructure, limited multimodal capabilities, and low security consciousness (Lau & Zhang, 2006). In platform logistics service dyads, users are less proficient than providers and lack standardized resources during the logistics outsourcing process. Consequently, their specific assets may provide limited support or even result in misunderstandings and conflicts, which is unfavorable to the establishment of mutual trust. Likewise, users will act with caution as their specific assets cannot be redeployed, which cannot directly lead to further operational or strategic information integration. Alternatively, users' specific assets can indirectly enhance information sharing by stimulating reciprocal investments from providers, in line with the reciprocal equivalence principle of SET (Cropanzano et al., 2017).

Through information integration (coordination) and resource integration (allocation), platform logistics providers realize efficient fluxes of information, resources, and services. This facilitates the seamless movement of capital and business operations throughout the supply chain, thereby reducing costs, enhancing responsiveness, and generating value for all participants. Concurrently, platform logistics integration enables providers to integrate profoundly into the vertical supply chains of logistics outsourcing enterprises, presenting highly integrated and comprehensive services to the entire supply chain (Luo & Wang, 2021).

Previous research has frequently concentrated on general information sharing, neglecting the unique strategic function of information integration as a coordination mechanism (Şahin & Topal, 2019; Wu et al., 2014). We propose that operational and strategic information integration play distinct roles in improving financial performance. Operational and strategic information integration serve as the basis for platform logistics integration, and it has been found that each exerts a distinct impact on performance, which expands upon the findings of recent studies (e.g., (Goswami et al., 2020; Valashiya & Luke, 2022). Operational information integration guarantees high efficiency in fundamental platform logistics service activities; however, it necessitates formal information systems that incur substantial costs (Evangelista et al., 2012; Olorunniwo & Li, 2010). Such costs may counterbalance the advantages of utilizing these information systems; therefore, operational information integration cannot directly contribute to financial performance. Conversely, strategic information integration between platform logistics service providers and their users is founded on shared values and long—term commitment and demands relatively lower fixed costs.

Furthermore, both logistics platform integration and location integration notably elevate the resource efficiency of platform logistics services, which is in line with previous research (Pearson et al., 2001). This indicates how the effective allocation of tangible (platform) and intangible (location) resources drives operational value. In fact, logistics platform integration encompasses the integration of an information platform, finance platform, management platform, and technical platform. The information system fosters transparency by sharing real time information among partners, such as the available warehouse space and the number of available vehicles. Companies can acquire financial support from financial institutions through financial platforms, which is particularly crucial for new companies lacking sufficient financial resources to expand or purchase facilities for integrating more resources to enhance their operational performance. Through the management platform, logistics companies in logistics parks with high-level infrastructure can receive free professional training, thereby enabling companies to integrate resources more readily within the park. With the assistance of the technical platform, companies can utilize advanced information and communication technologies to plan and control their internal operations and integrate external resources. Therefore, managers of platform logistics service providers should introduce the public platform system to enhance resource integration capabilities.

Logistics location resources exerts a positive impact on resource efficiency through its network externalities, which is in line with the findings of Ambrosino and Sciomachen (2012). The strategic advantage of integrating logistics location resources is reflected in the fact that a greater number of connections hold greater value, facilitating the coordination of the entire supply chain. Each platform logistics service provider occupies a distinct geographical position, suggesting that location is a heterogeneous and non—replicable resource. Through the interconnection of these distinct networks, providers can integrate the unique resources of other 3PL companies or logistics parks. Therefore, an appropriate location that complements the other logistics resources of platform logistics service providers can significantly enhance their ability to integrate internal and external resources.

6.1.4 Chapter Framework

This chapter examines platform logistics integration, which represents the specific manifestation of the logistics pillar within the four-pillar integration framework of this book. It elucidates how value is generated in the distribution domain through the interaction of governance, coordination, and allocation mechanisms. First, it tackles the challenges associated with information acquisition and resource allocation in platform logistics services. On this basis, information integration (serving as a coordination mechanism) and resource integration (functioning as an allocation mechanism) in platform logistics are proposed. Second, from the perspective of the SET theory, governance mechanisms are adopted as the approach for platform logistics integration. We analyze how the specific assets and mutual trust relationships between service providers and users influence the integration of operational and strategic information. Such information integration ultimately enhances financial performance and facilitates the efficient circulation of information, resources, and services. Third, logistics parks are employed as case studies to offer empirical evidence for the relationships among platforms, location resource integration, and operational performance, further clarifying the allocation mechanism and its contingency on firm capabilities. Consequently, the efficiency of resource integration in logistics parks is improved (Fig. 6.1).

This chapter centers on platform logistics integration, presenting economic governance and relational governance. It intends to build up the competitiveness of platform logistics information integration. Specifically:

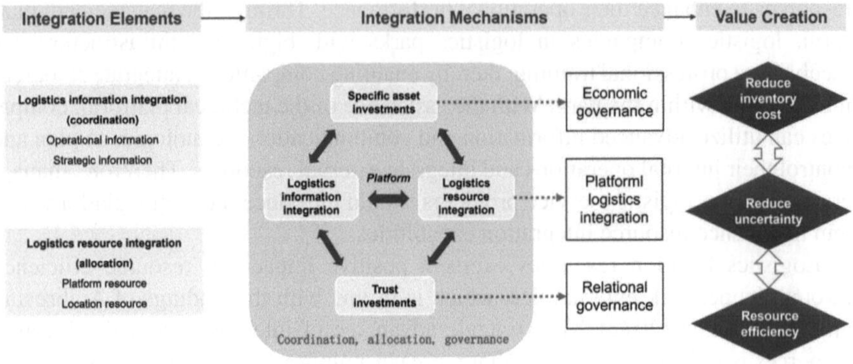

Fig. 6.1 Platform logistics integration conceptual framework

Governance of Logistics Service Providers: In Sect. 6.2, we focus on governance mechanisms to enhance the efficiency and competitiveness of platform logistics information integration (coordination). The SET theory provides a valuable theoretical perspective for understanding the relationship between platform logistics service providers and users. Specific assets, as an economic investment, serve as an economic instrument to bind them into a long—term alliance and ensure positive returns. Mutual trust is a relational investment with a long—term orientation. It maximizes profits by influencing the mutual perception of both parties and shifts the focus from self centered goals to mutual goals and benefits. However, the relationship between specific assets and mutual trust and its impact on the different outcomes of platform logistics information integration remain unclear, as well as whether mutual trust mediates the relationship between specific assets and information integration. This section explores the influence of specific assets of platform logistics service providers and users, as well as mutual trust, on operational, strategic information sharing, and financial performance, with the aim of maximizing the effectiveness of platform logistics information integration. This section examines the effects of specific assets of platform logistics service providers and users, and mutual trust on operational and strategic information integration and financial performance, aiming to maximize the effectiveness of platform logistics information integration.

Value Creation of Platform Logistics Resource Integration: In Sect. 6.3, the emphasis undergoes a definitive shift from relationship governance to the strategic orchestration of resources, delving into the core issue of how platform logistics resources are transformed into operational value through allocation. This section introduces and utilizes an integrated contingency and configuration theoretical framework to analyze this process. The contingency perspective contends that the efficacy of a logistics park's key resources—its integrated platform (tangible assets) and strategic location (intangible network assets)—is not inherent but contingent upon a crucial firm specific factor: its resource integration capability. This dynamic capability is theorized as the fundamental mechanism that unlocks the latent value of resources. In a complementary manner, the configuration perspective posits that superior performance does not stem from excelling in a single dimension but from attaining a specific, synergistic alignment or "fit" among strategic elements. In this context, it refers to the balanced, high level utilization of both platform and location resources.

Building on this dual theoretical basis, this section formulates and tests a research model. It posits distinct causal pathways: a direct influence from the platform on performance, a fully mediated impact from location on performance (via resource integration capability), and a partially mediated effect from the platform on performance. Empirically, a structural equation model (SEM) is employed to test these contingent, mediated relationships, and a two—step cluster analysis is utilized to identify the natural, emerging patterns of resource utilization among firms within Chinese logistics parks. The analysis aims not only to verify the significance of resources and capabilities but also to precisely define how (through mediation) and in what combination (through configuration) they jointly contribute to operational excellence. Ultimately, this section presents an evidence—based framework that transcends the simplistic view of resource possession, providing managers with a comprehensive understanding of how to utilize logistics parks not merely for their assets but as ecosystems for cultivating competitive capabilities and achieving strategic resource synergy.

Finally, we summarize the main contents of this chapter and look forward to future research.

6.2 Governance of Logistics Service Providers

6.2.1 Social Exchange Theory

The SET theory posits that successful social exchange stems from positive initiatives, reciprocal investments, and penalties for violations (Cropanzano et al., 2017). It has been demonstrated to be a valuable theoretical framework for comprehending logistics relationships (e.g., Huo et al., 2016; Moore & Cunningham, 1999; Shi et al., 2016; Wang et al., 2020). The SET theory offers a basis for investigating the governance of platform logistics relationships, elucidating how reciprocal investments and trust promote collaborative behavior.

The SET theory was initially applied to interpersonal relations and subsequently extended to elucidate interfirm exchanges that are not solely economic (Emerson, 1976). The fundamental postulate posits that the pursuit of rewards and the avoidance of punishments serve as the primary impetus for firms to engage in interactions (Cook & Emerson, 1978; Granovetter, 1985). Specifically, the greater the frequency of rewards associated with an exchange, the higher the probability of its recurrence. Conversely, when an exchange fails to yield the anticipated rewards or incurs unforeseen punishments, firms will proactively avoid or decline such exchanges in the future. The SET theory has also been employed to comprehend successful logistics relationships (Lai et al., 2012; Maloni & Carter, 2006; Moore & Cunningham, 1999). Logistics relationships develop through frequent investments and interactions, wherein both parties strive to establish mutually beneficial exchanges and evade unforeseen outcomes (Moore & Cunningham, 1999; Pulles et al., 2014).

Enterprise assets are the focal point of the SET theory. Specific assets encompass tangible and intangible assets, which represent economic investments and serve as an economic instrument to bind both parties in a long term alliance. Tangible specific assets refer to the fixed assets held by a firm, including logistics equipment, information systems, and other physical assets. These assets are transparent, possess a fixed long term capacity, and can be readily imitated by competitors (Barney, 1991; Grant, 1991). Conversely, intangible specific assets are scarce, non-physical, and future-oriented. They are related to a firm's utilization of its know-how, such as expertise, knowledge, and skills. Tacit knowledge is frequently acquired through human resources and organizational routines and plays a pivotal role in establishing sustainable competitive advantages, as it is difficult to comprehend, observe, and imitate (Grant, 1996).

The fundamental rationale of the SET theory posits that every exchange has a historical and a prospective dimension. Suh and Kwon (2006) discovered that trust perceptions are significantly correlated with the specific assets of both parties within a supply chain (Suh & Kwon, 2006). The prospect of above normal returns in future exchanges binds the two parties, leading them to act in a trustworthy manner. Reciprocal specific assets mirror the intention to make both parties mutually dependent and prompt them to be concerned about each other's well being, thereby establishing a framework that fosters mutual trust (Liu et al., 2009). Huo et al. (2018) ascertained that providers' specific assets reduce users' uncertainty and anxiety and contribute to the establishment of trust with users (Huo et al., 2018). Furthermore, specific assets can generate specialized knowledge, culture, and guidelines that enhance efficiency and signify a commitment from both parties to elevate their relationship (Demoulin & Coussement, 2020; Suh & Kwon, 2006). For instance, Yu et al. (2021) found that users' proactive specific assets prompt providers to recognize their capabilities, thus facilitating the construction of trust with providers (Yu et al., 2021).

According to the SET theory, information integration can be regarded as a partnership established and sustained through the provision of mutual benefits or penalties (Wei et al., 2012; Wu et al., 2014; Zaheer & Venkatraman, 1995). In an alliance, both parties are inclined to make economic and relational investments to uphold the alliance (Liu et al., 2009; Wu et al., 2016; Zaheer & Venkatraman, 1995). Consequently, in the following, we investigate these two governance approaches and their application in platform logistics integration. These approaches, namely economic governance and relational governance, form the core governance mechanism that facilitates effective coordination (through information integration) within platform logistics.

6.2.2 *Economic Governance*

Within logistics platforms, the relationships between providers and the users are maintained as both parties engage in investments that yield reciprocal advantages over a period. Specific assets represent an economic investment that is challenging to transfer and holds minimal salvage value beyond the specific relationship. This is because the majority of these assets, such as hardware resources or human resources, are designed or trained in accordance with the operational characteristics of both parties (Jell-Ojobor & Raha, 2022). The specific assets of platform logistics providers and their users serve as an economic instrument to bind them into a long term alliance and ensure positive returns. Such specific investments can effectively restrain the opportunistic behavior of both parties, as the termination of cooperation would lead to sunk costs.

Although service providers possess the expertise to enhance logistics efficiency, service users are obligated to invest in specific assets to guide and support the service providers. As per the 2019 3PL report issued by SCALA Consulting, 38% of 3PL service providers perceived their service users as "highly satisfied," whereas only 18% of 3PL users concurred with this view. Such a disparity in expectations indicates that providers should ascertain the actual needs of users. More crucially, users also need to allocate greater resources to logistics relationships and offer directions and guidelines to providers. For example, when users allocate information systems and human resources with logistics management experience, providers can promptly comprehend users' logistics requirements and subsequently meet these requirements through customized solutions. Additionally, the deliberate provision of specific assets by users renders it arduous for providers to terminate the outsourcing relationship (Law, 2018). This self imposed exit barrier implies that the logistics relationship is unique, which compels providers to fulfill their commitments (Dyer & Singh, 1998). This proactive locking in behavior of users assures providers that users will not renege on the relationship. Furthermore, users' specific assets impose a moral obligation on providers to reciprocate, and providers respond by making investments to uphold reciprocity (Huang et al., 2020; Muthusamy & White, 2005). Thus, economic governance, through mutual specific asset investments, establishes a credible commitment that promotes more in depth coordination.

6.2.3 *Relational Governance*

The SET theory posits that relational governance reinforces commitment, dependency, and long term orientation, consequently alleviating opportunistic behavior (Lai et al., 2012) and augmenting the overall welfare of the relationship (Giuffrida et al., 2019). Trust, commitment, and flexibility represent the three crucial behavioral dimensions. As an informal governance mechanism, trust is extensively acknowledged as the core element for maintaining relational contracts (Zanini & Migueles, 2013). Therefore, we focus on the role of trust in the 3PL integration process.

Trust is defined as the propensity to expose one's vulnerabilities, based on the expectation that the counterpart will perform specific actions (actions that are of crucial importance to the trusting party), regardless of whether the trusting party has the ability to monitor or control the counterparty (Mayer et al., 1995). Scholars regard trust as a morally just act marked by conscious reliability and positive expectations towards the other party (Zanini & Migueles, 2013). Relationships established on trust hold significant value, and all parties are willing to make investments in such relationships (Morgan & Hunt, 1995). Trust reduces transaction costs and risks by restraining opportunistic behavior among collaborators. Mutual trust is a long term relational investment. It reshapes the way parties perceive one another, redirecting the focus from self centered goals to mutual objectives and benefits, thus enhancing collective value (Li et al., 2014; Wu et al., 2014).

In contrast to traditional logistics outsourcing, which is transactional and function- based, platform logistics services are characterized by a high degree of customization. Consequently, users of these services find it difficult to discontinue their cooperation with current providers and switch to alternative ones (Huo et al., 2017). Therefore, the cooperation relationship necessitates an augmentation of relational investments, particularly in the form of mutual trust. In dyadic relationships, Moore and Cunningham (1999) posited that trust facilitates social exchanges within a logistics alliance. Mutual trust is established when both parties are assured that the other will act fairly, honestly, and take into account their welfare (Huo et al., 2017) A successful outsourcing relationship is forged through the willingness to share the latest information for mutual gains, and mutual trust serves as the cohesive force that binds partners together (Lotfi et al., 2013). Relational governance, with mutual trust at its core, mitigates the perceived risks associated with coordination (such as information sharing) and cultivates a collaborative environment that is conducive to both operational and strategic integration.

6.2.4 Logistics Information Integration and Performance Outcomes

Executives of platform logistics service providers ought to adopt embrace a SET theory perspective to promote information integration. Relying solely on reward motivation proves inadequate due to the fragility of inter relationships, and both parties may be hesitant to share information. It is proposed that executives encourage both parties to make economic and relational investments to enhance their capabilities and augment their willingness to establish open communication channels, thereby reducing information asymmetry and disruption. Economic governance and relational governance address both operational and strategic agendas. Collectively, they constitute the integrated governance foundation that enables and sustains effective coordination through logistics information integration.

Economic governance and logistics information integration. We argue that users' specific assets augment operational and strategic information integration in three respects. First, a high level of users' specific assets indicates elevated switching costs or penalties associated with pursuing alternative outsourcing relationships. Consequently, both parties opt to maintain or enhance information integration (Perry et al., 2004; Sambasivan et al., 2013). Both parties engage in operational and strategic information integration to attain greater cooperation. Second, in accordance with the SET theory, users' specific assets uphold a long term alliance as these assets mirror equivalent investments made by both parties. Therefore, under an atmosphere of reciprocal equivalence, users' specific assets prompt both parties to reciprocate in information integration. Third, user firms frequently dominate the outsourcing relationship, and their specific assets assist providers in comprehending their internal logistics processes and requirements (Suh & Kwon, 2006). Their economic investment conveys a positive attitude and serves as a strategic instrument for forging bonds with provider firms. As a result, providers are more inclined to engage in coupling behaviors, such as operational and strategic information integration.

For platform logistics users, they often find it difficult to acquire the specific assets of providers and find it costly to produce them in-house (Marchet et al., 2017). Therefore, providers invest in professional and complementary resources to engage in collaboration with users, including advanced and complex logistics technologies, knowledge, and experience (König et al., 2019). Nevertheless, providers also pose risks to users, such as conflicts and misunderstandings during the service process (Wang et al., 2020). Service providers aim to earn returns on their specific assets and maintain their alliance with users. Consequently, the specific assets of providers eliminate information integration barriers and may even proactively broaden the scope of information integration with users. Moreover, since the specific assets of providers have limited salvage value for alternative users, these investments serve as a penalty for relationship violation or termination, thus binding providers to the relationship (Young-Ybarra & Wiersema, 1999).

Relational governance and logistics information integration. Trust is defined as the cornerstone of a strategic partnership (Spekman, 1988, p. 79), as it embodies the positive beliefs of both parties that result in trustworthy responses or actions. The influence of mutual trust on operational and strategic information integration is direct, stimulates information integration, and creates conditions favorable for the sustenance of information integration. According to the SET theory, mutual trust shows concern about the other's welfare, and both parties are more likely to regard information integration as beneficial (Wu et al., 2014). Lai et al. (2012) discovered that trust restrains opportunistic behaviors in the relationships between platform logistics providers and their users, especially in uncertain environments (Lai et al., 2012). Furthermore, mutual trust enhances the willingness of both parties to take risks within the relationship, and both parties are less apprehensive about the risk of information leakage when participating in operational information integration (Liao et al., 2020). Information integration, particularly strategic information integration, necessitates frequent and intensive communication. Therefore, trust is a prerequisite for the sustained implementation of strategic information integration, which depends on complex interactions between users and providers due to their different origins, cultures, and values. Mutual trust can mitigate relational conflicts and enhance the confidence of both parties in engaging in strategic information integration by ensuring the similarity of values and goals (Wang et al., 2019).

Economic governance, relational governance, and logistics information integration. Collectively, it is posited that mutual trust serves as a bridge between specific assets and logistics information integration. The primary rationale is that mutual trust is tenuous in the nascent relationship between platform logistics service providers and their users, and both dimensions of information integration necessitate specific assets as an economic safeguard. Nevertheless, since both parties are entrapped in the relationship by mutual investments, neither can fully regulate the other's behavior solely through economic means. Consequently, they require mutual trust to fortify the fragile foundation of information integration. To some degree, mutual trust acts as a self reinforcing safeguard for specific assets. Second, specific assets are gradually embedded in social exchanges, which exhibits long term interdependence that fosters mutual trust. Specific assets also operate as a strategic instrument to offer a reliable and equitable mode of interaction requisite for the growth of trust (Liu et al., 2009). Therefore, perceptions of trustworthiness are crucial for initiating and sustaining information integration. This interaction indicates that economic and relational governance are complementary. Their combination gives rise to a robust governance system that effectively facilitates and enhances coordination (information integration) within the logistics domain.

Therefore, executives ought to cultivate an environment of mutual trust to leverage the advantages of users' and providers' specific assets in augmenting information integration. On one hand, mutual trust serves as a relational safeguard and establishes a conducive environment for both parties to engage in integration sharing through reciprocal and voluntary linkages. On the other hand, both users' and providers' specific assets can reinforce and complement mutual trust by strengthening economic incentives and penalties for breaching the relationship or terminating it.

Logistics information integration and financial performance. While the operational and strategic dimensions of logistics information integration are of significance, their impacts on financial performance may vary. On one hand, the operational information integration between users and providers can curtail inventory costs and lead times through the exchange of logistics information, including inventory, transportation, and delivery data (Liu et al., 2015). For instance, leveraging providers' information systems enables the tracking of product arrivals and departures, facilitating users' scheduling of subsequent steps and processes. Sharing capacity information mitigates shortage gaming, and sharing demand information enhances forecast accuracy. This alleviates the market bullwhip effect, reduces the pressure on warehouses, and averts additional inventory waste resulting from the bullwhip effect (Wang et al., 2016). Specifically, when user firms share plans related to packages, pallet configurations, and anticipated usage levels, providers can allocate equipment and formulate plans to meet cost requirements, thereby assisting users in reducing financial expenditures.

On the other hand, strategic information integration entails long term and in depth communication, which deepens the understanding of context—sensitive processes, culture, and technologies in logistics management. As a result, providers can identify logistical bottlenecks and offer customized and highly flexible solutions, such as downstream distribution network design (Marchet et al., 2017), This reduces users' logistics uncertainties and augments their profits. Moreover, strategic information integration involves logistics service providers from the early stage. Consequently, providers can gain a better understanding of operational processes, streamline the inventory and warehousing processes, and help users reduce resource waste and carrying costs (Youn et al., 2013).

In conclusion, this section elucidates how the governance mechanism (through SET) promotes coordination (through information integration), which subsequently drives financial performance, thereby completing a crucial value—creation pathway within the platform logistics integration framework.

6.3 Value Creation of Platform Logistics Resource Integration

6.3.1 Introduction

The strategic proliferation of logistics parks represents a significant investment in supply chain infrastructure, particularly in emerging economies like China, where they serve as key nodes in regional and national logistics networks. Yet, despite their growing prevalence, a critical question persists in both academic and managerial circles: through what mechanisms do these parks convert their physical infrastructure and geographical advantages into tangible operational value for the companies that operate within them? This question directly addresses the allocation mechanism within the logistics integration pillar. Conventional viewpoints often presume a direct link between superior resources and superior performance. This section challenges that assumption, advancing a more nuanced explanation: the effectiveness of resource allocation in platform logistics is not automatic. It is a mediated and conditional process, best understood through the integrated lenses of contingency theory and configuration theory.

Rooted in organizational theory, the contingency perspective posits that no single management approach is universally optimal; rather, the effectiveness of any strategic resource depends on the specific circumstances and capabilities of the organization. Applied to logistics parks, this means the value derived from a park's key offerings—its integrated platform (tangible services) and its strategic location (intangible network access)—is not uniform across firms. Instead, their impact is contingent upon a critical intervening variable: the firm's resource integration capability. Access to advanced resources is insufficient; translating them into performance depends on the firm's ability to deploy, combine, and leverage them effectively. Thus, effective allocation is not automatic but contingent on this firm-specific dynamic capability.

Complementing this view, the configuration perspective suggests that superior performance arises from the synergistic alignmen, or fit, among a set of interrelated strategic elements, not from excelling in any single element alone. Here, the key elements form a triad: (1) the logistics park platform, a tangible, explicit resource encompassing public information, management, technical, and financial services; (2) the logistics park location, an intangible, often implicit resource providing access to unique supply sources, government agencies, labor skills, and network opportunities (Freeman & Styles, 2014); and (3) the firm's resource integration capability, a dynamic organizational ability to combine and leverage both internal and external resources. The configuration approach asks: what specific patterns or "bundles" of these three elements are associated with the highest levels of operational performance? This perspective investigates the optimal allocation strategy—how resources should be combined and utilized.

Drawing on empirical evidence from Chinese logistics parks, this section systematically examines these dual dynamics. It demonstrates that platform and location resources, while essential, contribute to competitive advantage only partially or fully through the firm's integration capability. Moreover, it reveals empirically that the highest levels of performance are associated with a specific configurational state—one characterized by the synergistic and balanced utilization of both platform and location resources, which in turn fuels a higher-order resource integration capability. By integrating the contingency and configuration perspectives, we move beyond a simplistic input-output model toward a more sophisticated framework that explains not only that resources matter, but how, under what conditions, and in what combinations they collectively drive operational excellence within modern logistics platforms. This provides a comprehensive understanding of the allocation mechanism within platform logistics.

6.3.2 Hypotheses

The research model is theoretically anchored in the Resource-Based View (RBV) and Dynamic Capability Theory. The RBV establishes the foundational premise that sustained competitive advantage derives from resources that are valuable, rare, difficult to imitate, and non-substitutable (Barney, 1991). In the context of this study, logistics parks are conceptualized as strategic aggregators that provide tenant firms with access to precisely such resources: the integrated logistics platform and the strategic logistics location. While the RBV explains the potential for advantage residing in resources, our model extends it by emphasizing the process through which these resources are leveraged. We introduce resource integration capability as a critical, higher-order construct that determines how park-level resources are absorbed, combined, and utilized. This perspective aligns with the view that capabilities are a firm's ability to assemble and deploy resources to improve performance (Daugherty et al., 2009) and that resource integration results from complex patterns of interaction and coordination between resources (Hoopes et al., 2003). Thus, the model posits that the value of park-level resources is not automatic but is realized through the mediating mechanism of firm-specific dynamic capability. This perspective leads to hypotheses delineating how allocation (via platform and location integration) translates into performance, contingent upon this capability.

H1a: Logistics park platforms are positively related to operational performance.

A logistics park platform constitutes a tangible, codified resource bundle encompassing integrated information systems, management protocols, technical support, and financial services. IIndividually and collectively, these components serve as direct operational tools. Integrated information systems and logistics platforms have significant effects on operational performance in supply chains (Dyk & Maspero, 2004; Puertas et al., 2014). Management platforms improve the performance of channel members by providing a platform for integration across the supply chain (White & Pearson, 2001). Therefore, it is hypothesized that a higher degree of integration with and utilization of the logistics park platform directly enhances a tenant firm's operational performance, demonstrating a direct allocation-to-performance pathway for platform resources.

H1b: Logistics park platforms are positively related to resource integration.

Beyond direct tools, these platforms create an infrastructural environment that facilitates broader resource synthesis. Resource integration capability results from logistics platforms and relationship-building practices such as IT and supplier–customer relationships (Wang et al., 2016; Krysiński & Miller, 2017). With an information platform, IT infrastructure can create a higher-order integration capability (Rai et al., 2006). Through financial platforms, companies can obtain financial support to integrate more resources (Yuan et al., 2010). Thus, it is hypothesized that logistics platform integration actively cultivates and strengthens a firm's underlying capability to integrate resources. This suggests that platform resources also enhance the firm's ability to execute effective allocation more broadly.

The role of location is more complex, embodying the contingency view. A superior logistics location provides access to unique, often intangible assets: proximity to transportation nodes (highways, railways, ports), industrial clusters, skilled labor pools, and favorable government policies.

H2a: Logistics location is positively related to operational performance.

Logistics location integration provides access to unique, often intangible assets such as proximity to multi-modal transportation nodes, industrial clusters, specialized labor pools, and favorable regulatory policies. An optimal location can lead to reduced transportation costs and support better operational performance (Gao & Dong, 2012; Lium et al., 2009). While such geographic and institutional advantages can reduce nominal transportation distances and facilitate market access, in a complex, networked economy, these benefits are not automatically internalized as superior operational performance (e.g., higher order-fill rates or greater flexibility). Their translation requires active and purposeful managerial effort. Consequently, while a positive relationship is proposed, the hypothesized direct effect of location integration on operational performance is tentative and may be weak or non-significant, reflecting its conditional nature. This reflects the contingency inherent in allocation based on location.

H2b: Logistics location is positively related to resource integration.

The paramount value of a strategic logistics location lies in the network externalities it provides. It embeds a firm within a dense ecosystem of potential partners, suppliers, customers, and complementary service providers. This embeddedness dramatically reduces the search costs, contracting risks, and coordination efforts required to establish value-adding linkages. Many studies focus on location models with externalities that enable multimodal connections, which help enhance resource integration (Ambrosino & Sciomachen, 2012; Gao & Dong, 2012). Furthermore, valuable resources such as specific supply, government agencies, and unique labor skills help to enhance resource integration (Freeman & Styles, 2014). Therefore, location is hypothesized to be a powerful driver of the firm's ability to integrate: Logistics location is positively related to resource integration capability. This positions location primarily as an enabler of the firm's allocation capability.

H3: Resource integration is positively related to operational performance.

Resource integration capability is conceptualized as the firm's ability to identify, assimilate, and deploy both its internal resources and those accessible in its external environment. This dynamic capability enables a firm to optimally configure assets, respond with agility to disruptions, and innovate in its service offerings. Logistics resource integration may enhance performance by improving the accuracy of information and visibility of demand processes (Frohlich & Westbrook, 2002; Osmonbekov et al., 2009). It represents the essential organizational mechanism that converts static resource potential into dynamic, value-creating action. Hence, the core hypothesis is that a firm's resource integration capability is a direct and potent driver of its operational performance, placing the firm's allocation capability at the center of the value creation process.

Collectively, these hypotheses frame a model in which resource integration capability serves as the pivotal mediating mechanism. A key theoretical distinction is proposed: the value of logistics location integration is fully contingent on this capability (full mediation), while logistics platform integration contributes through dual pathways—a direct tool-based effect and an indirect, capability-enhancing effect (partial mediation). This structure formalizes the contingency argument and provides a testable framework for understanding how the resources of a logistics park are transmuted into firm-level competitive advantage. In essence, it models the allocation mechanism, showing how access to resources (platform and location) must be coupled with integration capability to unlock performance. The conceptual model summarizing these relationships is presented in Fig. 6.2.

6.3.3 Methodology

To subject the proposed contingent and configurational model to rigorous empirical examination, this research employed a comprehensive, multi-method strategy. The investigation was situated within the dynamic and heterogeneous context of Chinese logistics parks—an ideal setting characterized by rapid state-led development, significant regional economic disparities, and varied levels of infrastructure maturity. This intrinsic variance provides a powerful "natural laboratory" to explore the contingent effects of resources, as firms operate under meaningfully different external conditions. A meticulously designed survey-based study was conducted to collect primary data, which was then analyzed using complementary statistical techniques to address both the pathway (contingency) and pattern (configuration) aspects of the research questions. This methodology is designed to unpack the complexities of the allocation mechanism.

Sample and Data Collection. The study targeted companies operating within logistics parks across China. A total of 273 valid and complete responses were obtained from firms across 25 different logistics parks, strategically distributed in nine major Chinese cities. The selection of cities was purposive to maximize environmental and developmental heterogeneity, thereby capturing a wide spectrum of the contingent factors that shape logistics operations. The sample encompassed cities representing distinct regional economic models: traditional industrial bases

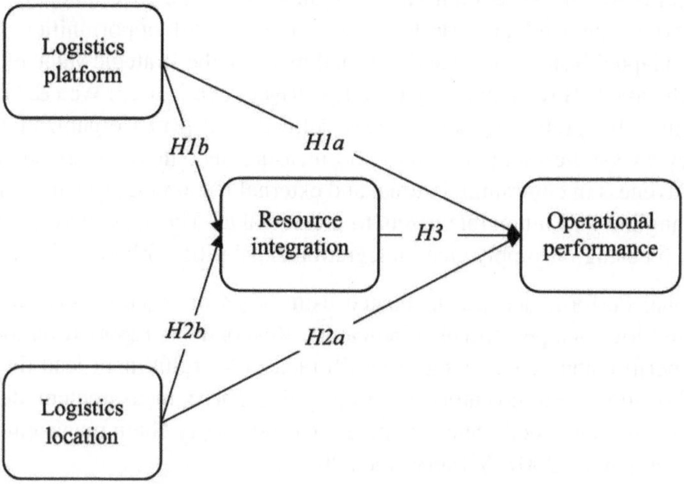

Fig. 6.2 Conceptual model

in Northeast China (Changchun, Haerbin); a major heavy industrial and inland transportation hub (Zhengzhou); politically significant and economically advanced coastal cities within the Bohai Rim Economic Circle (Beijing, Qingdao); and highly developed, globally integrated metropolises within the Yangtze River Delta region (Shanghai, Suzhou, Hangzhou, Ningbo). This deliberate geographical and economic diversity ensures that the findings are not artifacts of a single regional context but are robust across different stages of logistics ecosystem development. To ensure data quality and relevance, the key informants for the survey were specifically targeted as mid-to-senior level managers with direct operational responsibility for logistics, supply chain, or related functions within their firms, thereby guaranteeing informed responses on strategic capabilities and performance metrics.

Measures and Validation. All key constructs in the model were measured using multi-item, reflective scales developed through a rigorous process. Items were primarily adapted from well-established scales in prior literature, with modifications and refinements made based on expert interviews and a pilot test within the logistics park context to ensure contextual fit and clarity.

1. Logistics Platform Integration was operationalized as a second-order construct reflecting the extent to which a firm utilizes and benefits from four distinct, first-order service dimensions of the park: the information platform, management services, technical services, and financial services. The measurement items for this construct were adapted from seminal and contemporary works on logistics clusters and platform capabilities (Sheffi, 2012; Huo et al., 2014; Puertas et al., 2014; Kong et al., 2017; Wang et al., 2016).
2. Logistics Location Integration was measured to capture its multifaceted nature. Moving beyond simple geographical coordinates, the scale assessed a firm's perceived access to and advantage gained from a location's unique assets, including proximity to transportation networks, industry clusters, government policies and support, specialized labor skills, and business network opportunities. The items were adapted from scales that define and measure the strategic value of location-specific assets (Freeman & Styles, 2014; Rivera et al., 2016; Wen & Wu, 2017).
3. Resource Integration Capability was defined as a firm's organizational proficiency in synthesizing resources. Its measurement items assessed the firm's effectiveness in combining internal and external resources, as well as orchestrating tangible and intangible assets to create value. The scale was adapted from work focusing on supply chain integration capabilities (Zhao et al., 2011).

Operational Performance was evaluated using a set of objective-oriented, widely recognized logistics performance indicators. Respondents reported on their firm's relative performance concerning order-fill rate, order fulfillment lead time, operational flexibility, and inventory turnover ratio. These measurement items were adapted from established scales in operations and supply chain management literature (Devaraj et al., 2007; Vickery et al., 2003).

Constructs were measured using multi-item scales. Logistics Platform was operationalized across four dimensions (information, management, technical, financial).

Logistics Location extended beyond mere geography to include access to industry clusters, government policies, and labor skills. Resource Integration Capability assessed the firm's proficiency in combining internal and external, tangible and intangible resources. Operational Performance was measured via objective-oriented indicators like order-fill rate, fulfillment lead time, flexibility, and inventory turnover. All scales underwent a rigorous development process involving literature synthesis, expert interviews, pilot testing, and statistical validation for reliability, convergent validity, and discriminant validity.

The psychometric properties of all scales were rigorously assessed. After data collection, a series of tests were conducted. Exploratory and Confirmatory Factor Analyses (EFA and CFA) confirmed the unidimensionality, convergent validity, and discriminant validity of the constructs. Scale reliability was evaluated using Cronbach's alpha, with all values exceeding the recommended threshold of 0.70, indicating strong internal consistency.

***Analytical Techniques*:** To comprehensively test the dual aspects of the theoretical model, a two-stage analytical approach was implemented, aligning specific techniques with distinct research objectives.

1. **Structural Equation Modeling (SEM)** was the primary technique used to test the network of hypothesized causal pathways (H1a, H1b, H2a, H2b, H3). SEM, utilizing the maximum likelihood estimation method in LISREL, is uniquely suited for this purpose as it allows for the simultaneous estimation of all direct and indirect (mediated) relationships within the model. This enabled a direct test of contingent relationships, specifically the proposed mediating role of resource integration capability, and provided robust estimates of the strength and significance of each path. This tests the linear, contingent pathways of the allocation mechanism.
2. **Two-Step Cluster Analysis** was employed as a complementary technique to directly investigate the configurational patterns among firms, an objective beyond the scope of linear correlation-based methods like SEM. The analysis proceeded in two steps: first, a hierarchical cluster analysis (using Ward's method with squared Euclidean distance) was performed on firms' standardized scores for Platform Integration and Location Integration to suggest the appropriate number of natural groupings within the data. Second, a K-means cluster analysis was conducted to iteratively refine and definitively classify each respondent firm into a specific resource utilization profile or configuration. Subsequently, Analysis of Variance (ANOVA) was used to compare the mean scores of Operational Performance and Resource Integration Capability across the derived clusters. This method effectively answers the configuration research question by identifying which specific "bundles" or patterns of platform and location use are associated with the highest levels of performance, thereby revealing synergistic (or non-synergistic) resource configurations. This reveals the nonlinear, holistic patterns of allocation strategies among firms.

6.3.4 Results

The empirical analysis yields robust and nuanced results that collectively validate the integrated contingency-configuration framework, providing clear insights into both the pathways and the patterns through which value is created within logistics parks. The findings systematically address the core research questions, revealing not only that resources matter, but precisely how their influence is channeled and in what form their combination yields superior outcomes.

Testing Contingent Pathways: Structural Equation Modeling Results
The hypotheses pertaining to the direct and mediated causal pathways were tested using Structural Equation Modeling (SEM). The standardized path coefficients and their significance levels offer strong support for the proposed contingent relationships. First, the analysis confirmed that logistics platform integration exerts a significant, positive direct effect on operational performance ($\beta = 0.40$, $p < 0.01$), thereby supporting H1a. This finding substantiates the role of the platform as a source of tangible, direct utility, providing tools that enhance efficiency independently. In stark contrast, the hypothesized direct link between logistics location integration and operational performance was not supported ($\beta = -0.11$, n.s.), leading to the rejection of H2a. This result is pivotal, as it empirically validates the contingency argument: a superior geographical location, by itself, does not automatically translate into better performance, challenging deterministic assumptions. This confirms the differential nature of allocation: platform resources have a direct tool-like effect, while location resources do not.

Crucially, the analysis confirmed that both platform and location integration are significant antecedents to the firm's dynamic capability. Both logistics platform integration ($\beta = 0.24$, $p < 0.01$) and, more potently, logistics location integration ($\beta = 0.46$, $p < 0.01$) were found to have strong, positive effects on resource integration capability, supporting H1b and H2b. The notably stronger effect of location underscores its primary function as a network catalyst, whose value lies in enabling connections rather than serving as a direct tool. Finally, as hypothesized in H3, resource integration capability itself emerged as a powerful, direct driver of operational performance ($\beta = 0.56$, $p < 0.01$), confirming its status as a core competitive mechanism that translates resource access into realized gains. This establishes the central role of resource integration capability as the engine of effective allocation (Fig. 6.3).

Elucidating Mediation: The Mechanism of Contingency
To precisely delineate the nature of the influence pathways and formally test the proposed mediating role of resource integration capability, a series of mediation analyses were conducted using the Sobel test (Venkatraman, 1989). This statistical procedure rigorously assesses whether an intervening variable significantly carries the influence of an independent variable to a dependent variable. The results of these tests yielded a critical and theoretically meaningful distinction, fundamentally clarifying the "how" of the contingency process and providing granular insight into the differential roles of platform and location resources.

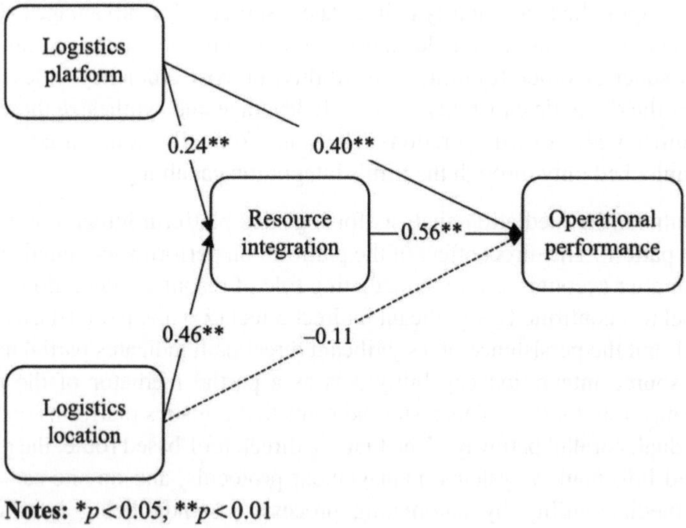

Fig. 6.3 Estimated structural equation model

Table 6.1 Mediation tests

Dependent variable	Logistics platform–operational performance		Logistics location–operational performance	
	Logistics platform	Resource integration	Logistics location	Resource integration
Model 1 (operational performance)	0.57** (0.058)		0.35** (0.080)	
Model 2 (resource integration)	0.54** (0.061)		0.49** (0.068)	
Model 3 (operational performance)		0.57** (0.058)		0.57** (0.058)
Model 4 (operational performance)	0.40** (0.058)	0.46** (0.056)	0.08 (0.077)	0.55** (0.064)
	Sobel test 5.9		Sobel test 5.5	

Notes: The number within parentheses is the standard error of the coefficient. $^{**}p < 0.01$. Source: Lyu et al. (2019)

The analysis first established the necessary preconditions for mediation. Logistics location integration showed a significant total effect on operational performance when considered in isolation. However, upon introducing resource integration capability into the model, the previously observed direct path from location to performance became statistically non-significant. The Sobel test confirmed a significant indirect effect ($z = 5.5$, $p < 0.01$), as presented in Table 6.1. This pattern of results fulfills the criteria for full mediation. Consequently, we conclude that resource integration capability acts as a full mediator in the relationship between logistics location integration and operational performance. This finding carries profound implications: it means the entirety of a location's potential economic value is contingent upon the firm's ability to integrate resources. The advantages of proximity, network access, and unique local assets remain entirely latent and fail to translate into superior order fulfillment, flexibility, or cost efficiency unless the firm possesses the dynamic capability to actively leverage and synthesize these external opportunities with its own operations. The value from allocating based on location is fully unlocked only through the firm's integration capability.

In contrast, the mediation analysis for logistics platform integration revealed a different pattern. The direct effect of the platform on performance remained significant even after accounting for the mediating role of resource integration capability. The Sobel test confirmed a significant indirect effect ($z = 5.9$, $p < 0.01$), as shown in Table 6.1, but the persistence of a significant direct path indicates partial mediation. Thus, resource integration capability acts as a partial mediator of the platform-performance relationship. This result indicates that logistics platforms create value through dual, parallel pathways. The first is a direct, tool-based route: the platform's integrated information systems, management protocols, and on-site services provide immediate utility by automating processes, standardizing interfaces, and reducing transaction costs, thereby enhancing performance independently. The second is an indirect, capability-enhancing route: by providing a shared digital and operational infrastructure, the platform environment itself fosters and strengthens the firm's inherent capacity for resource integration, which in turn boosts performance. Therefore, the platform's value is only partially contingent on this dynamic capability, as a substantial portion of its benefit is delivered through direct, readily deployable functionality. Allocation of platform resources yields both direct performance benefits and enhances the firm's broader allocation capability.

This delineation between full and partial mediation is the cornerstone of the contingency argument within the model. It empirically demonstrates that the two key resources provided by a logistics park follow fundamentally different logics of value creation. The intangible, network-based value of location is entirely conditional and must be actively unlocked through integration. The tangible, tool-based value of the platform, while also amplified by integration, retains a significant component of direct, unconditional utility. This nuanced understanding moves beyond simply stating that "resources matter" to explaining under what specific conditions and through what distinct mechanisms each resource matters for achieving operational excellence.

Identifying Configurational Patterns: Cluster Analysis Results

Moving beyond the linear causal paths examined through SEM, this study employed a two-step cluster analysis to empirically uncover the holistic, emergent patterns in how firms combine and leverage the two core resources of the logistics park. This method is particularly suited for identifying natural groupings within data based on similarity across multiple variables—in this case, firms' scores on Logistics Platform Integration and Logistics Location Integration. The analysis, following established procedures, first used hierarchical clustering to suggest the optimal number of clusters and then applied K-means clustering to definitively assign each firm to a group. This approach converged on four robust, distinct, and highly interpretable resource utilization configurations, which are summarized in Table 6.2 and described below. These configurations represent distinct allocation strategies.

Platform-Leaning Configuration: Firms in this group demonstrate a pronounced strategic emphasis on the park's infrastructural services. They exhibit high utilization and dependency on the integrated platform, including its information systems, management protocols, and technical/financial services. However, they show relatively low leverage of the location-specific network advantages, such as proactively building connections with local industry clusters or exploiting unique regional assets. Their strategy appears centered on operational efficiency gained through the park's internal tools.

Location-Leaning Configuration: This configuration represents the inverse posture. Firms here display high reliance on the intrinsic advantages of the park's geographical and network position. They effectively tap into local supply sources, labor pools, and transportation linkages. Conversely, they exhibit low engagement with the integrated platform services, underutilizing the shared digital and managerial infrastructure. Their strategy seems rooted in traditional, location-bound advantages rather than platform-enabled integration.

High-Resource Uniform Configuration: This group embodies the synergistic ideal proposed by configuration theory. Firms in this category exhibit high and balanced utilization of both platform and location resources. They fully leverage the park's internal service platform while simultaneously actively engaging with the external network opportunities its location affords. This pattern suggests a deliberate strategy of comprehensive ecosystem participation.

Low-Resource Uniform Configuration: Firms in this group show low utilization of both types of resources. They derive minimal strategic benefit from either the park's platform services or its locational advantages, representing a state of under-participation or marginal engagement with the ecosystem's core value proposition.

The identification of these four configurations empirically validates the premise that firms co-located within the same physical park adopt meaningfully different resource orchestration strategies. This sets the stage for the critical next question: how do these distinct strategic configurations relate to differences in firm performance and capability? The answer to this question, addressed in the following performance comparison, lies at the heart of evaluating the configuration perspective.

Performance across Configurations: The Synergy Evidence

Analysis of Variance (ANOVA) was used to compare the mean levels of operational performance and resource integration capability across these four configurations, as presented in Table 6.3. The comparisons revealed statistically significant

Table 6.2 Clarification of logistics resources

Resource pattern	Number of respondents	Percentage
Platform leaning pattern	56	20.5
Location leaning pattern	47	17.2
High-resource uniform pattern	73	26.7
Low-resource uniform pattern	97	35.5

differences, offering powerful evidence for the configuration perspective. Firms in the High-Resource Uniform Configuration demonstrated the highest levels of both operational performance and resource integration capability. This finding provides direct empirical support for the synergistic effect posited by configuration theory: supreme value is created not by maximizing a single resource dimension, but through the coordinated, high-level co-utilization of complementary platform and location resources. Conversely, the Low-Resource Uniform Configuration group performed the worst. The Platform-Leaning and Location-Leaning configurations occupied an intermediate performance tier. Notably, the Platform-Leaning group generally outperformed the Location-Leaning group, a result that reinforces and is consistent with the SEM finding that platforms possess a direct performance link which location lacks. This demonstrates that the most effective allocation strategy is a synergistic one, balancing both platform and location resource utilization.

In synthesis, the empirical results delineate a coherent logic of value creation within platform-based logistics ecosystems. The findings confirm that value stems from a dual mechanism: it flows through contingent pathways, where the impact of key resources is fully or partially mediated by the firm's resource integration capability, and it is maximized under a specific synergistic configuration, characterized by the high-level, balanced use of both platform and location resources. This integrated perspective advances beyond a simple resource-possession model, offering a nuanced framework that explains how logistics parks enable competitive advantage not merely by providing resources, but by creating an environment where resource value is activated by firm-level capabilities and amplified by strategic resource combinations. This completes the picture of the allocation mechanism within platform logistics, showing its contingency on firm capability and its optimization through synergistic resource combinations.

Table 6.3 ANOVA test

	Operational performance	Resource integration
1. Platform leaning pattern	3.2 (2, 4)	2.7 (3)
2. Location leaning pattern	2.8 (1, 3)	3.0 (2)
3. High-resource uniform pattern	3.3 (2, 4)	3.1 (1, 4)
4. Low-resource uniform pattern	2.5 (1, 3)	2.4 (2, 3)
Total	2.95	2.78
F	18.96^{**}	13.35^{**}

Notes: Numbers in parentheses indicate the cluster(s) from which that cluster is significantly different at $p < 0.05$. $^{**}p < 0.01$

6.3.5 *Implications for Platform Logistics Management*

The empirical findings of this study necessitate a fundamental shift in the strategic mindset governing platform logistics. Managers must therefore focus on enabling and executing effective allocation. For both the architects of these ecosystems—the park developers and operators—and their primary users, the tenant companies, the prevailing philosophy must evolve from a transactional focus on resource provision toward a dynamic commitment to ecosystem orchestration and capability building. This paradigm shift is grounded in the core revelation that the value of a logistics park is not intrinsic to its physical assets but is contingent upon the integration capabilities of its tenants and is maximized through the synergistic combination of its offerings. Managers must therefore focus on enabling and executing effective allocation.

For logistics park developers and operators, the implications demand a transformation from the role of passive landlord to that of an active ecosystem architect and facilitator. The primary strategic objective must transcend the mere filling of physical space to encompass the deliberate design of an environment that fosters and stimulates resource integration among tenants. This involves architecting interoperable technological platforms, particularly information and communication systems, that enable secure and efficient data exchange and collaboration between firms, not merely between each firm and the administration. Beyond infrastructure, operators must proactively curate a complementary tenant portfolio, strategically assembling a mix of manufacturers, logistics service providers, financiers, and technology firms to create a rich network of potential partnerships. To catalyze these connections, the institution of formal matchmaking forums, innovation workshops, and incentive programs becomes crucial. Recognizing the diverse configurations of tenant firms, as revealed by the cluster analysis, operators can further enhance value by offering differentiated, diagnostic-driven services. For instance, firms identified as "Location-Leaning" may benefit from intensive platform onboarding support, while "Platform-Leaning" firms might require facilitated network brokerage to connect with regional partners, guiding all toward the high-performance "High-Resource Uniform" configuration. Ultimately, marketing communications should reflect this evolved value proposition, emphasizing not just physical assets but the park's role in accelerating supply chain integration and amplifying a firm's resource leverage. The operator's role is to design the ecosystem to facilitate superior allocation by its tenants.

Concurrently, tenant companies must reframe their engagement with logistics platforms from a cost-centric real estate decision to a strategic investment in building long-term dynamic capabilities. This begins with a rigorous, ongoing audit of their utilization of the park's ecosystem, critically assessing whether they are fully leveraging information platforms for visibility, financial services for capital efficiency, and, most importantly, proactively building relationships with other tenants to access complementary resources and co-create value. The goal of this introspection is a conscious migration towards the synergistic use of all available resources. To operationalize this, firms must complement their technological investments with deliberate development of integrative management competencies, training supply chain professionals in partnership management, collaborative planning, and data analytic—thus evolving the logistics function from internal operations oversight to external resource orchestration. Consequently, the criteria for selecting a logistics park must be fundamentally re-evaluated. The decision matrix should prioritize the quality and diversity of the tenant community, the operator's proven track record in fostering collaboration, and the site's connectivity within broader multi-modal networks, weighing these strategic enablers of future integration more heavily than immediate, narrow cost savings. In this light, fees for platform services should be viewed not as an overhead but as an investment in capability-enabling infrastructure, with returns measured in enhanced agility, reduced operational risk, and competitive advantage derived from superior integration. The tenant's task is to develop the capability for effective allocation and choose an environment that supports it.

In conclusion, the managerial implications of this study advocate for a holistic, capability-concentric approach to platform logistics. For operators, excellence lies in orchestrating a fertile environment for connection and synergy. For tenants, advantage is secured by strategically selecting that environment and decisively investing in the integrative capabilities required to harness its full potential. This dual perspective completes the value-creation cycle, linking the design of the platform ecosystem with the strategic conduct of the firms within it. It underscores that value in the logistics pillar is co-created through sophisticated allocation, enabled by supportive governance and executed through dynamic firm capabilities.

6.4 Chapter Conclusions and Future Directions

6.4.1 Synthesizing the Framework of Platform Logistics Integration

This chapter has systematically constructed and empirically validated a comprehensive, multi-level framework for understanding Platform Logistics Integration (PLI) as the specific instantiation of the logistics pillar within this book's four-pillar framework. We frame PLI as a hierarchical strategic architecture activated through three core mechanisms: governance, coordination, and allocation. Specifically, information integration serves as the primary coordination mechanism, governing knowledge and signal flows. Resource integration serves as the core allocation mechanism, governing the combination and deployment of tangible and intangible assets (Sect. 6.1). This foundational distinction allowed for a sophisticated investigation that constitutes the chapter's core theoretical contribution: the successful bridging of micro-level relational governance with macro-level strategic allocation, offering a holistic explanation of how platform ecosystems create and capture value.

Section 6.2 examined the micro-foundational layer, employing Social Exchange Theory (SET) to analyze the governance of collaborative partnerships. It moved beyond viewing information sharing as a mere technical function, reconceptualizing it as a strategically managed relational asset essential for coordination. The research delineated how economic governance (embodied in transaction-specific assets that create mutual lock-in and credible commitment) and relational governance (embodied in mutual trust that reduces perceived risk and fosters goodwill) operate not in isolation but in a dynamic interplay. This governance complex was shown to differentially stimulate both operational information integration (e.g., real-time shipment data exchange) and strategic information integration (e.g., sharing long-term forecasts and innovation roadmaps), each with distinct pathways to enhancing financial performance. Thus, Sect. 6.2 detailed how the governance mechanism enables and shapes the coordination mechanism within platform logistics relationships.

In contrast, Sect. 6.3 widened the lens to the macro-strategic level, focusing on the allocation mechanism. Integrating contingency and configuration perspectives within the RBV and Dynamic Capability Theory, it developed and tested a model of how park resources translate into performance. The empirical findings were clear and consequential: the market value of a logistics park's offerings—its integrated platform (a bundle of tangible services) and its strategic location (a bundle of intangible network access points)—is not an automatic property. Instead, their value is contingent upon a critical firm-specific filter and amplifier: the resource integration capability. This dynamic capability was empirically proven to be the essential conduit. It fully mediates the value of location (which remains latent otherwise) and partially mediates the value of the platform (which also provides direct utility). Furthermore, the research employed cluster analysis to move from linear relationships to a typology of resource utilization configurations. The consistent superiority of the High-Resource Uniform configuration provided robust empirical validation for the configuration perspective. It demonstrated conclusively that peak performance is an emergent property of synergistic alignment—the deliberate, high-level co-utilization of both platform and location resources—rather than the outcome of excelling in any single dimension.

Therefore, the principal theoretical contribution of this chapter is a coherent, multi-level framework for PLI. This framework does more than catalogue factors; it specifies causal mechanisms (e.g., governance enabling coordination, capability mediating allocation) and structural forms (e.g., synergistic resource configurations) that link platform design and firm conduct to competitive performance. It connects the micro-relational question of how partnerships are governed with the macro-strategic question of how resources are allocated and transformed into advantage, offering a comprehensive and actionable understanding of platform-based competition in logistics.

6.4.2 *Charting the Frontier: An Expanded Agenda for Future Research*

The proposed framework, while robust, naturally illuminates a rich landscape of unanswered questions and new possibilities. It serves as a springboard for a multi-dimensional research agenda that promises to advance both theory and practice, particularly by exploring the interactions and boundaries of the governance, coordination, and allocation mechanisms within and beyond the logistics pillar.

Deepening the Organizational Micro-Foundations: A Capability Ecosystem. Future research must deconstruct and expand the "black box" of dynamic capabilities within platforms. While resource integration is central to allocation, how does it interact with complementary capabilities like absorptive capacity (for learning from platform coordination) or strategic agility? Do the relative importance of governance (e.g., trust) and allocation capability shift in hyper-volatile markets? Longitudinal studies could map the co-evolution of these capabilities with a firm's integration maturity within the platform ecosystem.

Contextualizing and Contingentizing the Model: The Role of Institutional Logics and Technology Stacks. The model's validation in a specific context invites crucial boundary-testing and enrichment. A vital stream of research involves cross-institutional comparative studies. How do variations in formal institutional frameworks—such as the strength of contract law, property rights, and regulatory regimes—alter the perceived risk and thus the efficacy of specific asset investments and trust-building? How do informal cultural-cognitive institutions—such as societal levels of trust (e.g., high-trust vs. low-trust societies), communication styles, and attitudes towards interdependence—shape the pathways of relational governance and trust-based coordination? Furthermore, the technological architecture and maturity of the platform itself is a key contingency. Research should examine how IoT, Blockchain, and AI redefine the costs, benefits, and nature of both coordination (information integration) and allocation (resource integration), potentially giving rise to new governance models.

Embracing Complexity Through Methodological Pluralism: Process, Evolution, and Networks. To capture the dynamism and complexity of PLI, future inquiry must embrace methodological pluralism. Longitudinal panel studies are needed to move from static correlation to causal inference and to trace the evolution of firm configurations, capability development, and performance over time. Complementary qualitative process studies—such as multi-case studies or ethnographic research within logistics parks—are indispensable for uncovering the lived experience of integration. They can reveal the political negotiations, routine practices, unforeseen obstacles, and managerial sense-making that survey-based research cannot capture. Additionally, the framework could be extended using Social Network Analysis (SNA) to move beyond firm-level attributes to map the actual structure of inter-firm relationships within the park. Does a firm's position (centrality, brokerage) in this network amplify or diminish the benefits of its resource configuration?

Converging with Grand Theories of Platforms, Ecosystems, and Strategy. PLI should be actively situated within broader theoretical conversations. A rich dialogue with digital platform economics and strategy is essential. This includes applying theories of multi-sided markets to analyze platform pricing, subsidization strategies, and the management of cross-side network effects between shippers, carriers, and service providers. It necessitates a study of data governance and value appropriation: who captures the value from the meta-data generated by integrated operations? Furthermore, research can explore platform envelopment and ecosystem expansion, investigating how logistics platforms might bundle or integrate with adjacent services (e.g., fintech, insurance, customs compliance) to create deeper lock-in and new value propositions, thereby reshaping competitive boundaries.

Confronting Grand Societal Challenges: Sustainability, Resilience, and Inclusive Prosperity. Perhaps the most urgent and impactful direction is to leverage the PLI framework to address pressing global challenges. Research must investigate how the governance and orchestration mechanisms of platforms can be deliberately designed for systemic sustainability. Can platforms internalize environmental externalities by enabling and incentivizing collaborative optimization for low-carbon logistics through better coordination and allocation? How can they be architected to facilitate circular economy flows, seamlessly integrating reverse logistics, refurbishment, and recycling into forward supply chains? Beyond environmental goals, the framework is vital for studying supply chain resilience. How do different platform configurations and governance models affect the collective ability to anticipate, absorb, adapt to, and recover from major disruptions? Finally, scholars must apply a critical lens to examine equity and inclusion. How do platform dynamics affect the distribution of value between large and small firms? Can platform design promote fair labor practices and contribute to inclusive regional development, ensuring that the benefits of integration are broadly shared?

In conclusion, this chapter has provided a foundational and integrative map for navigating the complex reality of Platform Logistics Integration through the lenses of governance, coordination, and allocation. The proposed research agenda charts a path forward that is both deeply analytical—probing finer mechanisms and contingencies—and ambitiously expansive—connecting logistics scholarship to pivotal debates in institutional theory, technology studies, platform strategy, and sustainable development. By pursuing these interconnected paths, the academic and practitioner community can ensure that the transformative potential of platform logistics is realized not only in pursuit of operational excellence but as a cornerstone of building more resilient, responsible, and prosperous socio-economic systems.

References

Ambrosino, D., & Sciomachen, A. (2012). Hub locations in urban multimodal networks. *European Transport, 51*, 1825–3997.

Barney, J. (1991). Firm resources and sustainable competitive advantage. *Journal of Management, 17*(1), 99–120.

Cheng, Z., Rai, A., Tian, F., & Xu, S. X. (2021). Social learning in information technology investment: The role of board interlocks. *Management Science, 67*(1), 547–576.

Choi, T.-M. (2021). Risk analysis in logistics systems: A research agenda during and after the COVID-19 pandemic. *Transportation Research Part E: Logistics Transportation Review, 145*, 102190.

Choi, T. M., Wallace, S. W., & Wang, Y. (2018). Big data analytics in operations management. *Production and Operations Management, 27*(10), 1868–1883.

Constant, D., Kiesler, S., & Sproull, L. (1994). What's mine is ours, or is it? A study of attitudes about information sharing. *Information Systems Research, 5*(4), 400–421.

Cook, K. S., & Emerson, R. M. (1978). Power, equity and commitment in exchange networks. *American Sociological Review, 43*(5), 721–739.

Cropanzano, R., Anthony, E. L., Daniels, S. R., & Hall, A. V. (2017). Social exchange theory: A critical review with theoretical remedies. *Academy of Management Annals, 11*(1), 479–516.

Daugherty, P., Chen, H., Mattioda, D., & Grawe, S. (2009). Marketing/logistics relationships: influence on capabilities and performance. *Journal of Business Logistics, 30*(1), 1–18.

Demoulin, N. T., & Coussement, K. (2020). Acceptance of text-mining systems: The signaling role of information quality. *Information & Management, 57*(1), 103120.

Devaraj, S., Krajewski, L., & Wei, J. C. (2007). Impact of e-business technologies on operational performance: the role of production information integration in the supply chain. *Journal of Operations Management, 25*(6), 1199–1216.

Dyer, J. H., & Singh, H. (1998). The relational view: Cooperative strategy and sources of interorganizational competitive advantage. *Academy of Management Review, 23*(4), 660–679.

Dyk, F. E., & Maspero, E. (2004). An analysis of the South African fruit logistics infrastructure. *OriON, 20*(1), 55–72.

Emerson, R. M. (1976). Social exchange theory. *Annual Review of Sociology, 2*(1), 335–362.

Evangelista, P., Mogre, R., Perego, A., Raspagliesi, A., & Sweeney, E. (2012). A survey based analysis of IT adoption and 3PLs' performance. *Supply Chain Management: An International Journal, 17*(2), 172–186.

Freeman, J., & Styles, C. (2014). Does location matter to export performance? *International Marketing Review, 31*(2), 181–208. https://doi.org/10.1108/imr-02-2013-0039

Frohlich, M. T., & Westbrook, R. (2002). Demand chain management in manufacturing and services: Web-based integration, drivers and performance. *Journal of Operations Management, 20*(6), 729–745.

Gao, M., & Dong, M. (2012). Analysis of logistics center location-selecting based on GIS: take Li County as an example. *Advanced Materials Research, 569*, 804–807.

Giuffrida, M., Mangiaracina, R., Perego, A., & Tumino, A. (2019). Cross-border B2C e-commerce to China. *International Journal of Physical Distribution & Logistics Management, 50*(3), 355–378. https://doi.org/10.1108/ijpdlm-08-2018-0311

Goswami, M., De, A., Habibi, M. K. K., & Daultani, Y. (2020). Examining freight performance of third-party logistics providers within the automotive industry in India: An environmental sustainability perspective. *International Journal of Production Research, 58*(24), 7565–7592.

Granovetter, M. (1985). Action and social structure: The problem of embeddedness. *American Journal of Sociology, 91*(3), 481–510.

Grant, R. M. (1991). The resource-based theory of competitive advantage: Implications for strategy formulation. *California Management Review, 33*(3), 114–135.

Grant, R. M. (1996). Toward a knowledge-based theory of the firm. *Strategic Management Journal, 17*(S2), 109–122.

He, P., He, Y., Tang, X., Ma, S., & Xu, H. (2022). Channel encroachment and logistics integration strategies in an e-commerce platform service supply chain. *International Journal of Production Economics, 244*. https://doi.org/10.1016/j.ijpe.2021.108368

Heide, J. B., & John, G. (1992). Do norms matter in marketing relationships? *Journal of Marketing, 56*(2), 32–44.

Hoopes, D. G., Madsen, T. L., & Walker, G. (2003). Guest editors' introduction to the special issue: why is there a resource-based view? Toward a theory of competitive heterogeneity. *Strategic Management Journal, 24*(10), 889–902.

Huang, S., Guan, X., & Chen, Y. J. (2018). Retailer information sharing with supplier encroachment. *Production and Operations Management, 27*(6), 1133–1147.

Huang, M.-C., Kang, M.-P., & Chiang, J.-K. (2020). Can a supplier benefit from investing in transaction-specific investments? A multilevel model of the value co-creation ecosystem perspective. *Supply Chain Management: An International Journal, 25*(6), 773–787.

Huo, B., Fu, D., Zhao, X., & Zhu, J. (2016). Curbing opportunism in logistics outsourcing relationships: The role of relational norms and contract. *International Journal of Production Economics, 182*, 293–303.

Huo, B., Wang, Q., Zhao, X., & Hua, Z. (2017). Barriers to third-party logistics integration: Empirical evidence from China. *Industrial Management Data Systems, 117*(8), 1738–1760.

Huo, B., Ye, Y., Zhao, X., Wei, J., & Hua, Z. (2018). Environmental uncertainty, specific assets, and opportunism in 3PL relationships: A transaction cost economics perspective. *International Journal of Production Economics, 203*, 154–163. https://doi.org/10.1016/j.ijpe.2018.01.031

Huo, B., Zhao, X., & Zhou, H. (2014). The effects of competitive environment on supply chain information sharing and performance: An empirical study in China. *Production and Operations Management, 23*(4), 552–569.

Hwang, T., & Kim, S. T. (2018). Balancing in-house and outsourced logistics services: effects on supply chain agility and firm performance. *Service Business, 13*(3), 531–556. https://doi.org/10.1007/s11628-018-00394-x

Jell-Ojobor, M., & Raha, A. (2022). Being good at being good—The mediating role of an environmental management system in value-creating green supply chain management practices. *Business Strategy and the Environment, 31*(5), 1964–1984. https://doi.org/10.1002/bse.2993

Kembro, J., Näslund, D., & Olhager, J. (2017). Information sharing across multiple supply chain tiers: A Delphi study on antecedents. *International Journal of Production Economics, 193*, 77–86.

Klein, R., & Rai, A. (2009). Interfirm strategic information flows in logistics supply chain relationships. *MIS Quarterly, 33*(4), 735–762.

Kong, X. T. R., Li, M., Yu, Y., Zhao, Z., & Huang, G. Q. (2017). Physical internet-enabled e-commerce logistics park platform. *IEEE International Conference on Automation Science and Engineering*, 406–411.

König, C., Caldwell, N. D., & Ghadge, A. (2019). Service provider boundaries in competitive markets: The case of the logistics industry. *International Journal of Production Research, 57*(18), 5624–5639.

Kosmol, T., Reimann, F., & Kaufmann, L. (2019). You'll never walk alone: Why we need a supply chain practice view on digital procurement. *Journal of Purchasing and Supply Management, 25*(4), 100553.

Krysiński, M., & Miller, P. (2017). The impact of an integrated logistics platform on the management of logistics. *Przegląd Nauk Ekonomicznych, 25*, 91–100.

Lai, F., Tian, Y., & Huo, B. (2012). Relational governance and opportunism in logistics outsourcing relationships: Empirical evidence from China. *International Journal of Production Research, 50*(9), 2501–2514.

Lau, K. H., & Zhang, J. (2006). Drivers and obstacles of outsourcing practices in China. *International Journal of Physical Distribution & Logistics Management, 36*(10), 776–792.

Law, F. (2018). Breaking the outsourcing path: Backsourcing process and outsourcing lock-in. *European Management Journal, 36*(3), 341–352.

Lee, B.-C., Kim, P.-S., Hong, K.-S., & Lee, I. (2010). Evaluating antecedents and consequences of supply chain activities: An integrative perspective. *International Journal of Production Research, 48*(3), 657–682.

Li, L., & Li, G. (2023). Integrating logistics service or not? The role of platform entry strategy in an online marketplace. *Transportation Research Part E: Logistics and Transportation Review, 170*. https://doi.org/10.1016/j.tre.2022.102991

Li, Y., Ye, F., & Sheu, C. (2014). Social capital, information sharing and performance: Evidence from China. *International Journal of Operations Production Management, 34*(11), 1440–1462.

Liao, K., Deng, X., Liao, Y., & Zhang, Q. (2020). Supplier empowerment: Mediating situational factors and perceived performance. *Journal of Purchasing Supply Management, 26*(3), 100611.

Liu, C., Huo, B., Liu, S., Zhao, X., & Chan, H. K. (2015). Effect of information sharing and process coordination on logistics outsourcing. *Industrial Management & Data Systems, 115*(1), 41–63.

Liu, Y., Luo, Y., & Liu, T. (2009). Governing buyer-supplier relationships through transactional and relational mechanisms: Evidence from China. *Journal of Operations Management, 27*(4), 294–309. http://www.sciencedirect.com/science/article/pii/S027269630800065X http://ac.els-cdn.com/S027269630800065X/1-s2.0-S027269630800065X-main.pdf?_tid=ea5d0968-39b2-11e5-82e8-00000aab0f01&acdnat=1438587810_e9bdd22ca9695d92d0b909e2398c698b

Lium, A.-G., Crainic, T. G., & Wallace, S. W. (2009). A study of demand stochasticity in service network design. *Transportation Science, 43*(2), 144–157.

Lotfi, Z., Mukhtar, M., Sahran, S., & Zadeh, A. T. (2013). Information sharing in supply chain management. *Procedia Technology, 11*, 298–304.

Luo, L., Liu, C., Zhao, X.-D., & Jeff, Y. (2015). Impact of Trust on 3PL Integration and Performance. *Journal of Beijing Union University, 29*(3), 74–80, 92.

Luo, H., & Wang, L. (2021). Study on the impact of third party logistics integrationon supply chain performance. *Chinese Journal of Management, 18*(3), 448–454.

Lyu, G., Chen, L. & Huo, B. (2019). The impact of logistics platforms and location on logistics resource integration and operational performance. *The International Journal of Logistics Management, 30*(2), 549–568. https://doi.org/10.1108/IJLM-02-2018-0048

Maloni, M. J., & Carter, C. R. (2006). Opportunities for research in third-party logistics. *Transportation Journal, 45*(2), 23–38.

Marchet, G., Melacini, M., Perotti, S., Sassi, C., & Tappia, E. (2017). Value creation models in the 3PL industry: What 3PL providers do to cope with shipper requirements. *International Journal of Physical Distribution Logistics Management, 47*(6), 472–494.

Maskey, R., Fei, J., & Nguyen, H.-O. (2020). Critical factors affecting information sharing in supply chains. *Production Planning Control, 31*(7), 557–574.

Mayer, R. C., Davis, J. H., & Schoorman, F. D. (1995). An integrative model of organizational trust. *The Academy of Management Review, 20*(3), 709–734.

Moore, K. R., & Cunningham, W. A. (1999). Social exchange behavior in logistics relationships: A shipper perspective. *International Journal of Physical Distribution Logistics Management, 29*(2), 103–121.

Morgan, R. M., & Hunt, S. D. (1995). The commitment-trust theory of relationship marketing. *Journal of Marketing, 58*, 20–38.

Muthusamy, S. K., & White, M. A. (2005). Learning and knowledge transfer in strategic alliances: A social exchange view. *Organization Studies, 26*(3), 415–441.

Newell, W. J., Ellegaard, C., & Esbjerg, L. (2018). The effects of goodwill and competence trust on strategic information sharing in buyer-supplier relationships. *Journal of Business Industrial Marketing Management, 34*(2), 389–400.

Olorunniwo, F. O., & Li, X. (2010). Information sharing and collaboration practices in reverse logistics. *Supply Chain Management: An International Journal, 15*(6), 454–462.

Osmonbekov, T., Bello, D. C., & Gilliland, D. I. (2009). The impact of e-business infusion on channel coordination, conflict and reseller performance. *Industrial Marketing Management, 38*(7), 778–784.

Pearson, G., English, J. M., White, M. A., & Cobb, M. H. (2001). ERK5 and ERK2 cooperate to regulate NF-κB and cell transformation. *Journal of Biological Chemistry, 276*(11), 7927–7931. https://doi.org/10.1074/jbc.M009764200

Perry, M. L., Sengupta, S., & Krapfel, R. (2004). Effectiveness of horizontal strategic alliances in technologically uncertain environments: Are trust and commitment enough? *Journal of Business Research, 57*(9), 951–956.

Puertas, R., Martí, L., & García, L. (2014). Logistics performance and export competitiveness: European experience. *Empirica, 41*(3), 467–480.

Pulles, N. J., Veldman, J., Schiele, H., & Sierksma, H. (2014). Pressure or pamper? The effects of power and trust dimensions on supplier resource allocation. *Journal of Supply Chain Management, 50*(3), 16–36.

Rai, A., Patnayakuni, R., & Seth, N. (2006). Company performance impacts of digitally enabled supply chain integration capabilities. *MIS Quarterly, 30*(2), 225–246.

Rivera, L., Sheffi, Y., & Knoppen, D. (2016). Logistics clusters: The impact of further agglomeration, training and firm size on collaboration and value added services. *International Journal of Production Economics, 179*, 285–294.

Şahin, H., & Topal, B. (2019). Examination of effect of information sharing on businesses performance in the supply chain process. *International Journal of Production Research, 57*(3), 815–828.

Samaddar, S., Nargundkar, S., & Daley, M. (2006). Inter-organizational information sharing: The role of supply network configuration and partner goal congruence. *European Journal of Operational Research, 174*(2), 744–765. https://doi.org/10.1016/j.ejor.2005.01.059

Sambasivan, M., Siew-Phaik, L., Mohamed, Z. A., & Leong, Y. C. (2013). Factors influencing strategic alliance outcomes in a manufacturing supply chain: Role of alliance motives, interdependence, asset specificity and relational capital. *International Journal of Production Economics, 141*(1), 339–351.

Sheffi, Y. (2012). *Logistics clusters: Delivering value and driving growth*. MIT Press.

Shi, Y., Zhang, A., Arthanari, T., & Liu, Y. (2016). Third-party purchase: An empirical study of Chinese third-party logistics users. *International Journal of Operations & Production Management, 36*(3), 286–307.

Spekman, R. E. (1988). Strategic supplier selection: Understanding long-term buyer relationships. *Business Horizons, 31*(4), 75–81.

Suh, T., & Kwon, I.-W. G. (2006). Matter over mind: When specific asset investment affects calculative trust in supply chain partnership. *Industrial Marketing Management, 35*(2), 191–201.

Tanskanen, K. (2015). Who wins in a complex buyer-supplier relationship? A social exchange theory based dyadic study. *International Journal of Operations and Production Management, 35*(4), 577–603.

Valashiya, M. C., & Luke, R. (2022). Enhancing supply chain information sharing with third party logistics service providers. *International Journal of Logistics Management*. (ahead-of-print).

Venkatraman, N. (1989). The concept of fit in strategy research: Toward verbal and statistical correspondence. *Academy of Management Journal, 14*(3), 423–444.

Vickery, S. K., Jayaram, J., Droge, C., & Calantone, R. (2003). The effects of an integrative supply chain strategy on customer service and financial performance: an analysis of direct versus indirect relationships. *Journal of Operations Management, 21*(5), 523–539.

Wang, Q., Huo, B., & Zhao, X. (2020). What makes logistics integration more effective? Governance from contractual and relational perspectives. *Journal of Business Logistics, 41*(3), 259–281.

Wang, L., Jiang, F., Li, J., Motohashi, K., & Zheng, X. (2019). The contingent effects of asset specificity, contract specificity, and trust on offshore relationship performance. *Journal of Business Research, 99*, 338–349.

Wang, Y., Wu, W., & Zhang, Y. (2016). The research on Chinese logistics mode of agricultural products transformation based on contingency theory. *Management & Engineering, 23*, 185.

Wei, H.-L., Wong, C. W., & Lai, K.-H. (2012). Linking inter-organizational trust with logistics information integration and partner cooperation under environmental uncertainty. *International Journal of Production Economics, 139*(2), 642–653.

Wen, W., & Wu, Y. (2017). Operation model summary and trend research of the highway freight logistics park in China. *Modern Economy, 8*(5), 745–752.

White, R. E., & Pearson, J. N. (2001). JIT, system integration and customer service. *International Journal of Physical Distribution and Logistics Management, 31*(5), 313–333.

Wu, L.-Y., Chen, K.-Y., Chen, P.-Y., & Tung, P.-J. (2016). Revisiting associations between specific asset investment and loyal and cooperative behavior: A complexity theory perspective. *Journal of Business Research, 69*(9), 3545–3552.

Wu, L., Chuang, C.-H., & Hsu, C.-H. (2014). Information sharing and collaborative behaviors in enabling supply chain performance: A social exchange perspective. *International Journal of Production Economics, 148*, 122–132.

Youn, S., Yang, M. G. M., Hong, P., & Park, K. (2013). Strategic supply chain partnership, environmental supply chain management practices, and performance outcomes: An empirical study of Korean firms. *Journal of Cleaner Production, 56*(1), 121–130.

Young-Ybarra, C., & Wiersema, M. (1999). Strategic flexibility in information technology alliances: The influence of transaction cost economics and social exchange theory. *Organization Science, 10*(4), 439–459.

Yu, J., Chen, F., Guan, K., & Zhang, Y. (2021). Building mutual trust in collaborative green NPD: Evidence from China's digital infrastructure. *Industrial Marketing Management, 97*, 245–257.

Yuan, Z., Zhang, L., Zhang, B., & Liu, B. (2010). Improving competitive advantage with environmental infrastructure sharing: a case study of China-Singapore Suzhou Industrial Park. *International Journal of Environmental Research, 4*(4), 751–758.

Zaheer, A., & Venkatraman, N. (1995). Relational governance as an interorganizational strategy: an empirical test of the role of trust in economic exchange. *Strategic Management Journal, 16*, 373–392.

Zanini, M. T. F., & Migueles, C. P. (2013). Trust as an element of informal coordination and its relationship with organizational performance. *Economi A, 14*(2), 77–87. https://doi.org/10.1016/j.econ.2013.08.005

Zhang, Y., Li, X., Wang, L., Zhao, X., & Gao, J. (2022). Financing capital-constrained third party logistic firms: Fourth party logistic driven financing mode vs. private lending driven financing mode. *International Journal of Production Research, 60*(9), 2963–2982.

Zhao, X., Huo, B., Selen, W., & Yeung, J. H. Y. (2011). The impact of internal integration and relationship commitment on external integration. *Journal of Operations Management, 29*(1), 17–32.

Chapter 7
Conclusions

This book set out to explain how platform firms create value through supply chain integration when the operating system is a multi-actor, customer-facing network. Across the chapters, we treated integration as an end-to-end orchestration problem: platforms must make autonomous participants behave as parts of one operational system, while preserving participation incentives, adaptability, and legitimacy. This final chapter illustrates the core insights, discusses the practical implications, and outlines limitations and future research opportunities.

7.1 Research Contributions

Contribution 1: A unified theory of platform supply chain integration built around a dual-layer framework and value-creation bottlenecks.

The first contribution is conceptual. We develop a coherent theory of platform supply chain integration that moves beyond fragmented discussions of platforms, ecosystems, and traditional supply chain integration. The book articulates a dual-layer integration framework. At the core layer, supplier integration and customer integration shape the two ends of the system: supply formation, demand formation, and matching efficiency. At the supporting layer, technology integration and logistics integration provide the coordination capacity and execution reliability that allow core integration to scale. This framework anchors integration in value creation by adopting a bottleneck logic: integration matters because it removes binding constraints that prevent platforms from converting network participation into efficiency, innovation, sustainability, and resilience.

Contribution 2: A mechanism-based explanation of how platforms coordinate heterogeneous actors while governing relational and systemic risks.

The second contribution is explanatory. The book builds an antecedents–mechanisms–outcomes logic for platform integration. On the antecedent side, we emphasize how resource and capability configurations, network structure, and external

B. Huo et al., *Platform Supply Chains 4*, Platform Supply Chains in the AI Era,
https://doi.org/10.1007/978-981-92-0133-4_7

environments shape feasible integration choices. On the mechanism side, we highlight two families of mechanisms and their complementarity. First, digital-intelligent coordination mechanisms convert dispersed data, activities, and decisions into real-time alignment, enabling sensing, prediction, and execution. Second, relationship governance and risk governance mechanisms discipline opportunism, reduce behavioral uncertainty, and limit risk spillovers that can turn localized failures into ecosystem-wide incidents. The key theoretical point is that these mechanisms interact: stronger digital coordination raises observability and accountability, yet it can also increase exposure, switching costs, and lock-in if governance and risk controls are underdeveloped. By explicitly modeling this complementarity, the book offers a tighter explanation of why some platforms achieve end-to-end coordination and others remain fragile despite high digitalization.

Contribution 3: A cumulative, multi-method research program that connects abstract integration concepts to measurable constructs and decision roadmaps.

The third contribution is methodological. Each pillar chapter decomposes integration into actionable design choices and proposes roadmaps to diagnose where value creation is constrained, identify the binding pillar, and select governance mechanisms and capability investments that relieve the constraint without damaging ecosystem participation. Empirically, the book emphasizes multi-source evidence and methodological triangulation. It combines primary and secondary data, and it integrates empirical testing with complementary approaches such as data mining, analytical modeling, and case-based evidence. This design strengthens internal validity and improves practical relevance.

7.2 Practical Implications

Platform supply chain integration is an operating strategy. Managers should treat it as a sequence of linked choices that connect the four integration pillars to concrete value outcomes. The starting point is diagnosis. Platforms often invest heavily in visible technologies or logistics capacity, yet performance problems persist because the binding constraint sits. For example, unstable supplier quality, weak customer participation, poor matching, or fragile trust can erode value creation. A practical way to begin is to map the end-to-end customer journey and identify where value is lost.

Once the bottleneck is identified, managers can design integration using a clear sequencing logic: supporting integration enables core integration. Supplier integration and customer integration define the core of platform value creation because they shape supply formation, demand formation, and matching quality. Yet these core forms of integration cannot scale without the backbone of technology integration and logistics integration. Technology integration provides the shared data standards, real-time visibility, and decision automation that make dispersed actions legible and coordinated. Logistics integration provides execution reliability and exception-handling capacity, so that platform promises translate into delivered outcomes. The implication is that platforms should avoid deep supplier or customer programs before the enabling infrastructure and execution routines are stable. Otherwise, growth amplifies variability faster than the system can absorb it.

Supplier integration should be managed as a transition from open access to a governed service system. Platforms create value when they reduce quality variability while preserving participation incentives for diverse suppliers. Operationally, this means disciplined onboarding, clear performance metrics, and structured routines for exceptions and service recovery. Governance design is central: the platform must deter opportunism and improve accountability, but it also must avoid pushing suppliers into short-term compliance behavior that undermines learning, innovation, and long-horizon investment. Effective supplier integration therefore pairs control with capability building by helping suppliers improve.

Customer integration should be treated as orchestration of customer participation. Customers in platform settings are co-producers of service outcomes: their search, selection, feedback, returns, and complaint behaviors shape demand quality and operational load. Customer integration creates value when platforms align interface design, incentives, and governance rules with operational capacity and ecosystem health. This requires coordinated choices across functions, because customer initiatives fail when internal integration is lacking. It also requires attention to cross-side externalities. Initiatives that increase conversion or trial can simultaneously raise fraud, returns, complaints, or supplier burden, damaging long-run ecosystem viability. Managers should therefore evaluate customer integration by its system consequences: whether it improves matching quality, reduces avoidable exceptions, and strengthens trust, rather than by short-run traffic metrics alone.

Technology integration should be built as an orchestration architecture. Its value lies in converting dispersed data and decisions into scalable coordination: making activities observable, comparable, and actionable across participants. This requires interoperability, real-time data governance, and clear accountability for actions triggered by algorithms. Technology integration also changes risk exposure. Stronger visibility and automation can reduce coordination costs, but it can increase dependence, switching costs, and reputational or regulatory exposure when failures occur. Managers should therefore treat data governance and algorithmic accountability as part of the operating model: who can see what, who is allowed to act, how disputes are resolved, and how the platform prevents technology-enabled opportunism.

Logistics integration is where platform promises become tangible and where systemic fragility often surfaces. In practice, logistics integration involves both information coordination and resource allocation across multiple service providers. Platforms need timely information sharing for forecasting and routing. They also need resource integration capabilities that allocate capacity dynamically under uncertainty, without degrading service reliability. The managerial implication is that logistics integration depends on governance mechanisms that support relationship-specific investments, joint problem solving, and credible escalation when disruptions occur.

7.3 Limitations

This book has several limitations that create opportunities for future research. First, platform supply chains evolve quickly. New technologies, new forms of algorithmic control, new data governance regimes, and new participant roles emerge continuously. Any framework risks lagging behind practice. Future work should treat integration as a moving target and study how platforms redesign integration when new technologies and institutional constraints reshape feasible governance and coordination choices.

Second, the book emphasizes structured integration pillars and bottleneck diagnosis, but it does not fully model long-run co-evolution and feedback loops. In reality, integration changes participant composition, which then reshapes data, incentives, and system risk. These dynamics can generate path dependence, lock-in, and unintended consequences. Future research could build dynamic models and longitudinal evidence on how integration trajectories form, when they become brittle, and how platforms regain adaptability after shocks.

Third, many emerging topics remain outside the scope of the book. Two are especially salient. One is geopolitical risk and cross-border institutional conflict, which can reshape supplier networks, technology choices, and logistics architectures. The other is platform globalization and outbound expansion, where integration interacts with localization, regulatory compliance, and legitimacy building in host countries. These contexts introduce new boundary conditions that may alter the efficacy of integration mechanisms developed primarily in more stable institutional settings.

Finally, while the book draws on multiple methods and data sources, empirical measurement of platform integration remains challenging. Key constructs such as quality of participation, governance credibility, and systemic risk spillovers are difficult to observe directly. Future work could develop stronger measures that combine operational traces, network data, governance documents, and behavioral signals to improve construct validity and to enable more precise identification of causal mechanisms.

MIX
Papier aus verantwortungsvollen Quellen
Paper from responsible sources
FSC® C105338

If you have any concerns about our products,
you can contact us on
ProductSafety@springernature.com

In case Publisher is established outside the EU,
the EU authorized representative is:
Springer Nature Customer Service Center GmbH
Europaplatz 3, 69115 Heidelberg, Germany

Printed by Libri Plureos GmbH
in Hamburg, Germany